I0418002

Building Solid
A Life in Stories

Joan Rudd

First published in the United States by Strudel Press in 2022

Book design by Paul Palmer-Edwards

ISBN: 979-8-9860489-1-8

To the memory of the mentors (visual artists and sculptors) that I found in the NW: Lloyd Reynolds, Frederic Littman, Manuel Izquierdo, Richard Beyer, and Phillip Levine

Contents

Autonomy

Act 2

Connectedness

Resilience

Resistance

Serendipity

Act 3

Perspective

Prologue

"If you sit in a hot bath, you think the whole town is warm." *Az men zitst in a heyser vane meynt men iz di gantse shtot varem.*

When my friend Miriam died, my grandmother gave me a new name. I understand now that it was to fool the Angel of Death. I was four years old. I have forgotten the name. I have known since that time that it was possible for me to die.

I remember that my grandmother held me near to her, then pushed me gently away as though to see me better. She considered the matter carefully while looking into my eyes with a concentration I had only seen associated with her anger. In this state of focus, she pronounced the name that we have all forgotten; even my mother could not recall it.

What I do remember are her other pronouncements: "You are spoiled! When I die, I shall watch you even from Heaven to see how you behave!" I was three. She pointed her finger at me. She was tall, rigid, on fire.

"Shame, for shame, for shame! Hissed through clenched teeth. I was six.

"And this one, this one will be a *rebbetzin* (a rabbi's wife, a teacher of little children), spoken gently and with great tenderness while my eyes filled with tears. I was five. I loved her.

When she was dying of cancer, suffering radiation sickness from the primitive therapies of the time, I had dreams of firestorms and destruction, all attributed to intestinal gas. I did not know she was dying until she was gone. I did not go to her funeral. I was nine. I had been sent away for the summer. My mother took me for a walk on the beach, alone, to tell me the news. My first question was whether she had told my brothers, how could we possibly tell them. She had already told them, but I had assumed it would be my role to comfort and support the "men." I was a little mother. My brothers were, in fact, older than I.

I have my grandmother's Passover dishes, her silver, her jewelry, her recipe for damson plum jam, and her bearing. She was Miss Odessa at seventeen, her hair in one long braid down her back. She was supposed to have been in love with a blue-eyed surgeon at the hospital where she became a nurse/midwife, but she married a red-haired Jewish accountant. They had twin beds. They gave generously to charity. They got some of the last ships' tickets out of Marseilles after the fall of Paris and got their two grown children safely out of Europe. Her sister, who would not leave her furniture, perished.

My mother's first impression of New York was of a woman walking a tiger (probably an ocelot) on a leash somewhere in Greenwich Village. During the War, my grandfather and uncle established a highly successful business manufacturing parts for radios, and soon, for televisions.

My mother was a vice president in that company, and held stock, but she was a pediatrician with three children, a husband, and a house to manage. My grandmother bought all my father's shirts right up until her death. With her own family grown, she took on ours. I was there every Sunday and frequently overnight on Saturday, too. The only recipe I got was the jam. We watched Molly Goldberg and pro-wrestling on the new TV, both of which my grandmother would react to as theater. She would move her head along with her neck like a Chinese dancer; her palm would support her chin and cheek while she swayed like a Jew in prayer, vocalizing, "Oy! Oy! Oy!"

My great-grandparents spoke Yiddish, my grandparents spoke Russian, my parents spoke French, and I, of course, spoke English. All the other languages remain, in some form, in my mind, brought forth in snippets under stress, tension, or in words of love. I spoke to my own babies in Russian I did not know I had. I curse in French. I am learning to find my own heart's way by studying Yiddish.

My heart has been lost and misplaced several times in my lifetime. I did not die at four of leukemia like my friend Miriam. I did not die at fifteen of mesenchymal sarcoma of the knee, either. But I fully expected to die. And when they told me they would amputate, and I would live, my rage gave me the strength to live, even as I was genuinely grateful that I would not die. My cousin, who was told to pray for my recovery, lost her faith in G-d over my amputation. It was so unfair. When I returned to high school, some of the girls screamed at the sight of me. One became hysterical and had to be led away. My grandmother's bearing came in handy. I held my head up when I walked on crutches. I learned to ride first an exercycle then a standard bicycle with an above-knee prosthesis. I hung out with two friends in particular, both the children of concentration camp survivors. They did not reject me, and we went through the usual pranks: cutting school, going to school in culottes (we were sent home to put on proper skirts), going to hootenannies, and to dances, playing guitar on the subway, raiding the refrigerator. Their parents had numbers on their arms, and I remember one of them sighing that with my recent loss, our childhoods were now over.

I also remember how the other one of my friends told me that her mother had said, "What a shame; now she will never marry." I had the wit to tell my own mother, who called the other one "an idiot." I asked my mother to look into the mirror with me before my bath, and I looked over my body with a sympathetic listener nearby. I announced that I was not ugly, that I resembled ancient statuary, that what was missing did not detract from what there was. That I was still beautiful.

My aunt's friend told me, in confidence, that I would be all the more attractive because of my difference. I believed him, mostly. My own father had been so scared of me since puberty that he said nothing on the subject other than, "What's dirty about sex?" and, "I know it is fun to have breakfast together, but that doesn't mean you should marry him."

But I did marry my first lover. My mother and grandmother won out in my early training. Then again, I was only nineteen. Pregnant at twenty-one. Divorced at twenty-three.

Act 1

Childhood

On the Existence of Witches

Of course there were witches. One lived with us, for starters, though just in summer.

Nanya had traveled with my father's family from Russia, her own three grown daughters left behind. Basically, she was a serf so far as I could analyze it later. There is no question that she saved my father's life, carrying him in a basket on the journey fleeing from St. Petersburg across the frozen river Neva and on to Finland. Once there, some men armed with a pistol came to take away my grandfather, Nicolai. Nanya flew down the steps in a rage, flapping her apron at the intruders and shouting, "You shall **not** kill the master!" And, wondrously, they left.

Nanya taught me to talk to God volubly, with her fist raised toward heaven, and to be afraid, terribly afraid, of cupboards and closets where demons and devils lurked. The pairing of a spirited and already anxious three-year-old with this virago was not a happy one, though the arrangement enabled my mother to go back to work full time when I turned three. If I did not behave, Nanya would warn, the demons would come out and get me! She had been the nanny to my father and for his next oldest sibling.

Even as an adult, I could trace some similarities in all of our world views, stemming no doubt from Nanya's tender care. We were all three of us more anxious than the other "siblings," were broader in our enjoyment of life, and controlling enough to create problems over the generations with our own kids.

At age eighty-four, that last summer, she had trouble making it up the stairs to the bathroom in time. "Poor soul," was my mother's attitude, and a downstairs bathroom was installed well before either of my parents reached eighty.

My paternal grandmother had seven children, one of whom did not survive childhood. Employing a nanny as soon as they could afford it was entirely logical. My own father assumed responsibility for her care in her last years, ultimately placing her in a Russian Orthodox monastery in Upstate New York.

The Country House

My father often told of putting five dollars into an envelope every day to save toward buying a place in the country. He found an old farmhouse sixty miles from NYC when I was about two, and we would go there every weekend, we kids traveling in pajamas on Friday nights until we got too big to carry in. We returned on Sunday nights, except after we started Sunday school, when we returned on Saturday nights.

Why was the country house so important in creating memories and security for me? It was a real house, like the ones I read about in books, with a staircase to the upstairs. My mother worked largely inside the house preparing meals and crying over having to do the dishes, and my father worked outdoors cutting the grass and planting trees. I knew where my parents were on the weekends, and I could find them.

My room had a child's-size wardrobe bought at some country auction and painted white by my mother. The wallpaper had a repeating motif of Dutch children in Dutch costumes: skirts and caps for the girls, and trousers and clogs for the boys. Long after the walls were redone, one figure of each gender remained glued decoratively to the doors of the wardrobe.

Home is a place that has the right feel.

The Battle for Control

I was sitting in a mud puddle, filthy from bottom to top, patting the muddy water, sliding my palms around in it. Smearing. This is what infantile anger looks like. It smears. I had been given a present of a plastic toy to play with in the mud. With a little spade for the hand, I filled the top with mud. Then, by pushing a sort of plunger, a perfect shuddering "brick" was extruded. I really liked this toy, but I never saw it again after that day. It must have been discarded after the epic mud session. Yes, the smearing session did follow some battle over toilet training. For a pediatrician, my mother, *olev-hashalom* (may she rest in peace), took a lot of risks with my well-being in service of "treating" me. I stole the infant enema syringe out of the medicine cabinet in the country house years ago, long after my mother's death. I could scarcely believe it still existed, a sort of existential threat even years after her death.

Leah

Leah was our housekeeper when I was between three- and eight-years old years old before we moved upstairs to a bigger apartment on the tenth floor. I don't remember much about the fifth-floor apartment besides Leah. My parents slept at night in the living room on a foldout bed, leaving the two bedrooms for us kids, my two brothers in one of them, and I all by myself in the other, smaller bedroom. During the day, all trace of my parents literally disappeared while they were away at work.

The heart of the home was definitely the kitchen, where Leah spent most of her time and me with her, before and after school days. She was a cheerful soul, industrious and polite to adults, warm with children. I must have been a trial to her. She had some difficult times with me, and I was not always nice to her. The adjective she used when I played some trick on her was to call me "nasty." Like a young character from a Dickens story, it was painful for me to be parted from her forever at age eight. I knew my mother was jealous of the bond and hid my longing for Leah, which resurfaced when I was fifteen. "I want Leah," I finally said. I wanted so much to see her again. It was arranged that she would be hired to "serve" at one of our large dinner parties, and I could go to the kitchen to greet her. She asked me anxiously, "You OK, baby? I heard what they done to you." And I was comforted that she knew and that I was still someone's "baby."

The "maids" of the era were tasked with supervising whatever was dumped on them: visiting cousins, schoolmates of divorced parents, squabbling siblings. I loved her warmth, and her welcoming lap defined safety for me. Hers was the first face I sculpted, quite unintentionally, the curves of her cheeks defining peace.

When I was eight, and the boys were eleven and thirteen, she gave notice. Her husband wanted his wife to be home to make his dinner instead of ours. For five years, she had stayed with us all day to do the housework and cook dinner as well. In addition, a second woman was employed to do the household laundry for our family of five. This was done in the basement in huge machines and hung on racks pushed in alongside a vertical, raging gas fire. The clothes then reappeared upstairs, dry and folded. Sorting three sets of boys' and men's socks fell to my mother, who would sit on her bed in a great pile of unmatched socks, cursing. As the socks wore and developed holes in the toes and heels, she put them aside.

She acquired from some woman's magazine the basic knowledge of how to make a braided rug out of loops of cut-up socks. Each loop looked like a slice of leek. She worked on that craft for a long time and did produce a rug, though she judged it to be not what she had in mind, was not proud of the finished work, and gave it away.

Anyway, Leah would take me to the park in the afternoons and sit on benches with many other housekeepers dressed in their gray uniforms with white collars and wearing sensible shoes. How they would cackle and laugh about "their" families and the things "their" children said! This embarrassed me no end, and after age eight, I both rode public buses to school and went around in Central Park with friends, but unaccompanied by adults.

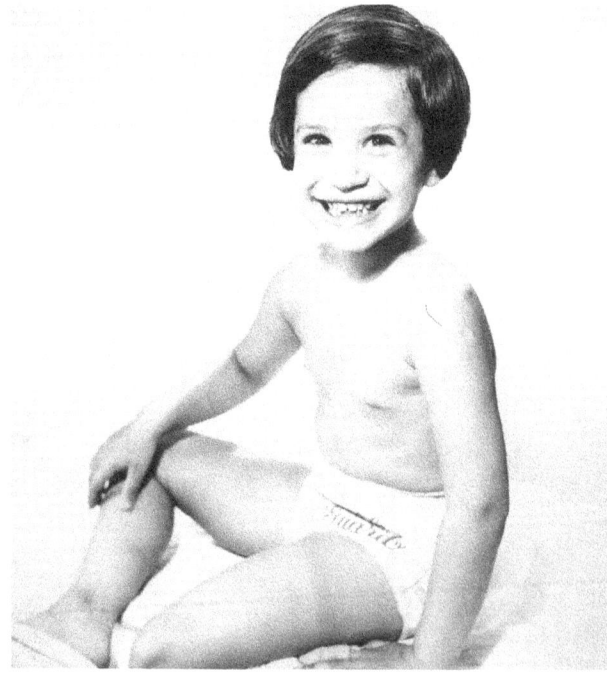

Pink Party Dress

If I wear men's clothes, then I have their power. I learned helplessness as a little girl with dresses that zipped or buttoned up the back. One could not dress or undress by oneself. The terrible defenselessness of this feeling remained.

When I was first photographed at my easel, age two or thereabouts, I was wearing one of my father's white shirts turned backward and buttoned onto me as an all-encompassing smock.

"If you want to tell stories, why don't you just write?" was the opinion of one of my art school friends. So here is a story:

The pink party dress was laid out invitingly on the bedspread. I was meant to get excited about putting it on for the children's photographer. He was hired to get portraits of all three of us at three, six, and eight years old.

Unfortunately, I would not cooperate. I understood that this picture was to capture an enduring image of me, and I was damned if it was going to be in frilly pink. Objectively, the dress was pretty, but I had another plan. I felt the most myself in a bathing suit, and not a girl's suit either. My briefs bore the word "guard," short for lifeguard, and I assumed several muscle man poses, flexing my tiny biceps with arms overhead and feet planted widely apart. The photographer was suffocating his snickers as my mother pleaded with me to put on the dress. I prevailed and was duly photographed for posterity in my lifeguard briefs and a big smile.

The Creators

I planted strawberries with my father on the site of the old chicken coop. The earth was somewhat claylike there. He pinched a bit of it into the shape of some mythical animal, pulling down each of four legs. My father made me something, a first gift of sculpting, of sculpture itself.

I don't think we saved these animals, rather making them anew each year when we worked the strawberry patch. Still, he made something tangible and gave it to the generally insignificant me as a gift. I was fascinated that he could do something clever with his hands, with his actual fingers. He could draw, too, though I only remember him doing so a couple of times. He could change the numbers one through five into shapes and figures: a swan from a two, a sailboat from a four. What a painless way to learn the numbers! And he could draw a daisy, which it turns out is a Yiddish illustration classic, and which he might have learned at school.

I found an illustration of "his" daisy in a Yiddish-English textbook printed in 1919 in the Jewish section of the Leeds Public Library. The daisy was exactly the same as his daisies, with the center on top and the petals coming out the sides—represented in deep space.

When I was about thirteen, one of my father's grateful patients volunteered to make a portrait of me, and I spent some number of afternoons at his studio having my portrait made in clay. The chaperones were a small fleet of assistants at their desks crafting fine jewelry and gold (clearly the sculptor's side, or most likely main, gig.) I learned that the process of serving as the model for sculpting was a process of being looked at lovingly for a very long time.

I still have the finished terracotta head of myself at fourteen. My father must have valued it because he hand-carried it on the plane on his last visit to me in Seattle. The sculptor's name was Louis Feron, and he left quite a legacy in the field of design, especially sacred objects. An interesting fun fact is that at the age of sixty-one, he married a young dancer later in the same year that he sculpted me.

Scandinavian-Type Bedtime Stories From My Father

A man from China, a fireman, and a Turk, along with a policeman, a sailor, a swordsman, and a swell guy with a top hat and tuxedo (with tails) all lived together peacefully under a bench in Central Park. They were only just so tall, like "brownies" in other cultures. The one with the top hat, "Moursielka" he was called, was mine. I had only to pass by the bench, and he would climb into my shirt pocket in order to accompany me on my adventures. He could also find his way, as needed, on his own, all the way to our apartment. If I had a very first dentist appointment, for example, Moursielka would have just gone the day before. He would describe the chair, the lights, the smells, and having to open his mouth wide. He made scary things seem simple. He was always available if I just imagined having him with me in my pocket, just over my heart. He was wise, and handsome, and young, despite the monocle he sported over one eye. He was my childhood hero and mentor: male, a century out of date, and dapper besides. Perhaps he was my father, who was known to have put on a dinner jacket in order to crash First Class on the ocean liner that brought him to America. Anyway, I think I got my heart from him. Moursielka is always with me, and I am happiest in a shirt with pockets.

A poem I wrote for my father in the late 1960s
Moursielka and the Turk in the shadows,
build them a bench to live under.
Wear pockets for them to travel in.
Moursielka, are you still in my pocket?
You have never left?
And the rent ticket of your tuxedo?
The Turk has disposed of it.
Mousielka, I have never seen your face.
I never thought of it, only of you small and strong.
Have you been there always?

Moursielka, each blossom is a bouquet for your bride,
Whom you will always marry.
The berries will make wine for your name days,
Pies for your company suppers.
Moursielka, when the great Yugoslav with
Potent yellow nose drop laughs,
Do not hide in the shadow of the peppermill.
A sneeze here or there when he grinds it
and he will catch you in his apron. It has pockets.
But in them are greater sneezes and huge laughs.
Moursielka, the chestnut tree spreads heavy.
Do not be under when the green nuts fall,
And do not stain your fingers with them.
Moursielka, could I see you in the old movies,
Caught like all the ancient smoke, halters, bosoms.
Now all hidden.
Moursielka, I would not give you wholly to my children.
The Turk, the Brownie, let them go to the dentist.
You live under the bench. I will come to you.
Moursielka, I never had long hair for you,
But I had the other knee, a larger,
No I suppose, still a smaller lap.
Moursielka, the rain drops make it difficult
To write. Ah, I write differently.
Mousielka, I am still the same, please stay.
Say you will live in my breast pocket.
Ah, but I have breasts now.

I Take the Elevator By Myself (Part 1)

My class went on a field trip and left me in the bathroom. I knew it was too quiet in the hall when I exited the bathroom, but I had not imagined the class would leave the floor altogether. I knew the short route to the large elevator and pushed the call button. When the doors opened, the space was full of towering adults. We were on floor five of Hunter College, where its elementary school was located. The principal's office occupied floor two, and the playground was on the roof. I knew I needed the principal's office, and I must have remembered from the school tour that I needed to go to floor two to find it. They were very surprised to see me there. I was complimented over and over again for my presence of mind in getting myself to where I needed to go and for taking the elevator all by myself. We all had elevators at home, so that part was not hard. It was an elevator filled with tall adults that almost stopped me. I was only five or six.

The Lamb

"Seek in suffering its meaning for your spiritual growth, and the bitterness will be removed from it." (Grandfather) Nicholas Goldberg-Rudkovsky from his Ethical Will, 1928.

My earliest strong memory of religious school and the family was the lamb I made in arts and crafts, perhaps age four. It was a beautiful lamb made of wooden spools and cotton, and the teacher had praised it highly. I had made it. I was a good maker. We went out to lunch—my parents, brothers, maternal grandparents—to a fancy restaurant after Sunday School. The lamb was left behind when we put on our coats to go home. Halfway there, I started to cry and then scream for my creation. No amount of pacification —especially the kind I got: "You'll make another, "it was just old thread spools"—helped at all. I was so upset we did walk back to the restaurant, and my mother, who was not timid, asked very timidly if the maitre d' could look for it. Impossible. All cleaned up. Garbage. Icy silence.

I never forgot.

But I have just now put two and two together about the small plaster lamb I gave my grandmother when I was six—a birthday of hers I had not been prepared for. Leaving for her party, I insisted I could not go without a present and gave her my toy. It reappeared quietly on my knickknack shelf, after her death, when I was nine. I cried and then screamed again. I had meant for her to have it always.

Early Birthday Parties (Joan)

My birthday parties as a child featured silliness, balloons, and an ice cream cake packed in dry ice from Grossinger's Bakery. They also featured party games that seemed designed for teaching survival skills, especially to observe and remember. My mother placed ten unrelated objects on a tray, which was covered by a cloth. We kids were each furnished with pencil and paper, but not for notetaking. This was a timed test. At a signal, the cloth was removed, and we were to observe the tray in silence. After thirty or maybe sixty seconds, the cloth was spread over it and the tray removed while we wrote down what we remembered. After three or four years of this annual game, I could accurately remember ten unrelated objects (thimble, eraser, etc.) Another table game was to identify and differentiate among fragrances: vinegar, ketchup, perfume, vanilla, beer. A tray with small amounts in opaque containers was passed around while we were blindfolded. Those children who could identify whisky were noted privately as to which child probably had an alcoholic parent.

Memorization as a discrete skill was not taught in American schools by the 1950s. In the '70s, when my older son created a comprehensive chart of superheroes and each of their powers, my mother's response to his homework was "such a pity, he could have learned all the kings of France."

Observing people was an acceptable way of passing the time, although my mother and I would come to different conclusions. Spotting a heavily pregnant young woman, for example, my mother would exclaim, "but she could not be more than sixteen!" Meanwhile, what I noticed was the diamond pattern of her dress stretched over the globe of her belly and revealing its exact shape. Years later, I saw an ancient Egyptian sculpture in a museum where the swelling forms of a woman were incised with a similar surface pattern.

The Arts and Crafts Man

For years, in good weather, he would sit, centered on a park bench, in the same general area each time, his paper shopping bags perched as sentinels both beside him and at his feet. The children could not get too close to him even if they wanted to. We did not know his name. "Hey, Mister!" was probably the closest we got.

Still, we swarmed him to watch his amazing hands at work or to beg for art supplies. He recognized no one who did not speak nicely, politely to him, and more importantly, we each had to promise to finish the art project. If we were not dedicated to this work, then godlike, he would withdraw his help and give no more instructions or supplies.

What wonders he himself could make out of nothing! The most impressive one, for sheer drama, was a palm tree made out of rolled newspaper, then slashed this way and that with scissors, and unfurled. It was deemed too complicated for us children, and moreover, it required his scissors. We young children were sent to gather discarded popsicle sticks, seven of them to be exact. For some of us, this meant buying popsicles so as to have at least two beautiful, clean, freshly licked sticks.

The arts and crafts man would briefly caress a stick or two we brought him to demonstrate with, and, quite suddenly, he would weave the ends of six of them into a sturdy Star of David with the seventh stick woven in to hold it with. Proudly we showed these to our black nursemaids or our white mothers. "Ugh! Dirty! Where did you pick up so many? From the ground? Phui!"

With every star completed, though, there was a smile from the man. Jewish children lived! (in New York, maybe, but were alive!) His own accent was thick, indistinguishable to me from the many European accents I was surrounded by in New York in that era. He was undoubtedly a refugee, a survivor of some sort.

One wintry day as it was growing dark, my mother approached the man.

"I see you're not well," she said in her best doctor voice. "We will walk with you."

He protested mildly and would accept no help with his shopping bags. But he let us accompany him. He was clearly short of breath. We all walked slowly out of the park toward Central Park South. There, he turned for the tall, fancy Essex House building, tipped his hat to my mother, and went inside.

We never ever saw him again in the park. My mother thought he had probably died. Apparently, he had the appearance of someone with advanced heart disease. He was heavy, he was old, he was unutterably sad except in summer, when he sent us to fetch seven popsicle sticks for the stars. He dressed well, all in grays: a gray fedora, a gray overcoat, a gray suit. It is possible his shirt was white and his shoes black. He appeared to be a gentleman, dignified in dress, like an uncle or an accountant or something.

"I'll be damned," my mother kept saying. "I just knew it!"

"Knew what, Mommy?" I wanted to know.

"That he was probably very rich," she said. "Only the very rich can be so eccentric, so I wanted to see where he lived."

Passovers Past

At the time, the goal was to see if Aunt Helen would drink enough wine to sing opera. It was wondrous to me as a little girl that such a powerful sound could burst out of the equally short woman across the table from me.

By contrast, at the Passover table on my mother's side, the children were segregated to a card table at the far end, relegated to "the children's table" until each reached the age of predictable behavior. There was one year when we cousins all agreed on what to demand as a ransom or gift when any one of us would find the Afikomen. This is a ritual half piece of unleavened bread (matzoh), folded into a napkin and hidden away until the end of the meal and prayer service in order to keep the children's attention on the events. My rather formal grandfather was a bit unbent with the good humor called for by the situation. He was prepared to offer us whatever treat (chocolates?) (rolls of brightly colored Life Savers?) we asked for. When we demanded that we go to Chinatown NOW, he was both surprised and offended. We had just celebrated our own history and culture, and now so eager to see and eat from another? He said: "No." We said: "You promised anything we wanted!"

The compromise reached was that we would go to Chinatown another time, and we did. (I hated fried rice and all the dead animals hanging in the shop windows.) We did receive some treat that Passover night, but I don't remember it, just the feeling of solidarity amongst my big brothers, cousins, and me. We were a force to be reckoned with.

I Prayed for Wisdom

When I was about seven, the question of wisdom came up. It was part of a Sunday school lesson about "riches," of all things.

The question was posed whether it would be better to be rich or to be wise (the two together was not one of the choices). Aspects of wisdom were discussed, and the story invoked of King Solomon awarding the baby to the more compassionate mother. I don't remember the examples for riches, but it was a left-leaning, labor-oriented school, so rich people were probably painted as filthy capitalists.

Should I pray for wisdom or riches ("If prayer really works, if there really is a God?" I asked myself at age seven.) Anyway, having silently chosen one or the other, we were given a brief period to pray for it. For our whole lives. And I chose wisdom, the thought having come clearly and immediately. Wisdom, of course, because with wisdom, one could always get riches or a living anyway. And riches alone, I knew, did not lead to wisdom.

Prize for Drawing

I won a prize for drawing when I was seven. There was a children's art competition at a community center near Vails Gate, and I wanted to enter it. My parents were upset and downplayed it. My father wanted to know what the curves and squiggles I had drawn "meant." Answering their questions "why" I had done this or that, I responded, "Because I felt like it." Such freedom. Heady freedom. It was typical of my style at the time: interconnected balloons, like talking in a comic strip, and in each balloon another feeling. The feelings were represented by colored stripes: yellow, maroon, pink, purple, blue. One balloon I turned into a Mickey Mouse face and another, a yellow one, contained a Jewish star. My mother did frame it, and it hung at the country house for many years.

The judges' comment was that it was "original."

White Linen (Part 1)

White Linen is the name of my favorite Estee Lauder perfume, but the sentence fragment has many more layers of early meaning to me. I was taken to the Museum of Natural History in New York City very frequently at very young ages while my grandparents still lived in an apartment with a doorman and a canopy literally just across the street. My brothers were three and five years older, so large, hanging whales suspended from the ceiling and long-dead mummies held no particular terrors for them. For me, on the other hand, the mere idea that the wrapped still figures were actually dead bodies was simply impossible to bear. I did appreciate some doll-like ancient figures polling wooden boats while wearing short linen skirts.

More Than White Linen (Part 2)

In the 1950s, my mother stockpiled canned milk before a threatened strike of milk deliveries in NYC in that year. "My children are going to have milk!" she said emphatically. She said the same thing when the issue of milk with meat meals came up. I probably owe my strong bones to those pudding- and cheese-based dishes; potatoes au gratin, rice pudding, "gogol mogul" (hot milk poured into egg yolk beaten with sugar until light in color), and of course, "camel's milk" (watered evaporated milk), a drink that would always bring comfort.

I was bottle fed on evaporated milk after I stopped growing on breast milk alone. I was the third child, and an unplanned one at that. At least I was a girl, after two boys. The planned brother was the only one with a really secure bond to both parents, and he was named after someone who died in France, a boy named Pierre who was a soldier in WWII, and had been an eighteen-year-old private student of my father's.

Waste was another great generational subject. In honor of her parents, my mother never threw out string, nor the peculiar wood and wire handles that could be affixed to a parcel wrapped with string. Perhaps every household has a "junk drawer," but I loved ours for the stories that came out of it—of war and shortages, of flight, and resettlement.

There was bread pudding, too, not just rice. My mother, like her father before her, could not throw out bread. "I have seen men willing to kill for a crust of bread," he was reported to have said.

The braided rug made out of old socks was a combination of European shortages and pioneer sentiments. A great reader of women's magazines, my mother hated to waste fabric too. With three sources of worn-out boys and men's socks, she would cut the tubes into circles, braid and then coil the resulting strands. She actually completed one braided rug before moving on to some other handicraft.

I was very impressed with that rug project and with the new French curses I learned while she made it.

White Linen Three (Part 3) Why carry all those tablecloths?

My mother's mother must have brought some of those tablecloths from France, perhaps even from Russia. I have a linen apron, too, with crochetwork joining the front panels which is almost certainly from Russia.

The obvious use for white tablecloths is to put them on the table, especially for holidays. I am reasonably certain, however, that they held a deeper (atavistic) meaning.

When my mother was in medical school in Paris, she was quite fascinated with the culture of ancient Egypt. There might have been an exhibit showing at that time, but I do know she wrote at least one of her medical school senior theses on "Pregnancy Tests in Ancient Egypt." This involved the interaction of urine and barley, as I recall. The reason my mother wrote many theses instead of just one was that the male students had either joined the army, been drafted, or dropped out of sight into the Resistance. By finishing the coursework of their absent friends, the ladies were making it possible for everyone to graduate on time. She left Paris with her family for the south only one week ahead of the fall of Paris in June 1940. They eventually reached Marseilles and from there, after several months, obtained passage to New York. It was my father's family who sponsored their entry into America.

Whoever she left behind in France, my mother married my father within a couple of months. She wore a navy-blue suit as befitted a lady doctor. Among her possessions were a length of navy-blue linen and also one of white linen. They carried very little on the flight from Paris. So what was the deal with the linen?

"I thought I might need it to make clothes," she said when she passed the fabric on to me. This white linen, to me, was always a winding sheet fabric for our shrouds. Like the Shroud of Turin, which may be over 2,000 years old and may be only 800 years old, I too had noticed that Egyptian tomb figurines were still dressed in their little linen loincloths after 3,000 years. Linen lasts. Traditional Jews bury the dead in linen shrouds. I think the tablecloths were to ensure a decent burial, even in a foreign land. And, indeed, the only communal purchase I know of made by the Society of The Fellows of Odessa is a good-sized Jewish cemetery parcel in New Jersey, where there is room even for my generation.

To Entrust a Child with Fire

To entrust a child with a match, with lighting fire, is no small thing. Her sense of her own power increases with every candle lit until she believes she can create light. Creating light is the basis for creation, for a creative life, for love, for children.

Among some of my old art books, I found a folded length of gold foil paper. In my childhood, such paper was used for making the "flames" above the paper Hanukkah menorah Scotch-taped to the dining room mirror.

As an adult, far from home, from parents, from firstborn child, I was still saving gold paper to make flames, to make light, in my new home and for my second child (son). Some years later, I was hospitalized with a broken hip over the start of Hanukkah, during his senior year of high school, and he brought paper flames to me, Scotch-taped to an actual, silver-plated menorah with short, pretend, paper candles as well. I cried over the sweetness of this gesture: to kindle flames, to keep the fire, even in the darkest night of pain.

Carousel of Days

While both grandmothers were alive, I was always freshly washed, dressed, and combed to see them. My mother's mother took me shopping for a pink (naturally) party dress for my oldest brother's Bar Mitzvah. It was a dream dress for me. Pink organza, very delicate and floaty.

It had a flattering collar, as I was getting chubby, and a long organza sash. When she asked the price, my grandmother heard the saleswoman say "fifteen."

"Alright," she said, hesitating a little.

Then the saleswoman corrected her that it was "fifty."

"Fifty!" my grandmother repeated, fingering the clasp on her purse. Turning to me, my grandmother shook her finger and intoned, "You will not tell your mother." And I didn't.

Grandma Weinberg sometimes visited Grossingers' Bakery on Sunday afternoons, often with us in tow, to buy cakes and cookies for teatime with her.

Besides the cakes, I was struck by how Mrs. Grossinger and Mrs. Weinberg greeted each other formally as well as affectionately as "Mrs." It was Europe in New York. And we grandchildren were introduced and admired, and our growth duly noted. This made me feel known, and somehow safe. The thing I most remember was the ritual exchange of family news: "how is the family?" and "how are the grandchildren?" and even more so, the nut cake, the babka, the black and white cookies, thumbprints, and the bakery boxes tied with red and white striped string. I still have a piece of that string in my miscellaneous drawer.

Another treat was to walk to the carousel in Central Park. There too, I was aware of my junior status as I was placed first on the static "carriage" seat, eventually allowed a standing horse, and finally, bliss, a horse that went up and down on its pole, as well as round and round with the carousel. What was it like for my maternal grandparents to see three grandchildren (or sometimes all five of us on my mother's side) going round on gaily painted horses? Alive and well and noisy. It must have been like Paris had never fallen.

After an adulthood of assimilation in France ("to live like God in France" is an actual Yiddish proverb), my grandparents reverted to being much more religiously observant in the United States, both at home and in the Orthodox synagogue where my grandfather prayed. He took my cousin and me there, separately, when we were younger—less than nine years old—to see a service when we would still be permitted as little girls standing in the men's section. I remember that the velvet of the Torah cover and the Ark curtains was red, the color of blood. Our own Reform synagogue had royal blue velvet everywhere, but I have a belief now, based on the bedspreads used for times of childbirth that I saw displayed at the Jewish Museum, that red velvet served a purpose in joining the idea of passion to piety. The field of pious red was spread out perhaps so as not to be afraid of blood, and also somehow to dissociate red from a Victorian style (of red velvet décor in a bordello).

Entertaining at home, in any of our households and at the country house too, involved as big a table as possible. All of my grandmother's dishes and silver came in sets of twelve, and for Passover we were sometimes more than that. Having a big table in the country meant lots of extra work for my mother, carrying dishes out from the kitchen. My father would sit at the head of the table, expansive and amused by everything. If their friend Jules was among the guests, he would play his mandolin and I admired the live music being played informally and out of doors. Jules and his wife, Rosette, pals from medical school, never had children of their own. But after their deaths, it was discovered that they had sponsored any number of orphans to come to the United States and had paid for their educations. I learned to play the mandolin as an adult in their honor.

But when I was about seven, one time when there were at least five of us kids there at the country house; I got fed up with no one paying attention to little old me.

"You'll be sorry when I am gone", I often thought to myself.

I was the youngest of ten cousins, and as such was often in the way, or not allowed to play. There is a heart-wrenching home movie that shows a game where four to five cousins would run away from me, laughing. I would then chase them, falling behind on my little, short legs. Then they would turn and move toward me and, as I stopped crying and began to smile, they would run past me again, fast, so I could not possibly catch up. Four of them are deceased now. The oldest and the boldest. Little old me is still here.

I was a fan of the comic book character Little Itch, an intrepid soul, a young witch in training. Who knows where I got the idea to run away? I put some things in a kerchief, tied it on the end of a big stick, and left home. I was going down the road to see the elderly farmer who sold us our corn in summer. He would want me. He lived alone in a one-room house with a wood burning stove. And I was sure he could use a little company. I had previously been inside with my father who periodically took Old Man Wester's blood pressure and listened to his heart with a stethoscope (I am pretty sure he lived well into his nineties).

Anyway, the more I thought about it, the better of an idea it seemed. Just two of us and his cat. Of course, the cousins told on me and my mother came running down the road to catch me. I had not gotten very far yet, and his place was only about a quarter of a mile away. Tearfully, I let her walk me home, but I made sure I got her ear about feeling left out. It was hard to be the youngest. Perhaps my resolve to strike out on my own brought me eventually to the West Coast, but at the time it resulted in ever more indoor board games in which I could be included as a player.

In my room in the city apartment, I had a desk of my own. Apparently, I had a high tolerance for being confined, as long as I had something to do. My first desk was covered with a layer of "contact paper" so I could paint and do projects, which made a mess. Also, when I was sick with a cold or fever, a bedside table would be rolled over/under so I could have a surface to work on. I often got new craft kits when I was sick, which might have been the wrong message. I liked new crafts. I suppose I was easier to deal with when I was sick if I was busy.

When well, ice skating at the rink in Central Park was a favorite activity. The perfect knitted snowflakes on my sweater were crafted by my mother, but I perfected a "spiral," which is a figure-skating pose standing on one leg and raising the other behind me, with arms outstretched, leaning forward, in perfect form. I was flying.

In the city, outdoor games had city themes. People usually don't believe me when I tell them how one of my friends and I had a game called "Run from the Exhibitionist." There were always several of them in Central Park, behind trees near 83rd Street. The game was to run along the path until someone flashed us, then run back to the "home base" tree and slap it. I don't think we told anyone else about this. After a few times, though, it turned into a boring game. We were ten.

The public buses held another even more unpleasant kind of man, "frotteurs," who would rub up against you or try to touch you through your clothes. I asked what I was supposed to do about this and my mother advised stomping on their feet. In my opinion, little girls should not have to ride on crowded public transportation until all men are handcuffed to the rails.

I was also wised up to addiction by panhandlers begging for handouts. I always felt sorry for them and would have been an easy touch but for the warning I did receive that these desperate people were probably heroin addicts.

The park, across Central Park West from our apartment, was an endless source of exercise and entertainment. I customarily climbed over the stone wall to get into the park, much more interesting than the official entrance a couple of blocks down. There were some huge formations of original Manhattan bedrock, at that time largely free of garbage and broken glass. We climbed them, sure footed like little goats in our rubber soled Keds. Then the joy was to slide down the sections forming natural slides and feel the contour of the rocks directly through our bottoms. In the country too, a neighbor had a shed whose roof we were permitted to climb on and then slide down, recreating some of the thrill of the park with the additional danger of falling right off the edge. I lobbied unsuccessfully for a pair of leather pants (lederhosen) when we passed through Switzerland the summer I was ten. It would have saved a lot of the cloth pants which wore through while sliding on shingles or bedrock.

There were also the greater-than-life size bronze sculptures in Central Park that children were allowed to climb around on. One was of Hans Christian Andersen with his inviting lap and giant bronze book. The other sculpture was of Alice in Wonderland, and that one was more difficult to ascend. My friend got her period for the first time while climbing Alice and suffered greatly from embarrassment that nothing should show. I helped her tie her sweater over her rear end and walked behind her all the way home to ensure that no one could look at her from the back. I think that was the last time we climbed on Alice.

By the time we were fourteen we could no longer run in the park. This was before Title IX, and a policeman would stop us to say that "young ladies do not run," and to go home before we got into trouble. I suppose it was all our young breasts that bothered the policemen. Running is healthy!

On the weekends in the country, I could usually count on resting in the fabric hammock strung up near the garage near the orange tiger lilies. We read a lot of comic books (I liked Little LuLu, as well as Little Itch) and also made raids on the local library. I particularly enjoyed biographies, real or imaginary, usually of men, as well as the exploits of Cherry Ames, Nurse (more than Nancy Drew, Girl Detective). Some of our neighbor friends were forbidden to read comic books and would join us sitting low in the hammock to read them on the sly.

We had a swing set, too, with a ladder and sort of trapeze on it as well. Later, after we grew up, my father put in a modest swimming pool, professionally done, not just a muddy hole. The pool was meant to attract guests and most importantly grandchildren. My most vivid memory, though, is of another of my friends arriving hot and sweaty from the city. She stripped off her pants, shook hands, and murmured "bonjour" to one of our female guests while already half naked, and then ran shrieking to the pool while peeling off her shirt and bra. As she jumped in, the adults all excused her behavior as unavoidable.

Another feature of attending junior high and high school at 68th and Lexington Avenue was the proximity to museums, especially the Metropolitan Museum on Fifth Avenue. In eighth and ninth grade, a couple of us literally hung out at this museum, free at the time. I made many stone friends, especially among the Etruscans and the Greeks, the curvaceous Italian sculptures and some of the French ones. We humans sat quietly with paintings too, as they tended to have benches before them. Warm and dry, we exchanged confidences during the short winter afternoons.

The Passover Nut Cake

One of my friends was really interested in horses when we were about eight or nine years old. I was invited to go riding with her in the ring at the old Central Park stables, off Central Park West, where I lived. While I liked the idea of riding horses, I was not nearly as good at it as she, nor did it mean anything special to me. And my mother really disliked the smells of horse and stable, so it meant a bath, a complete change of clothes, and more laundry for the household.

Anyway, I was to eat lunch at my friend's house after riding and maybe stay for supper too. Presented with a peanut butter sandwich on whole-wheat bread, I picked it up and then put it down.

"It is Passover," I said, "and I cannot eat bread."

"You are keeping the Passover," gaped Mrs. G., "but isn't your mother a doctor? Wait, I will telephone her."

After a mommies' call full of bonhomie and even some giggling, I demanded to know what my mother had said. I was told that she said they had been sending me to Sunday School and that I had picked up all sorts of ideas. Mrs. G. promptly invited me to supper and was enthused about how she was going to make us a Passover sponge nut cake, something she had not even thought about for many years.

Humming, happy, with more affect than I had ever seen on her, she cracked seemingly endless eggs, seven or eight, I think, to add to the freshly ground nuts and sugar. This cake obviously brought her deep satisfaction and a connection with happy memories from before WWII and her safe arrival to New York to start a new family.

As an adult, I used a family photograph to paint a mural of post-WW II children dressed in Purim costumes. This was to illustrate a war time song (Moments of Hope or Minutn fun Bitokhn) by Mordechai Gebirtig. My birthday parties had become annual costume parties for many years when I was a child, as Purim was always close to my actual birthday.

My friend never got over preferring horses to people. You can see her here on the left, holding on to my cat for dear life. (I am on the far right.)

Uncle by Marriage

I put the metal jacks in the freezer until they were nice and cold. I had time to collect my rubbery, slimy, fake night crawlers from my expedition to town. No one had remarked on their purchase in place of my usual bag of cat's eye marbles.

Then I short-sheeted his bed. I learned how to do that at summer camp when I was nine or ten years old. To short sheet a bed, fold the top sheet back upon itself and tuck it in so when sliding into bed, one gets stuck halfway. Then I arranged the worms and icy jacks in his bed and went to my own bedtime well satisfied with my plan.

The scream, the shouts, and the fury in French awakened me from a calm sleep, and in the morning, I had to face my mother's deceptively calm questioning. Had I done this? Had he done something? Why was I so angry at this uncle (from my aunt's marriage)? Eventually, I blurted out that he would take my visiting pal up onto his lap while he looked at his magazine with nude pictures, and he would pat and tickle her, and she would squeal. I didn't like it. I didn't like him. He was subsequently banned from weekends at the country house.

When he had first come to America, and his English was even worse, he had been sent to the store to buy toilet paper. Since he would not say the word toilet and could not pronounce the word paper, he came back with a shaker of pepper. The family assumed from then on that he was a fairly useless individual.

To Throw Like a Girl

Is there really something about a girl's elbow that makes it impossible to throw a baseball? I was constantly taunted by my brothers that the reason I could not throw anything but a slow and wobbly ball was that I was a girl.

Now I think it was all bunk, just a reason to keep me in my place: frustrated, helpless, weak. I showed them, though, what the power of persistence is. I could pogo-stick longer until the skin was abraded off my soft hands. I could bounce a ball and turn my leg over it for endless songs and rhymes. And I will likely outlive them both, the harassers of my youth, the boys.

Years later, when I threw a screwdriver at the wall hard enough to make a nice hole in the sheetrock, I decided that I now could throw. I only did something like that once, and there was a reason. I would have to leave my beautiful Portland studio in order to move to Seattle (to marry Joe).

Fencing Badge

My brothers were rivals for attention, for achieving (parental) goals, for charm in addition to attractiveness. As for me, crying and whining are the privileges of the youngest child, always the baby.

Somewhere along the line, fencing equipment was purchased for the "boys." Possibly in France. Uncommon then in the States, the kit included masks that looked like rodent cages, the padded vests with Nehru collars and long sleeves, padded gloves, and the foils themselves. The idea was to regularize their fights and aggression. But, like other aggressions, I don't remember the sport taking. Just as with the Bar Mitzvah books on Jewish philosophy, the piano lessons, the puppetry sessions, and interest in tools in general, it fell to me to inherit the equipment and to master the craft.

At the time, I was a Girl Scout in a troop managed by a lady who was an avid amateur fencer. In a pique of boredom with the standard scouting badges for cooking, camp craft, etc., we took a vote and decided to create a fencing achievement badge with embroidered patches to match and go on our sashes. These sashes, reminiscent of those worn by Queen Victoria, with royal insignia, were worn over our uniforms and allowed a rapid calculation and evaluation of another's worth, at least as measured in merit badges. I held four, and fencing was the fifth.

Our scout meetings came to be dominated by our fencing sessions. Foils, doublets, and masks were shared and lent to those who did not have their own. A weekly participant in movement classes and dance, with the redoubtable Mrs. Kohlberg of the Upper West Side, and a frequent bicyclist, I had the thighs and quadriceps to match. I loved advancing right foot forward, right arm extended, and allowed to simply charge at my opponent to see if she would cower and retreat.

This was tremendous training for learning the game of Manhattan aggressiveness, and I was good. Once engaged with the opponent, came that dance: the feint, the blow striking inside her foil and lunging for a touch of the foil on the official quadrant of her padded jacket. There was only one girl who could beat me, and that only sometimes. I was the acknowledged best fencer of the scouting group. And fencing taught me to go for the kill.

Androgyny, or Why I Wanted to be Santa Claus

In elementary school, the annual holiday show put on for parents and relatives always closed with the appearance of Santa Claus, just like the Macy's Thanksgiving Day Parade in New York. My oldest and fatter brother, "Nick," in fact, did a beautiful job in sixth grade. When my next older brother was in the same grade, svelte and graceful as he was, he was also cast as Santa.

Naturally, I wanted to be, assumed I would be, could not imagine not getting to be the star of the play: Santa. I was totally gob smacked to hear that I could not be Santa because I was a girl. Santa had to be male? Who says? He was a sexless figure, no? A fake beard? No problem, I could wear a fake beard and a pillow in my pants. The teacher/director held fast in the face of my insistence that it was a family TRADITION to be the Santa if there was a Rudd in the sixth grade.

Unswayed and becoming a bit fussed, the teacher replied that perhaps I could be Mrs. Santa. My distress increased at this sop, and I cried over the idea of just being someone's WIFE.

I was asked if there was any other character I would like to act and I proposed a pirate.

With relief, the teacher seized on the idea that there would be a sword fight, a sort of fencing exhibition, between me and another friend from Girl Scouts, where we had created and achieved badges in fencing. Our leader was a recreational fencer and thought it good for us to learn to fence and become more assertive. So another Scout and I were dressed as (MALE) pirates in—horrors—torn jeans and striped shirts, and allowed, like the pirates in Peter Pan, to engage in a short duel covering plenty of stage room. No one ever mentioned that I had been bought off of the impossibility of playing a male role by being offered a male role (OK, there may have been female pirates too). The whole performance was aggressive and not at all faked. I was, in fact, probably the best fencer in the troop, with the possible exception of another daughter of refugees from the Nazis, who could put up a fierce battle with the occasional illegal, unsportsmanlike move.

Teach us to be more assertive in life, hah! A couple of years later, I demanded to learn how to shoot a rifle, a skill my brothers had learned at summer camp.

Little Girl in the Elevator

Other interesting people lived in our building. We would meet them in the elevator. My mother was not shy about noticing things about them, nor about speaking out. She deduced that the middle-aged man carrying flowers was going to see his girlfriend on floor eight, as he seemed to do every Tuesday. She also accosted a young and somewhat frightened mother and even more frightened young daughter.

"Why do you dress her as a doll?" my mother demanded. "She cannot move in those kinds of clothes. She is a child! She needs to be able to move about! She will be so much happier. Believe me, I know. I am a pediatrician."

Europe by Freighter, Twice

We had to climb up the side of the freighter using a rope ladder. It looked like a fishing net or one of those rope adventure things you might see at playgrounds these days. We three kids, ages ten, thirteen, and fifteen, had no problem with it and my mother gamely followed. The crew had a little more trouble with my diminutive and fearful aunt, who protested, but may have been simply carried up. We were all on our way to Europe, and at a nominal rate.

Another aunt worked for a shipping company whose executive, "GeoGeo," could permit passengers on a space-available basis. We went to Europe twice this way, once when I was ten and again when I was thirteen. Sending three Manhattan kids to summer camps in Maine cost more than either of these trips. On board, we ate with the "officers," a steady diet of eggs fried in olive oil for breakfast and boiled beef for dinner!

Anyway, I got to see the Louvre and the Winged Victory, and we picnicked all over France. My mother drove the rented Peugeot, my oldest brother sat up front and played the man, down to ordering the wine(s). I learned to eat in the European style, with the fork held in the left hand throughout cutting and eating. I ate one of the best meals of my life in the south of France, trout of all things. After enough cathedrals (for which I had to don a lace mantilla) in Paris, Chartres, Rouen, visiting even the very square where Joan D'Arc was burnt—and castles of all sizes, but most of them smelling of urine in the corners, we simply refused to get out of the car for any more of these sights.

We were all satisfied by books and bookstores, and soon acquired enough of them to need a large additional suitcase for our purchases. I was allowed to read whatever I wanted and read both my own selections and theirs, a number of which featured Nazis. I read *The Hunchback of Notre Dame* and also experienced the joy of assembling a picnic every

day for our lunches. We would first visit a boulangerie (bakery) and then a deli for meats and a vendor for fruits. We would then literally stop at the side of the road in the countryside, trespassing on a corner of some farmer's field, and using my mother's pocketknife in turn, would make our own lunches.

I admired my mother's sheer competence in running our trip as she navigated all over France for a whole month. She found local pensions on the way for us to sleep and a restaurant meal with (watered) wine every evening. Our luggage, including the trunk of books, was piled high on the roof of the car, fastened with ropes (she and my oldest brother, the Eagle Scout, could tie knots). In case of rain, all this was covered with plastic held by bungee cords. Over time, the plastic frayed and flapped in the wind.

We must have looked like a kind of a clown car stuffed with people as we flapped into some village. People came out to look as if we were advertising the arrival of an entire circus!

After a month, my father flew in to join us, and our aunt flew home. From France, we went to Switzerland to see the Jungfrau (elevation 13,642) and the Alps, just a day or two without winter clothes!

We went on to Italy and a stop on the island of Capri. I remember that side trip in particular because there I saw a life-size sculpture of a seated man, hauled out of the sea after some 3,000 years and sitting at the edge of the clifftop's path. (It was most probably a Roman copy of a Greek original, sited in an area where emperors had summer palaces.) I caught up to my parents and insisted that they retrace their steps to really see it again. "Look! He is sad!" I marveled that a little American girl, so many years after the sculpture had been made, could recognize, identify, and empathize with a human emotion contained in an inanimate material. It was suddenly clear to me that art, of all human endeavors, transcends time. I believe that was when I formed the wish—without any particular skills yet—to become an artist.

Our second freighter trip to Europe was three years later. I was to stay a month with a French-speaking family in Megeve (French Alps) to learn French, hopefully with a Parisian accent like they had.

Childhood | 67

The plan was fine except for the two British boys my age who were lodging there for the same purpose. We went to the local swim club all day every day to swim and sunbathe. Once in the swimming pool, someone bumped into me by mistake and said, "Bitte." (Excuse me.) This was the first time anyone had ever addressed me in German, and I froze, unable to even nod, much less say anything, due to my terror. On some level, I had not put together that Germans still existed. The gentleman was possibly Swiss German anyway. Our motley crew did have to speak French at dinner, but after dinner, no speaking at all was allowed as the master of the house would sit at the cleared table to write in his daily journal, so absolute silence was required. I was much impressed by the long row of past journals. Who, if anyone, was ever going to read them?

Eventually, my parents and middle brother collected me, and we went off to an international medical meeting in Rome. My father's fluency in Russian, French, and English, as well as expertise in rheumatology, made him an ideal participant in this kind of thing. For the first time, I was conscious of young waiters stopping their work to watch me cross the breakfast room in my snazzy Italian razor-cut hair and my long, tanned legs contrasting with my white, short shorts. I hated that intrusive watching. It felt like I was prey for their gaze.

At the close of our stay in Rome, however, the meeting ended with a dinner at the sixteenth-century Villa d'Este. After dinner, I left the group to start climbing some graceful trees ringing the center of the gardens. These trees had smooth, gently angled branches with clean, whitish bark. Some branches were low enough to catch ahold of from the ground. I kicked off my sandals and delighted in climbing first one and then another. I was wearing a knee-length, full-skirted dress with a sash that probably came undone, swinging along with the lightweight skirt as I climbed around.

Before my parents made me come down, I enjoyed testing my flexibility against the strength of the branches. I chortled with my own sense of power. It was a moment of glorying in my body. I do not remember the sound of my chortle, but I remember the feeling.

As I climbed higher, to the highest I went that evening, I noticed an old man below and underneath me. His hands were in an attitude of prayer, and he exclaimed, loud enough for me to hear and also to take in, the single word "Bellissima!" (lovely) as a sort of a benediction.

Experiments with Death

Marksmanship using .22-caliber rifles was a skill taught to boys at summer camp in that era. Girls took archery and learned to play tennis. When my next older brother demanded a rifle of his own to practice during the year, there were some long discussions about safety. The four-and-a-half acres behind our country house actually did offer some space for stray bullets, and hay bales were purchased and stacked into a wall. We practiced both archery and riflery there. Maybe this explains why I admire Wonder Woman. I became quite successful at target practice with both.

The land sloped down to some woods and ended at a year-round creek, known as Murderers' Creek because of a history of local Indians coming up from the creek to annihilate the new settlers. Hostile Indians in the woods merged in my mind with evading all who would try to kill me.

We were all of us kids shown the Alain Resnais film *Night and Fog*, with graphic footage from the concentration camps: corpses, a vacant skull with a fly protruding from an eye socket, and all. My mother marched on the Sunday School principal's office to protest the traumatization of the entire student body, but the damage was already done.

Anyway, my brother promised not to kill anything with his new gun, and he pretty much spontaneously stopped blowing up his plastic model airplanes and battleships using firecrackers. This had been his favorite pastime. A day came when he begged to kill something, just once, just to see what it felt like—anything, a bird or one of those woodchucks constantly making holes in the lawn. He did kill a woodchuck and was very remorseful about it after. My mother suggested that at least he should study it, dissect it even, so the death would not be in vain. Together they placed the dear woodchuck on a board and opened the ventral surface, I suppose with a knife, in order to identify its organs. I did not watch that, but they called me over to see the mammalian-like parts inside. Then they got into an argument about whether they were looking at a uterus or a bladder. One of them pressed on it with their forefinger, and piss flooded the board! Poor woodchuck. I suppose we buried it.

Years earlier, we kids and the cousins had buried a dead bird to answer the perennial question of whether there was or was not a heaven. A couple of days later we dug up the hole, and the bird was gone! This confused me for many years.

The cat died years after the homemade wine episode and was buried at the edge of the property. I was allowed to use nail polish to paint her name and dates on a nearby stone. I never tried to dig her up. Nor did I ever use nail polish. I wonder whose it was?

There was also a memorable day when we were playing with the ax out of sight of the grownups, demonstrating how one swung an ax up with force in order to swing it back down. My oldest brother managed to catch his own chin. The wound appeared to be on his neck because the blood dripped down from his chin. I ran up the hill to the grownups with my next-youngest cousin. We were so out of breath when we arrived that only I could speak. And all I said was "Nick" (his name) "the ax." The grownups came to swift attention, probably thinking the worst, and ran down the hill with us to give aid. I had never frightened them to such an extent, but they could still think and act in a crisis.

My father had a phobia about fire. When his family fled to Finland in 1919, they sometimes saw blood on the sides of the white birch trees in the forest, and there were many fires in various buildings before they reached safety at their own country house. In upper New York state, my mother set out to cure him by repeating a controlled fire. Cement blocks were purchased and stacked into a sort of grill at a good distance from the house. We burned any trash or paper garbage and ate roasted marshmallows at the same time. None of us kids grew up afraid of fire. I don't know if it helped my father.

Kitchen Chemistry

Keeping three active children occupied at the country house was both harder and easier than at the NYC apartment. Projects that made a mess were usually carried out in the country house kitchen. The plaster Indian chief with feather headdress, cast in a flexible rubber mold, was memorable for its impact on my future interest in sculpture.

Every horizontal surface was covered in newspaper, and all the directions were followed about soaping this and suspending that. My casting turned out nicely, but my brothers quickly lost interest in the events. Despite the newspaper, there was a tremendous mess to clean up.

Another childhood kitchen experiment involved fermentation, as my mother tried to turn some fruit into wine. The overly large jar was left on the table waiting for our return the following week. When we returned, it was to find the jar exploded, and shards of glass mixed with fermented and rotten fruit all over the floor. Our housecat (named Moishe Pipik), who traveled with us to and from these weekends, fell upon the spilled "juice" and lapped up a great deal of it. She then started to walk in an ungainly manner, and we all commented that she was "walking drunk." We let her outside and followed her next door, where the neighbor, another doctor, had tried to build himself a swimming pool by having a hole excavated in the yard. Naturally, this filled up with rainwater, turned to mud, and froze solid in the winter. When the cat reached the ice, still trying to escape our hands, she fell, splayed out, while we howled with laughter. The image remained for me of the drunk cat and her attempts to maintain her dignity, which in turn caused her to hold her head up, and then her feet went out from under her.

The storm cellar doors in our house led to a dry old basement with a built-in workbench. We had a few tools: hammer, saw, ruler. I commandeered it for my own use. I went to a progressive elementary school where girls took "shop" as well as "art." I enjoyed building things and with weekend access to a workbench and vise, I sawed and hammered both a table and a bed for my doll(s). I was not the slightest bit interested in dressing these dolls at the time, even though it was what most of my little friends did with theirs.

Back in the city apartment, papier-mâché projects were permitted as this involved only flour and water, no plaster! I made puppet heads, once turning in a standalone head with a little painted "blood" on the neck as my school project on the French Revolution. That one earned me a comment on my guidance card. Everyone else seemed to be making models of a guillotine. I also had carpeted my puppet head with scraps of real mink pelt taken from our family sewing box.

One Halloween, I decided to dress as a devil. Blowing up a big balloon, larger than my head, I covered it in papier-mâché and later painted it red with some kind of paint with fumes. I suffered a lot inside the costume because I couldn't breathe. The rest of the outfit was OK, just a red sweater and red PJ pants. Interestingly, the name assigned to me by my Yiddish teacher as an adult had a double meaning. Just by changing the pronunciation of Taybl to Tayvl, he, therefore, knowingly called me both a dove and a devil.

"Artists who design characters are poised to later tell stories." I forget who said that.

Science also was not neglected, although it was only the one brother who went into medicine. Whenever anything went moldy in the apartment refrigerator, it had to be trotted down to my parents' medical office on the first floor and examined under the microscope there. I was interested visually, but that was about it. To enliven our lab sessions, my brothers would taunt me about the skeleton in the closet. I did not believe them at first. Unfortunately, there really was a teaching skeleton in the closet, and I was afraid of closets and of skeletons for a long time. I walked out of the first movie theater I was allowed to go to at age eight. (Before that age, we were considered unable to distinguish between imagination and reality.) When Tarzan's parents turned up as skeletons in a cave, I headed for the lobby until it was over.

Physical Strength

The First Dutch Doctor

The first Dutch doctor was a friend of my parents—my father's really—I suppose from some international meeting of rheumatologists. Hans was a survivor of the Japanese prison camps in Indonesia, where his parents perished when he was a young teenager. Repatriated, he became a doctor and a charming man, though he smoked like a chimney. When my parents remonstrated with him about it, he replied that he had few pleasures, and that smoking was one of them.

I don't recall if he had children, although a marriage and later a divorce were mentioned. What I do remember is him catching me by surprise with a huge kiss as I was lounging and talking on the telephone from my parents' bedroom. Hans would have been on his way to the bathroom, and I suppose it was a sort of crime of opportunity to climb on the bed and kiss me with such ferocity. I didn't fight back; in fact, I think I met his forcefulness, or I would have ended up flat on the bed, which was scarier.

I did not tell, ever, even though I was only fourteen.

A year later, when he visited the States and us again, he tackled the problem of my uneven leg length. He called for cardboard, a pencil, a pair of sharp scissors. Using the insole of my offending shoe as a pattern, he cut out a wedge of cardboard to even up my stance. My parents had been helplessly fluttering about the issue, complaining about the new prosthesis. Hans just took over and fixed the immediate problem with such simple materials. It made a tremendous impression on me that he wanted to fix me up with his own hands, could do so, and made my parents look so foolish and helpless.

I was sad to hear later when Hans died of lung cancer; my parents just shrugged.

I am fond of a series of romance novels by Betty Neels featuring heroes who are Dutch doctors. In the real world, once while flying internationally and waiting at Sea-Tac Airport with a large suitcase, I met another Dutch doctor. My husband, Joe, was still parking, and the only way I could move this large suitcase was to kick it. I was fine with that, although I suppose it did not look very dignified. A pleasant-looking professional man with overlong hair came over and asked politely, "Please, Madame, may I help you?" I let him move the suitcase, and as he turned away I was delighted that his shoulder bag had the initials from the Dutch airline KLM.

The Dybbuk and the Gift of One Last Dance

As a teenager, I loved to go to dances, as well as the feeling of being held for the slower ones. The foxtrot was still being done in 1963; once, the rabbi chaperone asked me to dance. He was the assistant rabbi, hailing from the Bronx, as anyone could see from his choice of fabrics. His shirt was patterned white on white, and his suit some sort of new fabric, also nubbly, and not wool. Two strikes against him. But he was tall and surprisingly masterful.

He danced me. He dared me to follow in speed, complexity, and precision. I, in my olive-green knee-length corduroy jumper and lavender oxford blouse, was swept away. I don't remember my shoes, but they must have been flat or low heeled, and I was fleet of foot as well as surefooted. The distance he kept between our bodies was totally decent, and all I felt was the fabric of his long, swinging jacket.

There was air and space inside the grip of the dance embrace. I had never felt so free and never so submersed. I gave over my will to him, to the dance. Three of us were dancing, and one was death disguised as a dybbuk. It was invisible in amongst the fabric flowing with the dance music.

I did not understand for many more years that, at fifteen, it was the most extraordinary introduction to sex any young girl could have had.

A few months later, when both the senior and the assistant rabbis came to visit me in the hospital, my dance partner's face held a wry expression. He literally could not move his face. After the homilies expressed by the senior one, the junior one remarked that he had never met such a dancer, that he had tried every complicated move he knew and that I had faultlessly followed his lead. He shook his head at the wonder of it, of the sequel to our dance being the loss of my rightmost leg.

I think the rabbi(s) visited every congregant in hospital, but in my case, I know my mother had called them. I had expressed concern that my leg have a proper burial in a Jewish graveyard. I had the wit not to mention resurrection to my mother, but I knew that I needed all my parts. She called the rabbi to check, and when it proved to be true, she questioned how her child could possibly know such a fact. I do not know how I knew that "rule," but I did, and it was already too late. After pathology, such a remain would have been burnt, becoming a part of the omnipresent soot lurking on all the windowsills of Manhattan, from all the incinerators of all those people in all those buildings. The horrors of giving a body to be burnt have never left me.

In recent years there was a community meeting to discuss the probability of locating a hospital incinerator nearby, and I was a vocal opponent. I was the most incoherent I think I have ever been in public, sudden tears choking my plea not to be rained on by discarded body parts.

The Books, Not Chocolates, That They Gave Me, Two Years After Age Thirteen

At fifteen, I was finally gifted with all the books everyone thought I needed. Because it was not a Bat/Bar Mitzvah, these books were about other subjects, but from many of the same "guests" as if had I become a Bat Mitzvah. My parents had told me at the time that I could not have a Bat Mitzvah because I would be having a wedding. (I had replied that in that case, I would like a typewriter for my thirteenth birthday in compensation!)

The three books I really remember were *Siddhartha* by Herman Hesse, *The Fire Next Time* by James Baldwin, and *Michelangelo, The Early Works*. Spirituality, anger, and beauty were to comfort me on my way out with my illness. Except, I did not die but took those gifts away with me on my life's journey, which soon involved leaving New York.

Professor Green of Hunter College

Professor Green, a biology professor at Hunter College, thought I was really smart. He was in my hospital room visiting his niece, who was in the other bed, recovering from her osteosarcoma. We made each other miserable. She was only twelve. And she did die a few years later. There was often a clutch of relatives visiting her, and so her uncle, Morris Green, would drift over to discuss philosophy with me. He was fairly homely and very intelligent and understood that I considered the spiritual dimension of my suffering to be its major lesson. It was he who gave me the *Siddhartha*. I think he understood that I required bolstering of this nascent spiritual strength. He also invited me to visit him at his lab in the college after school sometime to see how a biologist works. I did do that, and my mother was much relieved that his pleasant fiancee was also present at our meeting. All I really remember were the white lab coats, an air of peace, and a deep interest and passion in whatever it was that he and Miss Fiancee were researching. Dedicated passion, spirituality, peacefulness within that bustling great college edifice set a new standard for me of what grownup life might be like. In the end, I found myself my own biologist when I was nearly forty and remarried. I wonder what happened to Morris Green.

Flying out West

When I first arrived at Reed College in Portland, Oregon, I felt great relief that there were not a lot of girls running around with Peter Pan collars and pageboys because that was Bryn Mawr, and that was not me. I did feel like I fit in in terms of counterculture stuff in that the socializing that I did the last two or three years of high school included a lot of folk singing and wearing of Mexican embroidered peasant stuff. We were just ahead of the curve of the Summer of Love and all of that. When was that? '67? I started Reed in '65.

But to be without makeup, wearing embroidered clothes, and willing to go barefoot, that was my scene. I mean, that was "alternative" when I was in high school, but it was mainstream at Reed. So appearances were no problem.

Once in a while, I'd get tired of being sort of folksy, and I had a jumper, which is a dress-length, sleeveless garment that has a scoop neck. Under it, you can put any kind of turtleneck or top and knee socks or tights. My jumper was black and white with different colorful splotches so you could wear it with different things, and I had a red turtleneck with red knee socks and a green turtleneck with green tights. It was one of my outfits from high school in which I looked like a nice girl.

And whenever I would wear that at Reed, sort of as a break from being barefoot and in jeans, some teacher or some dean would come over and say, "What a pleasure it is to see someone ..." I can't remember what they would call it. I don't think they said "dress like a girl," but it was something on that order. And I appreciated the compliment, although it wasn't who I was all of the time.

There were a few surprises among the makeup of my entering class. I found the people who came from the Northwest to be incredibly sporty. They had been skiing all their lives; they already knew how to drive, and some of them had cars. This was completely foreign to my existence. I had been doing interesting things in the subways for years, leading folk singing and whatever. But the idea that some of these people had been driving family cars since sixteen was just incredibly foreign.

There were the westerners, and there were a few easterners. Well, actually, there were a fair number of easterners. Probably a quarter of the class were easterners. But I could not always tell who they were at first. And then the biggest surprise to me was southerners. I just remember one southerner in particular. I had known black southerners in New York, especially our housekeeper, but I'd never met a white southerner. And I thought they were from another planet. I couldn't believe they were talking like that on purpose.

Roast Beef

There I was, a new freshman, and a sophomore chatted me up over lunch or in the quad or somewhere. And it turned out that what he really wanted was he wanted me to come and cook dinner. So I was mystified by the whole thing. But I'm pretty direct, and I asked. And it turned out that what it really was, was that they missed home cooking, and he and his roommates had purchased a four-or five-pound roast—raw roast beef. And he had been dispatched to campus to find a girl who looked like she knew how to cook. And I was the candidate.

I just thought it was a very funny story. I did not know him previously. I think he picked me because I looked friendly. Because, well, I bet he picked me because I looked like a relative. He was a nice Jewish boy from Chicago or Cleveland or somewhere. And he figured a girl like me would know how to cook. But the thing is, he didn't know we had always had a housekeeper. Actually, I didn't know squat about cooking at that time. But I knew how to read a cookbook. So I told him how to use a cookbook.

But I thought it was funny. It was the funniest pickup story I had ever heard. I was kind of flattered, you know. An upperclassman was so interested in me.

Drinking off Campus

A group of my friends, pretty much the same group of people but in the second year, held a dinner party off campus, and the goal was to get drunk. And I thought that that was sort of silly. But I was invited. But what they didn't know about me was that when I drink too much wine, I don't throw up, I don't get silly. I sing. And moreover, I sing in French, Russian, Hebrew, and English. And I don't stop. And they could not shut me up. And I ended up ending the party because they couldn't stand it anymore. One of them picked me up like a sack of potatoes, put me across his shoulder, and carted me back to the off campus apartment I shared with the other girls. And I've always thought that that was the sweetest memory, that they would look after me and take care of me even though they were heartily sick of me.

No, it is Emergency Money

Well, I'm so dumb; I mean, I just never got it. They knew, my parents knew what the going price for an abortion was in 1965. I didn't. I mean, a conversation about my brother's friend never got far enough for me to find out. I guess it did, somehow, for them to know.

So I had this money, and I was not to touch it except for an "emergency." I kept it in my bank account, and I didn't touch it.

I guess I told a few people about it because I just thought it was so odd, and I was waiting to be enlightened. And nobody ever enlightened me about why my parents gave me an emergency fund of six hundred dollars until it happened that somebody needed it. And somehow then, "Well, Joan's got it, and she'd probably lend it to you."

And, I was asked suddenly to do this thing. And I had some questions and fears about who this person is, and will it be safe, and will she be harmed? I extracted some various promises. And there was an adult involved. The mother in question couldn't be involved, but a friend of the family was going to do the shepherding—and so I was assured that there was an adult involved and assured that they were going to leave if things did not appear hygienic and modern and safe.

But I felt guilty about it for the rest of my life. And it had huge repercussions at the time and also later on. It led to incredible misery for a whole bunch of people and lifelong sequelae, some directly related and some not directly. These various sequelae gave me a lot of respect for the significance of the event. I don't even know what my position is. I'm not opposed to the idea, and I've never had to do it. But the fact that one action leads to other repercussions is really true. And I see that now about a great deal of my Reed experience.

More About Reed

I'm sure things change over the years, too. And I think who they admit is probably different, and how they're supported is probably different. And there are more women faculty, and there are more young faculty, and there are more faculty with children, and all that helps.

But there was a real moral vacuum when I was there, and it was really scary for a lot of people. I found it scary.

It doesn't sound like a moral question, but when the dean of students, Jack Dudman, complimented me on wearing nice girl clothes. I mean, what was so exceptional that he had to comment on it? Now I came to Reed to avoid the Bryn Mawr Peter Pan collar with the circle pin and the flip, the pageboy hairdo. But the idea that people might want or need some order or discipline in their lives still holds. That is part of why Lloyd Reynolds and the art history, graphic arts, and calligraphy thing was so important for me because it gave me a structure. I took it on as a structure.

What I mean is, other people took other structures. Some took drugs. Some took sex. Some took playing hearts or bridge. But, you know, the "free love, atheism, communism" slogan was very much in vogue when I was at Reed. It was printed on the sweatshirts! I think that the free love stuff led to a lot of confusion for a lot of people. And atheism is okay as long as you actually care about your fellow human beings. But sometimes, doing whatever you want harms other people.

And the communism thing I thought was just plain silly. I mean, first of all, I had lived on a socialist kibbutz. I had worn used clothes that were issued to me. I had done work that was required of me, even though it was physically very difficult. I actually had a tremendous idea of what socialism was, and that's still important to my life. But not communism. I mean, I think it was always kind of tongue in cheek, the whole red-baiting and McCarthy era references.

So there are pieces of it that make some sense. But especially having raised two sons now in the Northwest, this is kind of an outrageous thing to say, but I don't belong here. I've never belonged here. I've been in the NW for more than fifty years now if you count Portland and Seattle. I belong here only in relation to some people some of the time.

It's a long time to stay if I've been feeling that way all this time.

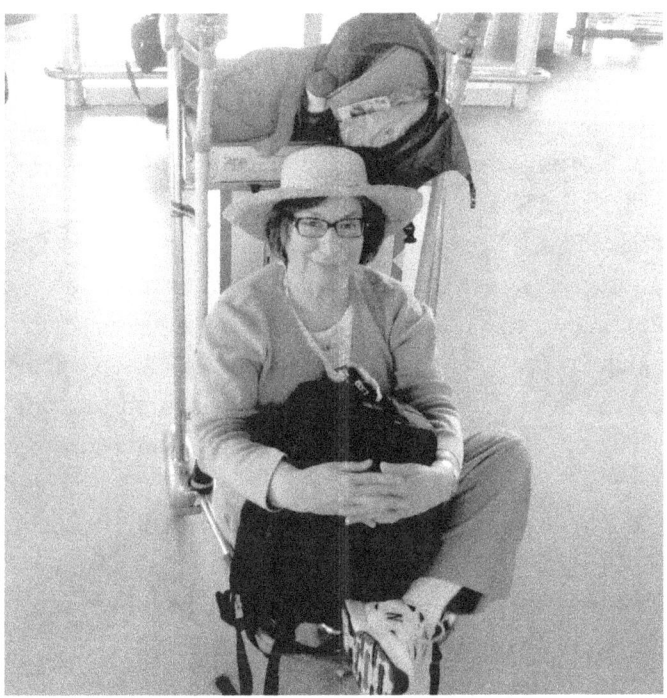

Losing and Finding My Soul

What about starting to lose my soul at Reed?

I think it has to do with fitting in, and it has to do with aping other people or not doing so. I mean, there were friends of mine who were really surprised and sad to hear that I was leaving. I think what happened was I learned how to use my right brain with calligraphy practice. I learned how to "be the tree". I learned how to watch trees grow. There was a lot of book learning that I didn't want. There was a lot of experiential learning that I did want.

To be a student at Reed was really very hard and very stressful. So, part of how I survived academically that first year was to avoid the evening socializing altogether and study in the mornings. And that's fine although my roommate objected to the radio on a Gospel station waking us at 4 AM. I suppose I did some variation of that the second year, when I was off campus. But I kind of gave a whole bunch of things my best shot. I worked hard and I got through biology and chemistry. I tried psychology; I didn't like it. The professor actually kept his own baby in a Skinner box. I tried political science. I mean, the only thing I really liked was the art and art history with Lloyd Reynolds. When I told him that I thought I was losing my soul at Reed he took me quite seriously. He replied that if I knew that now, then it would be better to leave.

Also, if you look at what else was going on in my life, like the trip to Israel—by this time, it was two trips to Israel because, at seventeen, I did the trip with the youth corps and worked in an immigrant village. And at eighteen, I did a second trip and worked on a kibbutz the whole summer, or most of the summer, and got a real sense of living a different way. So, I guess I couldn't see staying at Reed. Because, first, to do a creative thesis at Reed, only some people got to do them. You had to major in English at that time. Then if you were lucky, you'd get to do something that involved your hands. And I knew I could graduate college in other ways.

So, I did exactly what I wanted. I did intensive language. I did Middle East studies. I did enough art to really understand that art was what I wanted to pursue. I finished and I got my official first bachelor's from Portland State. I didn't do the two years at Reed, then the four years at the museum art school. I did a year and a half at Reed, a half a year of Arabic in Monterey, a year and a half at Portland State. I actually graduated early. I graduated in March of what would have been my fourth year of college. And I did very well at Portland State taking twenty-one credits instead of fifteen.

And then I had my first son after I finished college the first time. I think back to Professor Panny's wife nursing their baby in front of me. At that point, I didn't know. I mean, I still really didn't know if I was going to have a full life. And I wasn't going to miss it. So, I finished college, went traveling, and I had a baby. Okay, young marriage doesn't always work out. So, I went to work.

But why did college and marriage involve losing or finding my soul? I guess, like I say, it had to do with being really, really aware of how short life is and wanting to spend it as I wanted to, and not spend it wrecked up. People were getting into scarier behaviors around me, too. Riskier things. I don't recall much drugs. Other people do, but maybe I didn't have those kinds of friends.

I think it was a metaphysical thing, a political thing when I talk about losing my soul. The parts of me that I wanted to nurture and nourish didn't seem to be valued, other than these "ministering moments" I spoke of in relation to other students. Or, you know, writing poetry or calligraphing somebody else's poetry. Getting involved with beauty, I guess, even though that sounds corny. Getting involved with beauty was the thing that made me feel like I was saving my soul. That I had a soul, that life was worth living, whatever. And when study didn't involve that feeling it was not interesting.

What happened later at Portland State, the reason that the art came to dominate was that my first husband said, "The only days you're happy are the days you have art classes. So why not do more of those?" So I did. I switched the balance between the Middle East certificate program and the art the other way, so I was doing just a little bit of the Middle East program and the rest was all art classes.

And then, after my first son was born, when he was two, I applied to art school but was turned down because I had a two-year-old. These were retro days. And the next year, there was a new dean, and my parents had told me they would pay for a professional school, any kind. They had in mind law, medicine, or teaching. But I held them to it. And they were good enough, really, in retrospect, to pay for four years of art school. It was an eight-hour day program which I did in six, because I had a young child, and I didn't want to leave him in daycare that long. But I did very well, and I did all four years, a BFA in sculpture.

And I am an artist—an artist being somebody who makes art.

Arye and Rachel Kalev (z"l)

When I went to Israel the second time and met the movement therapist Arye Kalev, I learned some ways I could fix some of my aches and pains myself. He analyzed the way in which I had been overextending my calf muscles, my back, my neck. He taught me exercises to stretch my back and how to massage my own calf muscles and foot. I owe the continued strength of my foot and proper alignment of my remaining leg to Arye.

Those personalized exercises meant that even though it is extremely rare for a person of my age and challenge to still have a straight back, I am still strong and straight. I hope they knew of my gratitude though I was not great about keeping in touch as the years passed. Now I write their oldest daughter on the various holidays and she has asked for the use of one of my drawings to advertise her movement classes for children!

One of the floors of their Center for the Art of Movement was canvas-covered straw for practicing martial arts without injury when you fell. I was allowed free run of this for when there was not a class in session, and I reclaimed my body's movement in this safe space. It was their encouraging tone and actions that endeared them to me so much. Rachel welcomed me into their home and mothered me, as did her own mother, who lived with them. I thought of them really as an additional set of parents. I grieved deeply when their son in the army was killed in one of the first terrorist explosions. It was inconceivable to me that someone could die so senselessly at only nineteen.

My First Husband Was a Long Distance Runner, Quite a Good One

Originally my first husband went to university on a track scholarship and had dropped out to train with a pre-Olympic coach in California. When we got married in New York, apparently people kept pressing money and checks into his hands. Arriving at the hotel for a one-night honeymoon, I begged to be allowed to at least put on my new nightgown, a garment heavily influenced by Walt Disney's ball gown for Cinderella. It was mostly white, with blue ribbons threaded here and there among the lacy cut-out bits and, what I clearly remember, firm blue bows attached all around the perimeter. But the thing was, he was not at the moment the slightest bit interested in my appearance but instead was jumping up and down on the bed and throwing the money up in the air, allowing it to rain on him while shouting, "We're rich! We're rich." I should have known right then we were in trouble. Actually, I did know, but I was meant to be safe, free of sin with my sexuality—in short, married.

What We Did With The Money, or Reading in the Country

We wanted to buy some undeveloped land in the country with our wedding money as an investment, I suppose, but mostly to have some place outside the city—not that Portland was particularly bustling at that time (1968). For a while, we had a share in a rustic cabin, which allowed us to "go to the country" one or sometimes two weekends a month. This was somehow not enough, so we looked for our own place, joining forces finally with another couple to afford half of a quarter section, or eighty acres of previously homesteaded land in the Lewis River valley, in Clark County. At the time, we did not know that the area had a history of utopian and communist communities and that the locals were disposed to lump all newcomers into the labels: Jews, Commies, Hippies. Actually, we were sort of all three, mostly without the drugs. Once when the local dealer came around our city commune, he was met by a shirtless Lew and another communard practicing Yoga, who told the hapless dealer that "we are holy men" and not to bother coming back. Our country communards actually were what we later called "stoners," but they did that mostly on their own, and in spite of it, were fairly industrious. There are photos of Lew and me, though, and baby Ben, sheltered only by a large, clear plastic tarp over a tree branch, with Lew lying on the bed reading a book.

The weekend that the others wanted to start digging at the site of the spring, in order to create a water delivery system, we drove up, and Lew unloaded a folding, plastic lawn chair/recliner and his library book. With a heartfelt sigh, after a long week of teaching high school, he got into the chair with the book. "What are you doing?" demanded one of the others. "There is so much to do here. What about the water collection system?" And Lew looked up and said something like: "You go to the country to rest."

After the Purple Dress I Wore for the Divorce, Walking the Toddler in the Park

We flew into Manhattan nearly straight from the meadow in the Lewis River valley. Wide-eyed, my toddler accepted my parents' apartment until we reached the glossy, white-tiled bathroom. At this, he let out an unholy shriek and clung to me. It was too strange, too white, too clean, too smooth. Definitely, the toilet was too big. It was nothing like peeing in the woods, though I had trained him to use a pot to sit for the other necessity. My mother remarked, dryly, that she supposed we could walk him in the park. I was not sure if she was kidding. Anyway, she went to a neighbor who sometimes had a visiting grandchild, and she borrowed a sort of kiddie insert for the adult toilet, a blue rim with a smaller opening and a wonderful blue plastic duck's head, sort of like the knob on a saddle, to grasp onto. Thankfully, this compromise was acceptable to all. It was somewhat novel to wear clothes altogether, as we had all spent the early part of summer largely in the nude, daytime at least.

She Gained, No She Lost

"Let's face it; she'll never be pretty." So my exercise instructor insisted.

I was nine years old and did not even get it, at first, that the older ladies and aunties were discussing me and my prospects until my mother hissed, protectively, "Pshhhhh." I was, I am afraid, customarily referred to as the "little elephant" in these movement classes.

At least I learned how to stand on my head in these sessions, and a few stretches, and I felt beautiful in my tight fitting dance leotard.

"She gained!" "No, she lost!" was a frequent party game, dispute, and refrain among all the old ladies, auntie figures, and real aunts. Here I am at 9, and at 17.

Personally I liked stripes and plaids and also flowers on my clothes. My favorite outfits, worn until too worn-out looking, were often given to Goodwill before I was ready to lose their "protection." Once, I was left without any outfits at all that I felt truly OK in when wearing them. That was a miserable time for me to be scrutinized by all the relatives.

Smoking vs. Vegetarianism

"I did not go to medical school in the 1930s so that you could iron your husband's shirts!" my mother expostulated when I detailed some of my duties as a wife in the late 1960s. I was also baking our own bread, sprouting our own alfalfa seeds, making our own yogurt, and, yes, making a baby (my first). How I made my mother suffer over our "healthy" vegetarianism! At the time, my physician parents each smoked two packs per day...

When the child was three, and we went to visit for Thanksgiving, the roasted turkey was revealed in all its customary dead-birdness. Shrieking, our little son ran from the room and would later consent only to Cheerios as his Thanksgiving dinner. I cannot remember what I ate that evening, but more than forty years later, this older son remains a vegetarian.

Bulvan

"We have to pretend to be stupid because they really are." A saying from another one of my aunts, (a practicing divorce lawyer), about men in general

I demanded to know the word my mother would use to describe my art-school boyfriend to the aunties. I badgered her because I knew she would find a single word, in some language or other, to sum up her opinion (read, judgment).

Finally, saying that she did not even know which language it was, she came up with "bulvan" (a brutish person).

Actually, it is Russian but is also used in Yiddish to describe a coarse type of person, not part of the intelligentsia.

Yet, when he spontaneously cleared the table after a meal together, she was flabbergasted by his nurturing and helpful behavior in the kitchen. Also, she observed how well his two boys played together with my only child. She left advising me not to produce a little girl before I was through with art school. He did see me through art school, but we parted sometime around then. He was having continued financial problems with his business. One of my nearly life-sized sculptures of a seated man came from a drawing I did of him in despair.

I had offered a studio tour to my congregation sisterhood, and they had come to see. The most voluble was the sweet wife of the rabbi, whose response to another nude male torso cast in concrete was, "Oh, is it anyone I know?" And, to the full figure sitting despondent, she said, "Oh, yes, financial troubles; I have seen this before."

Unfortunately, my friend was stockpiling pills on his mantelpiece for quite a long time. Then one year, on his birthday, when I dropped by with a homemade cake, I found him unconscious and lying on the floor on top of an empty pill bottle. He was still breathing; I could still act, and I called the police. He went to the hospital by ambulance, and he recovered. I don't think he ever forgave me for calling 911, and I think he was seeking temporary oblivion rather than death. I was advised by the ER to confiscate his collection of pain pills, and I did so, though he never mentioned it.

Ski Racing: I Become an Athlete

In college, I had asked interesting-looking people to carry my food. Then my act got totally blown because it turned out there was a sophomore who walked on the kind of crutches I used—forearm crutches—who carried his own tray and balanced himself while carrying stuff, which is hard to do. It's tricky, because if you mess up, you lose your whole lunch tray. You can sort of balance yourself if you make yourself very rigid and carry something like that and walk. But it's not easy.

Anyway, he would just go to the closest table. He didn't try to cross the whole lunchroom. So that kind of blew my helpless act for a little while.

And then my mother wanted to know if I'd become special friends with this guy.

"Why?" I said. "Why would I?"

"Well, it just seems," she said.

And then he told me that his parents had the same reaction—that there was a woman at college, a freshman with only one leg. And, moreover, she was a member of The Tribe. Another Jewish person. Because, as it turned out, this guy was also Jewish.

First of all, he was dating, of course, the only German exchange student on campus. And I wasn't interested in getting too involved with anybody.

What I did do, I introduced him to three-track skiing (one long ski and two ski tips mounted onto crutches). I did it first, and I can't remember how I got started with it or why I went the first time. But I can tell you that I was the first female in national competition for amputee skiing when it first started. It started at Timberline Lodge with a couple of vets. And somehow, I got involved in that. There was a PE credit requirement when I was at Reed—that was what the roller skating I did was—but I don't think the skiing was anything for credit. I probably saw a sign for it at the artificial limb shop. The skiing happened mostly on weekends, so it was mostly working people.

Anyway, it sounds all very fancy—the first woman in a national competition—and it was. But what it really speaks to is my pigheadedness because I didn't yet know how to turn when they held the national championships. And so, there was no way I could do a slalom. I did the only thing I could do, which was to fall down at every gate. And got up and got myself pointing the other way. It took me nine minutes to finish the course, but I didn't invalidate any gate. And I was declared the female national champion. It was kind of cool.

And then, some years later, quite a few years later because I was over thirty and concerned about becoming old, I took some lessons, and I went to Winter Park, Colorado, two or three winters in a row. And I was first the bronze winner and then the gold winner in my age category for women in the slalom. There was an actual group of competitors by then. I had been skiing once or twice on two legs prior to Reed. It's actually easier on one leg in a lot of ways because you can't cross your skis. As someone put it at the nationals, all skiers have handicaps. We don't have rigid ankles, our feet are not long enough, and our arms don't reach the ground. We just all use different devices to make up for those deficiencies in skiing.

So was I the only woman? How many other women were competing? The first time, on Mt. Hood, it was only me. That's why I was the winner.

Winter Park and Then Banff

After winning first the bronze and later the gold in the "C" class women's slalom at Nationals in Winter Park, Colorado, I was encouraged to go to the International races held in Banff, Canada. In order to afford it, and also as a means to psych myself up that I was worth it, I made the rounds looking for sponsors. Some surprising local businesses (car repair, dry cleaner) I frequented each chipped in something, and so did my synagogue. It may also be that those were just some of the ones I asked and that I do not remember who exactly got me to the $500 point I needed. Like approaching the talented and gifted program coordinator for a job while carrying with me a cloth template for a cast concrete flamingo, people responded to a visibly inconvenienced athlete in ski clothes who was looking for a race.

After "C" class, there was only a combined "A" and "B" course on a black diamond, expert slope. I had never been on one and was terrified. I did a trial run parallel to the marked course on the day before, helped by a single slug from someone's portable wineskin. On the day of the race, the first initial of my last name dictated a late start, when the slalom had already been carved into significant ruts. This would be both a guide and a hindrance, as any deviation would mean a fall. Somehow, like drawing, like welding, like calligraphy, I focused on staying upright and on the track before me. I concentrated, I swear, as hard as I had ever done, both before or since. I made a single run, at a respectable speed, with no falls though much fear, and lay down in the snow weeping with relief, just away from the finish line. Not far from the end. Soon, of course, I had to pee, and it was too far to ski back to the lodge!

And worse, it had just been announced that in order to qualify at all, a second run was required. I did the second run, I fell repeatedly and got up each time to finish the course. The ruts were hip-deep by this time. But the combination of one bad and one good run was not enough to even place in the race. Driven by the idea that I was there on other people's money, I had felt I had to try, even though the previous day's exploratory run had shown me it was hopeless. I vowed never to do anything on anyone else's money again, a vow I managed to forget in 2014, when I did a Kickstarter type campaign to raise money for an epic exhibit and then had to actually produce the show I had raised funds for!

After that earlier gold medal win, a slalom I had completed in 27 seconds, I was to have had a medal hung around my neck while standing on a box in front of everyone, but I asked someone to collect the medal for me and changed my flight for Manhattan. I could just make it for my oldest nephew's Bar Mitzvah, and now I had something to celebrate! I had nothing vaguely suitable to wear, so I wore my velvet jumpsuit with matching sash, which was actually bought from the lingerie department. Everyone thought it was very original. My family was happy to see me, and there is a wonderful photo of my father holding up my arm as if to declare me, finally, a winner.

Adventures in Prosthetics

When I still had aluminum underarm crutches, I once carelessly put one crutch down a sewer grate, fell over the top of it, and bent it to a forty-five-degree angle. Sitting on the curb, I could not stop laughing. It was such a ridiculous position to be in. I would not be able to walk the two blocks home, and still, I laughed and could barely speak when a passing gentleman took in the scene, bent the crutch over his knee to about twenty degrees, and gave it back to me. I walked home.

"You did a really good job on that one," I said to the prosthetist. "He is walking really well." I was looking at a handsome young man striding down the corridor down from my fitting room.

"He ought to," replied my tech guy. "He is missing an arm."

Some weeks later, when presented with a new endoskeleton limb with a cosmetic foam cover, my powers of observation were tested again.

"This is another left leg," I said, leaving it unsaid for the moment that I required a right one. "What the ..." and then he tried to bullshit me about all the curves, which clearly went in the wrong direction. I finally won out with my anatomical knowledge about the ankle, where the interior process is always higher than the exterior one.

The mix-up was partly my doing, as I had provided a plaster cast of my remaining left leg to work from (not replicate!). In my garage workshop, I had gathered all the materials I needed in hand's reach. I had settled my extended leg into a box, drawn a horizontal separation line on my skin, buried my leg halfway into wet plaster, and let it set. I had thoroughly Vaselined my leg and cast myself ankle to thigh, leaving aside the complexities of my foot, which would be a standard rubber one anyway. Placing the second top half of plaster was a bit nerve-wracking even though I had applied plenty of release agent to the surface before encasing the lower half. Thoroughly captured in setting plaster which heats slightly as it dries, I wondered if my husband would be able to hear me if

I got into trouble extricating myself from the mold. I thought not. I had a chisel and mallet at hand and tapped at the seams. The top half lifted off just fine, and with a little wriggling, I got my leg up out of the bottom.

My work was not done as I then had to recoat the interior surfaces, reattach the two halves, and fill it full with yet more plaster. When set, I chipped off the mold, and there it was—a left leg, recognizably my own. This is what I brought into the prosthetics shop and passed on, via the boss, to the hapless Vietnamese helper to copy. Lost in translation was to copy it to make the mirror image, the right leg. The relationship between boss and helper was one that allowed for no uncertainty or questions, and I guess the poor guy did not think for himself about the purpose of the exercise. He just followed orders and copied it.

Tumbling to the facts around prosthetics was often difficult for outsiders. At the National Inconvenienced Sportsmen's Ski Races one year, there was a charming double amputee who held a whole table full of skiers mesmerized while he recounted that he was broke and sleeping in his car to economize. He was a good-sized guy with the broad shoulders of an athlete. We all teased him about how he could possibly be comfortable in the back seat of his jeep. It took quite a long silence for most of the single amputees at the table to get it—that without his two prosthetic lower legs on, he was not really very tall. He finally supplied the punchline himself so that the few idiots remaining could share in the joke. Sometimes, there is nothing to do but laugh.

Janis Joplin and Hypothermia

Had Janis Joplin not died, I probably would have. Her death demonstrated to me that it was possible to die of an excess of passion. At the time, I did not understand her use of heroin or alcohol, but I did understand the pain and the raw screams in her voice.

My river kayaking lessons were also a flirtation with mortality. Capsizing in a pool was nothing like doing so in a raging river. I had sent my clothes and contact lenses on ahead with the van and planned to kayak with only my swimsuit on. I quickly capsized twice, got to the river bank, emptied the boat, got back in, and rejoined the group, but I understood that I could die under one of these rocks I could not see. I firmly told the guide that I was in danger and that I could not continue unless I was permitted to follow him as he navigated each rock. I did not capsize again, I did not drown, and I am here to tell the tale. Not panicking counts. Actually, we learned that at my summer camp, made to jump in the lake fully clothed and shod with firmly tied shoelaces. Then we were not to panic, but to untie our shoelaces, remove our footwear, sweatshirts and pants, all underwater, and come up swimming and breathing! I repeated that exercise a couple of years ago just for fun, and it is a wonderful training against panicking.

Ukraine

Antisemites were particularly virulent there. Then again, where did they not kill babies and children, and hurt women? The world has had cruel peoples and territories for a long, long time.

The legacy of "making business" with bribery and of officials playing falsely is still very strong in Ukraine. Knowing how to play these games is a survival skill.

Personally I am good with knives now, but when I first started sculpting, I could not get near a sharp edge without cutting myself accidentally. One has to learn how to be safe around sharp edges and crooked people.

Miscarriages

What I remember is hearing the voices of two of my neighbors, chatting with each other outdoors. I was lying flat, prone on the ground, behind a gate to our garden. I was beyond crying and holding onto the earth itself. It was a third miscarriage, and I felt *in gantzen* (altogether) forsaken. Until then, I did not know that grief could take the form of losing one's hold on gravity. Perhaps it was gravity that brought me to a still surface. From there, the voices of the women chatting was a way back to living in the world. They were clearly alive, and perhaps I was, too. There was nothing that could not be borne in community.

Some days later, I spoke with one of them about the failed pregnancies. To my surprise, she herself had two miscarriages before giving birth to her two sons. She told me how common the event was and how people did not talk enough about this experience.

I started to look for statistics on frequency, and indeed, miscarriage is common. This knowledge did not remove the grief, especially in view of my professor husband's opinion that a simple biological event had occurred (which he did not seem to incorporate as an emotional event). Still, the idea that other women had experienced the same sorts of feelings helped me feel less alone with them. I also searched for, and found for the occasion, a Yiddish woman's prayer (*techina*) in a 19th century book I found at YIVO in New York City.

Eventually, I purchased an heirloom rose bush and asked the unemotional partner to dig the hole for it. This he did, and we planted "miscarriage rose." It bloomed for the first time for the subsequent successful pregnancy (my younger son), and it blooms every year

Crying out to God: Why Mothers Get White Hair

Raising my hand and arm toward the ceiling, I cried out to God to help me. I pounded my fourteen-month-old between the shoulder blades just as we had been shown in infant CPR. I had draped him across my lap, face down, and hit him until he started to breathe.

Moments before, he had been lying on his back, babbling to me, when he suddenly swept a little hand under the edge of the sofa, scooped up a penny, popped it in his mouth, and apparently swallowed it before I could even react. His facial color went a deep blue very quickly, and while I remembered instructions on how to dislodge foreign objects, I was completely terrified.

Calling out for God's help made me breathe, focus, and continue to act. He was breathing and pinking up, but the penny had not been disgorged. I picked him up and went off for an X-ray.

The doctor's office was fairly casual because the baby was breathing and content. After the X-ray, they whisked us to the ER across the street to have the penny extracted under general anesthesia. The penny was stuck upright in the esophagus. Had it fallen flat, it would have blocked the windpipe. We were very lucky, I was told, that it had not fallen from its position. Of course, it got upright and off the windpipe by my blows to the baby's back and my strength and presence of mind, which just may have come from the hand of God.

My friend Naomi made a necklace for me featuring the now-corroded penny, but I have never worn it. My toddler son, successfully coming out of anesthesia and eating an icy popsicle to soothe his sore throat, was enough. He enjoyed that popsicle, and so did I. We could have lost him. This upsets me even now. Mothers, look under the edges of your furniture!

This was no retreat into the primitive past with religion as the conduit. This episode in my life was an integration of body, mind, and spirit.

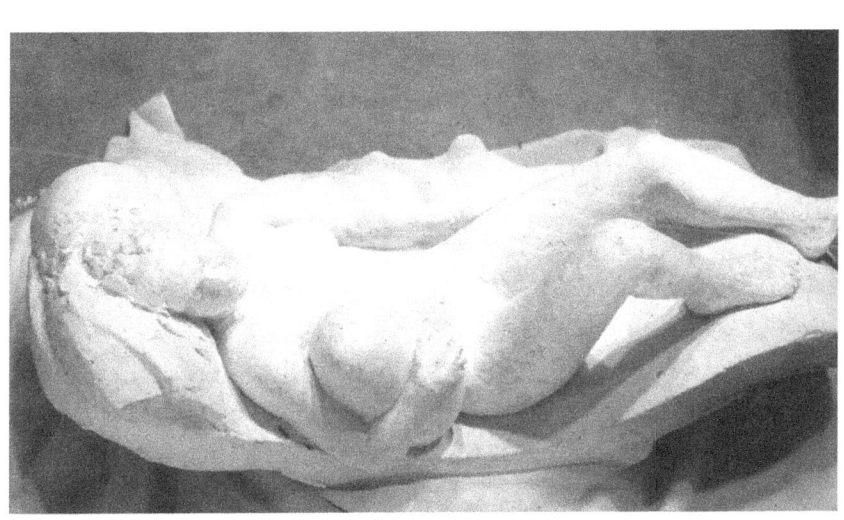

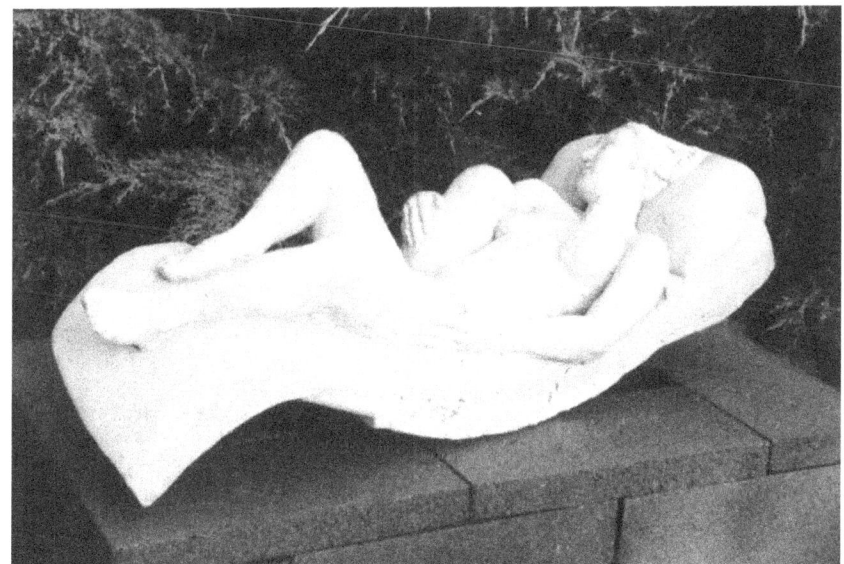

Witches' Disassociation in Times of Crisis

Nanya's eyes were blue—my first witch, full of terror, speaking on familiar terms with her God, miming the demons ready to spring out of closets and cupboards, fear-inspiring (not fearful) even into old age as she wet her pants climbing the stairs to the only bathroom at age eighty-four. No wonder my father feared her fate and installed a main-floor bathroom. My father died at eighty, anyway, aiming for it on purpose. "It is not good to become too old," he said.

Perhaps the most frightening thing about disassociation is when I accidentally scraped the back of my hand against multiple sharp points—a ragged, raw cut edge of wire diamond mesh—and it did not break the skin. I was therefore able to identify that I was sometimes in a "state" when working. So dissociating, getting into a "state," is useful to warriors, to women in childbirth, to survivors.

Finding Each Other by the Root

I've also had some impact on bringing people together who wanted to find each other. At the first conference I organized in Seattle in 1997 about Yiddish language and culture, we put up a giant map. We had people put a pin or stick a dot or something on it. It was very, very interesting to see that the entire Jewish area of Eastern Europe is well represented in Seattle. All those areas that were decimated in the Holocaust, there are still some descendants. And it was a very important feeling for all of us who attended that first conference and came to subsequent conferences to sort of reunite. We organized the tables in the dining room by region. People were doing lots of, "Where are your relatives from? Where are your relatives from?" It was really exciting to find each other alive and well in the NW.

The Sailing Trip

I wanted to participate in more outdoor recreation but generally felt disadvantaged doing so with other people. I saw a sign pasted up somewhere for a sailing lesson from a known organization for the differently abled. I presented myself at the dock and, somewhat reluctantly, was waved "bye-bye" by Joe and young Zach.

Out on the lake, it was deliciously cool. The calm man at the stern gave simple, pleasant directions to the crew of four to do this and now that. I was even given a chance to steer mid-lake, the wind blowing in my hair. I looked around and thought up theories as to who these people were. The calm captain was surely from the organization of the able-bodied taking us out. The woman with terrible tattoos up and down her arms certainly, and hopefully, was a recovering addict. The guy with sunglasses had some unknown malady. A quiet fourth helped with the sails. I was the fifth, and I got to steer again as we came to the dock.

The calm captain was less calm as we nearly rammed it full tilt when someone didn't follow his instructions. I was steering, and I naively aimed right for it. As we disembarked, there were lots of surprises. The calm captain was lifted into a wheelchair, as he was paraplegic. The woman with the tattoos was the social worker with the organization and was taking care of us. The man with sunglasses was blind. Good thing I aimed for the dock. However someone might have explained what "bringing her around" actually meant when I nearly hit the dock straight on!

Broken Promise to Me

"Falling down one can do on one's own. To get up again takes many helping hands." *Aropfaln ken men aleyn ton. Tsu oyfshteyn nemt a sach helfindi-ke hent.* Yiddish proverb

Who knows what I mean by broken promise there? Let me describe the tributes made in clay by each of my two young sons: "Best Mom" and "I Love You" written across these medals. I really do my best, am my best, will be my best. What does that mean? Never to disown them, even when I feel like it? To be a dispassionate presence, an eternal verity, a scent, an embrace? After I distanced myself from my own mother after my cancer at age fifteen, I did not really let her reach me until a visit when my dog had gone missing. I let her hold me briefly to comfort me. I snuggled in for a moment to her open arms. I was already age thirty-one, and she died the next year. Dispassionately, without an embrace, she had earlier allowed me to bring her a cup of tea, to serve her. She wished me "Adieu," and for the first time, I understood what it meant—that I would see her again only with or within God. This is a concept so terrifying and so comforting as to be nearly paralyzing. Where was she going?

Many years later, when my father died, and then recently, a brother, I understood that the concept of the "Wings of the feminine essence (known as the *Shekhinah*) of God" is, of course, related to the embrace of a mother. The opening of the arms and baring of the heart area is an archetypal symbol so powerful as to transcend language, time, and even culture. Hold me and be held. Of course, "No" is another answer. Don't touch. Go away.

And never hug over the threshold because it is bad luck. I did exactly that with this daughter-in-law I did not know if I wanted. I was so eager to show acceptance I did not feel that I hugged her at the door. Soon enough, she said they would not be seeing me anymore and has managed to enforce it with my older son. That is his broken promise. They have not visited in almost fifteen years. Yesterday my son called my remaining brother and asked for "support on this," that what I have been doing is "wrong." What have I been doing?

I put an old photo of son and daughter-in-law, taken from his twenty-fifth high school reunion gathering and available on the web, into my annual holiday letter. I stated that they could choose to be distant, but like the alumni association, family would always be there. What a crime! I called her by her name, referred to her as his wife, accorded her the status owed to her, and received: opprobrium. Of course, from their point of view, they must have experienced it as yet another unforgiveable boundary "violation" for which I must apologize.

Conceptual Art

I really was laughing up my sleeve when my older brother—who's very sophisticated, lived in Manhattan his whole life, is interested in art, has a career in advertising—looked at a sculpture with a Yiddish proverb for a title. The sculpture fits the proverb, and the proverb fits the sculpture. Yet, he couldn't figure out which came first. He said, "I get it! It's a conceptual piece." And, I mean, that's true, but give me a break here, I knew what I was making when I made it. I had an idea in mind. And just because you can read my idea, that's good. That means I succeeded (below *Shtarkayt in Eynhayt*, Strength in Unity). Language was part of the art!

Photo: Alex Strazzanti

Autonomy

Mashed Finger

When I was pretty young, maybe seven, I caught my left index finger in the car door as my middle brother suddenly slammed it. Needless to say, I howled. My mother hurried over. We were parked in front of our building where my parents' medical office was located, as well as our apartment. She sent me upstairs with the rest of the family while she collected supplies from the ground-floor office. Really fast, she put together a tray with a sterile cloth on it and on which were all the supplies she would need to fix my finger.

I was so very impressed that she could think and act at the same time and had the skill to act on someone she was so close to. I have a scar and deformed nail on that finger still, but I have a clear memory of how capable my mother was.

When I graduated from art school after four fairly tough years as a single parent raising a very young child, my parents delayed their visit for another year. They then saw my garage set up for the first time as a studio, with my tools clean and laid out in order by groups and by sizes, clean and rust-free. From that moment, my mother said she took me seriously because she saw how I took care of my tools. I had a profession that's even similar to a "fixing" occupation, but my profession dealt with building from scratch.

Weights and Measures

Miss Pappas, in home economics class, taught us how to make spanakopita decades before real men ate quiche (with bits of green vegetable in them). We had to keep a notebook of our recipe assignments and results, just like for a science class. I baked some muffins without noticing the difference between teaspoon (tsp) and tablespoon (tbsp) and trashed one of the ovens with the overblown results. I never made that mistake again and still take good care to record methods, quantities of materials used, and any color tests in lab notebooks in my sculpture studio.

In my school's junior high school homeroom, we also learned how to measure money: the difference between stocks and bonds and the pitfalls of compound interest. Years went by before I studied any of that again, but the basic lessons stuck and were empowering. Women could expect to independently understand money.

The biggest challenge of my high school years was my relationship with authority and my rebellion against the enforcers of that authority. I was threatened with immediate expulsion if I ever left school in the middle of the day again. That first particular occasion was a dustup with a PE teacher who refused to allow me to play basketball while hopping. (The alternative was a 13½-pound fiberglass prosthesis.) I left the building, right out the door, and went to visit my youth group rabbi to unload my grievances. His office was in the limestone-clad "Love Thy Neighbor as Thyself" building, then owned by the Reform movement of Judaism, on Fifth Avenue and 65th Street in Manhattan. He heard me out, briefly but lovingly patted my behind while remarking that I had such a nice one and advised me to go on home. When I got there, the school principal was on the telephone line, and I was in big trouble for causing her to worry about the possibility of being assaulted in the park.

Twice more, then accompanied by a friend, we escaped the building without getting caught by climbing the ladder up from the balcony of the tenth-floor gym onto the roof. From there, it was a simple matter to cross over to the college roof and go down their elevator to the street level. A block away was Madison Avenue, with all its delights of window shopping.

The second expedition was cut short by running across our Latin teacher, who pretended not to see us. Since no one wanted to get him into any trouble, we stopped going out. We were clearly more respectful of others' needs than they often were of ours.

The next year I had relearned how to ride a bicycle and often rode to school in good weather, which necessitated pants (forbidden) or a highly practical "skort" or "culottes". Again I was threatened with expulsion, and again, just for show, I changed into a skirt after arriving in my skort. However, I knew this was totally idiotic, completely out of proportion, and had nothing to do with common sense or practicality. Upholding the school dress code had everything to do with "them" and nothing to do with "me." This became my standard in all things: if something was only to benefit or please "them," then "I" could certainly nix it.

Today this kind of independence of thought is sometimes called "oppositional defiance," but for me, my very survival depended on it.

Childbirth

The forsythia outside the window of the hospital was blooming when I was giving birth to Ben, my first son. This was in early February, a bit early for the Northwest. Forsythia has always had a meaning of the coming of spring to me. My dad used to cut some of the apparently dead branches in December at the country house, bring them into the warm, city apartment, and they would push out green leaves and then yellow flowers in a display of light and hope.

The actual birth was straightforward, and although I objected, there was an episiotomy (better than a tear). I sat up for much of the labor, and the nurse kept trying to push me horizontal. I did not consciously think about gravity, though it is obvious now. I did have to lie in stirrups for the actual delivery, but I experienced the final waves of contraction as my world's biggest orgasm ever to date and went over the top with it—cries of joy and the unrestrained noises of a working animal.

Nursing protocol whisked the baby away too soon and later bore him off to the nursery. I had to produce nearly a complete meltdown to attract enough staff to get the baby back.

"What does she want?" asked the attending physician over all my crying.

"She wants the baby," answered the nurse grimly.

"Well, give it to her!"

And so I got the baby back in my room and in my arms, but the pain of that separation would remain with me always.

My second childbirth, twenty-three years later and after three miscarriages, was also straightforward, though four weeks early. After a threatened early labor at twenty-eight weeks, my doctor had told me to hold out for thirty-six weeks minimum. So I followed instructions. It was very textbook, actually. I made a pot of soup and maybe even cleaned the kitchen. And in some order, I walked by Lake Washington, at Matthews Beach, and sat and then lay down on a large sloping rock. It was a perfect shape for a birthing bench, with plenty of room to catch a baby or even to let it fall to the ground. I read somewhere sometime that there was a birthing stone known to the local Native Americans at that beach. But I was just looking for a clear spot to sit down.

There was a passerby who was very agitated by my very pregnant state and kept asking to go for help, but I shooed him away. I had come to the lake for strength, to concentrate my mind for labor. I knew what effort was to come, and I wanted to practice emptying my mind across the liquid of the waves.

Then, or maybe first, more likely first, I went to the mall, straight to the perfume counter of a large department store, and sniffed samples until I identified Shalimar, the essence of my mother. I sprayed some on a paper sampler and took it with me. Now I was ready, although my mother had died thirteen years before, now she was with me. Indeed, during the "transition" phase of labor, my mother and my grandmother appeared to me as corporeal images, massed together near the foot of my bed, ready to assist if needed. This frightened me as I assumed seeing them meant I was dying.

And I "heard" my mother say to my grandmother, "We are frightening her. We had better go." And then their images disappeared.

And I gave birth. No orgasm this time, and a nasty, though small, tear. What with patients' rights, the doctor had obeyed my request for not doing an episiotomy. Note to self: a tear and stitching hurts worse than a neat episiotomy. And the sensation of tearing is one of unbearable bursting and a sense of traumatic injury, as indeed it is.

Erotic Smells of Plaster Hold for a Lifetime

Skipping forward to sculpture training, I learned to use enameled basins for mixing plaster, and was actually told by an orthopedic surgeon (a cousin's husband) that I was doing the work of an orthopedic surgeon—supporting the wrists and ankles against breakage throughout the process by making strong armatures for the piece and using metal and plastic inside the molds.

The smell of wet plaster and of cement all became associated with the great pleasure of using these materials. Even the smell of the "release agent," ordinary green soap applied to the inside of the molds.

Textures. Dry hands. Smooth tools. Plaster slipping off the tool. Smoothing off plaster.

Knife thrills. Rotary cutter for fabric. Paring knife. Fettling knife. Pottery needle. Scalpel.

The Beach

Our trips to the beach on the Oregon coast were a vacation from money, from worry, from grocery shopping and bills, repairs, and taxes.

I would rent something simple for a solid week and immediately set up an arts-and-crafts corner in case of inclement weather. I would buy enough food for the whole week, so I would not have to go to the store even once. Then I rested, really rested—a week of Shabbat-like days where I could lie down whenever I felt like it.

Ben and our shepherd mix dog were equally free to run as much as they wanted. I could lie down but still enjoy watching them run this way and that on the beach, launching and then following Ben's colorful kite. In late August, the weather was usually ideal at the beach for kite flying and for wading.

We did not try to swim in the great Pacific. It was enough to outrace the tiny wavelets advancing onto the shore after a big wave crested further out. It was the sound I loved, the intense quiet of the wild covered over with the ongoing hum and drone of the holy ocean.

I will always be here, the ocean said to me. *I have always been here. I am here even when you are not. I am always here.*

When Ben got married twenty years later, he did so on an Oregon beach—I suppose the most spiritual place he knew. Maybe I gave him that with those summer weeks of freedom.

If it was cold or rainy, we could always amuse ourselves with puzzles, games, and, especially for me, art projects. We both played with watercolors straight from the box, painting imaginary scenes. And in our little isolated family, like the pioneers, Ben knew he needed to be useful, ferrying groceries, anticipating, and then fetching whatever had to be carried. We really were a team.

Traveling Alone With a Child (Written About 1977)

When I first separated from my husband, I imagined that I would take off to explore new cities and meet new circles of (single) friends. Like most suddenly single women, I found myself immediately isolated and excluded from my social circle.

The next four years were a complicated swirl of depression, part-time jobs and part-time daycare for a very young child, and eventually, full-time school for both of us. It was difficult enough to maintain a home, a schedule, a way of life without considering further upheaval! In fact, the idea of traveling anywhere terrified me. I was afraid of driving any distance, afraid of feeling any greater loneliness or withdrawal from society than I already was feeling.

Of course, I eventually made new friendships and revived some of the old ones. My confidence expanded as I discovered I could cope and grow by myself. But there were still things I did not have the "heart" to do. One was vacationing. I started small: an afternoon's outing, an overnight, a weekend. I even took myself to the beach for a week (and rediscovered a peace I had forgotten so completely, I felt reborn). But I still drew the line at distance. With the exception of visiting my family—destination known, plane fare paid—I stirred very little from my own territory. My city was relatively small—small enough, anyway, that I ran into familiar faces most everywhere I went. I thought it was the kindness of known faces that sustained me.

I knew somewhere in my mind that the outgoing, comfortable self was still partly buried and that I needed a complete change, at least for a while. Traveling is liberating because it is possible to try on any self at all—for "size" and for response. Anyway, I love to talk to strangers, always have, and feel a lot safer about it if the contact is predefined by the transient situation.

Anyway, I rather methodically began to prepare for a month's absence during my school vacation, but before the main holiday crowd: June 3-July 3. I got a friend to take the dog and water the plants. I got the car tuned up and checked out. I cleared my desk (for the first time in a year). I assembled camping equipment and clothes:

- One (2) person tent with floor and mosquito netting
- Two ensolite pads
- Two sleeping bags
- One battery-powered reading light
- One campstool
- One mess kit
- One burner propane stove
- Two (for easier carrying) small Styrofoam chests
- Three nesting plastic bowls
- Silverware and spices
- One plastic 2-gallon jar
- One 5-gallon plastic water carrier
- Two flashlights, insect repellent, first aid kit, second-hand guitar

A triple A (AAA) triptik guide Portland to Santa Fe and return via the Southwest, starting out with the Oregon Trail (going in reverse).

The only real mystery confronting us was why we were sometimes not served in restaurants or denied registration at a motel. They told me they were either "waiting for the man to come in and be seated" or concerned that I might be being followed by a violent man "who would bust up the place". I was a woman traveling alone with a child, that is all. We were fine.

The Fuller Brush Man

I had time, and I was also very lonely. There were few door-to-door salesmen in my childhood, though I did remember a Fuller Brush man at the country house. It was amazing to see all their wares swiftly unpacked from suitcases and demonstrated before your eyes. I didn't hesitate to let a salesman with company ID into my Portland home. He was personable and talkative, and I treated him with politeness and genuine interest. I even bought a small brush I still find invaluable in my studio some forty-five years later.

At the time, as the salesman packed up and prepared to leave, he became suddenly grave. He warned me that I was much too trusting and that he could have done "whatever he wanted to do here."

"I just got out of prison," he said meaningfully, "but you treated me like a human being." At that, he choked up a bit and left.

What of value did he see in my living room? A threadbare, though once valuable, "oriental" rug, a paucity of furnishings, a guitar, me, myself, no match for his strength, I am sure. But I was not afraid of him. He had a mission to sell brushes, and I had bought.

The Piano Tuner

Middle-class Jewish families of my time acquired pianos as soon as they could afford them. This was somewhat for show, but more importantly, to test for Horowitzship (prodigies) among the children. One of my father's brothers was such a prodigy, and I think my older son might have been one.

We had gone to a musical while on a visit to NYC, and a few weeks later, I overheard him remember and pick out the theme song on someone else's piano. Directly, I acquired a secondhand piano for him and lessons to go with it, but I would have done better to let him pick things out and play on his own.

He learned enough about music in high school to sing in a chorus in college and afterward, to sing (and also juggle) with the choruses of first the Seattle and then the Portland opera companies. The private lessons he wanted as a young teen were drum lessons and a drum set of his own. He earned his pocket money all through college, playing drums with various bands.

The used piano I bought him when he was seven was badly out of tune. The piano tuner I hired happened to be blind. As he did his work, I sat on the sofa and dozed. It was so comforting to have another adult in the house. The tuning required a lot of striking the same or similar tones up and down the scale as he adjusted the strings.

"Well, you really must trust me," he said when he was done. "You fell asleep while I was here."

Now, how did he know that? I suppose he heard me breathe, maybe even snore, slightly. I felt utterly safe being lulled to sleep by tones of music.

Which Body to Inhabit

I dressed for a date in a slip. Just a lacy slip instead of a dress. We were not going to go anywhere, I was sure. Just off to bed.

The remarkable thing was that I had spent days in "men's clothing"—pants and rough shirts for the studio—and little or no time on appearance. Quite abruptly, I put on a dress-length slip and glanced in the mirror, feeling a tremendous disconnect between my power inside and the appearance of fragility outside. Clearly, I was choosing a costume and a feminine identity to make love with a man. Like a man of the era, I was also choosing to be sexual on my own terms and pretty much without strings.

Recreational sex was not invented along with the birth control pill. I am sure it had been around for the ages. But powerful women, even seen as "butch" by some, held a certain attraction, of wildness, I suppose—something animal, something energetic. We certainly never used the word passion. Yet I think that is what it was: a sort of misspent or possibly well-spent passion that could have gone toward some other obsession and often did.

It took days, weeks, sometimes months to carry out the sculpture works I made at the time. Wrapped up against the cold in many layers of clothes, working to my physical limits, a date was a change. A hot bath would ease the muscle aches. A simple slip became a ballgown and poof! I was a woman again.

Adventures With Joe Before Zach (Joe: Part 1)

My coworkers never quite believed the travels I was suddenly undertaking: London! The south of France! Even with a French postmark on a French postcard, they doubted the validity of my story.

It was, in fact, both unbelievable and totally predictable that my scientist fiancé was invited to meetings all over the Western world and that he wanted me to accompany him. Sometimes this was really basic, like a dorm room at the University of Nottingham (not exactly Claridge's in London). Nottingham was the first time I took buses and went exploring by myself during the days when Joe attended his meetings. The town is built in an area of soft sandstone, and I was fascinated by store spaces simply carved into the ground or surrounding cliffs. I went to the Robin Hood museum but, even more important, a craft museum, where I was able to trace the evolution of the form of the "English" style ceramic pitcher, a subject I was as much interested in as Joe was in the evolution of the human species.

Our trip to the south of France was to the private estate of an extremely rich benefactress of the Human Genome Project. Here again, my five-hundred-dollar wardrobe, purchased with the sale of my company stock just before I met Joe, came in handy. I also knew, or could guess at, the prevailing culture at the estate, so I dressed every evening for dinner and spent at least part of my time continuing to embroider my trousseau. I was now up to flower-bedecked pillowcases with crocheted edges.

I have a mental picture of myself in a crisp, pink-and-white, vertical-striped blouse, with a pink bandana tied jauntily around my neck. I was sitting on a sofa, waiting for the dinner gong, while embroidering. One of the sous chefs went to get the master chef with the tall hat to come and take a look. He emerged from the kitchen, made a French sound (sort of an "aw!"), and then "C'est jolie ca!" (That is so pretty!)

The actual lady of a house was an absolute ruler. There was one evening where she apparently thought that dinner had been sufficient, and, lifting her hand, she sent the carts bearing salads for sixty people back to the kitchen. She also took enough of an interest in me to order a rental car with automatic transmission for me, so I could go see museums of the Nice area while Joe was in his meetings. Terrified at first by the other cars going 125 kilometers per hour on the motorways, I nevertheless got myself out of the lavender fields of the estate (where I had, in fact, been perfectly happy) and went to see wonderful art.

On a Saturday without meetings, Joe and I went exploring and out to lunch with another couple, from Harvard no less. They seemed quite interested in getting to know me, and I think I talked a lot about my various enthusiasms. The next day, the wife sought me out to tell me that her husband had cried (and he never cries!) about meeting me. Apparently, he had never actually talked to anyone with a disability and had thought that a prime purpose of the Human Genome Project was to "get rid of people like me."

"But she's wonderful!" he said, and then started crying, "and she even speaks French," he wailed!

The next time we went to Europe, it was London and then Edinburgh. In London, there were the wonders of the British Museum and a lasting impression of a hideous enlargement of a bronze of Albert Einstein done straight from the maquette. The head was recognizable, but the larger-than-life size body was like a pile of loose clay.

In Edinburgh, I was shown the castle and all the sites and fed an enormous Sunday dinner by our hosts, consisting of ham and three vegetables. I was actually so distressed about eating it, I later made a version of my dinner plate in painted plaster.

When Joe wanted me to accompany him on a trip to Germany, I bartered for a trip to Israel at the next opportunity. I cried all the way into Germany on the train from Belgium. No amount of being urged to look at the scenery could distract me from my reality of passing into Germany by train. We even saw police waylay, catch, and beat a brown-skinned stowaway on the train. Then they arrested him.

For Christmas-Day dinner, we were served an unidentifiable stew, salad, etc., and our hostess mocked me. "You are not a Jew. You didn't even ask. I gave you pork." So that was that. I have not eaten pork nor shellfish since, no matter the hostess, nor returned to Germany.

It was at this point that on a routine trip east (New York and Washington DC), we went to the Hirshhorn Sculpture Collection and Garden. It was actually not my first time there, but I knew I liked the place.

My son Ben was grown and gone to college. I was indoors, surrounded by wonderful sculptural forms in warm-looking bronze, in stone, and cold metal. I wandered outside and suddenly saw a small boy, maybe six or seven years old, jump over a hedge just because he could. I was surrounded by the most beautiful sculpture in the world, and none of it was as beautiful as one living child jumping. It was not that I wanted to give up sculpture, and I did not. The overwhelming feeling was that I did not want to give up being the mother of a moving creature who was a delight to my eye.

A subsequent trip to Denmark was less difficult on the dietary side. There was always fish, like twenty-two kinds of herring, for breakfast. But most fraught for me was my feminist agenda. In Copenhagen, it was particularly obvious, but everywhere it seemed women were either whore or Madonna, bad girl or good girl. In the big city, tarted-up females were everywhere, but so too were stolid housewives with plastic shopping baskets and sensible clothes. And blunt cut bobs of hairdos, always with bangs cut in like tidy five-year-olds. Could one not be elegant without aping an over-the-top Dolly Parton look?

The smaller town we were going to, Aarhus, boasted two art schools, and I arranged to visit the sculpture departments. That was fun for me to see how things were both the same and different. I did see a student modifying his plasterwork with a hatchet, and that made a tremendous impression on me to see, even though I had read that Rodin did the same thing.

So many art graduates in one town meant that even the most modest grocery store had a beautiful window display. I so enjoyed window shopping, as if the windows were paintings, which they were in composition, color, and texture. When we left Denmark for Sweden by ferry, we saw another difference in national character. There was a soccer game on, and when the Danish team won it, we braced for shouting and high fives. Instead, the Danish youth nearby simply turned slightly pink with pleasure, a very buttoned-down response.

Romantic Love

"Ironically, the gendered nature of traditional Jewish instruction enabled some women to have access to modern ideas earlier than many men within their communities." — *Jewish Women in Eastern Europe*, by Paula Hyman

Yiddish songs serve as historical sources for "the struggles and victories" of Jewish women, as well as expressing "joy and suffering, interests and concerns."

In the poem "The Saxophone Player" by Beyle Schaechter-Gottesman, the poet assumes that romantic love is the cause of the musician's plaintive music: "Did she leave you, or did you chase her away?" The poet feels the "outcry" of the musician and identifies herself with the pain. She begs others to give him money in hopes that he will "be quiet" and describes his playing, while, "The night embraces me," as, "An echo that stretches without end." For a woman to understand and write about romantic pain, she must have experienced it for herself at some time, within or without marriage (late twentieth century).

The other poem presented in a class, "Mother, What Do You Want of Me?" is also concerned with romantic love, but in this case, the anonymous poet of the "Folksong" is from an earlier era and is still under the actual control of her own parents, who "drive you away from me!" The poet addresses both her mother and her beloved: "Where are you, my soul?" in a lament about being separated from her "friend." She first asks her mother, "Why do you torture your child?" about this enforced separation from her beloved or possible unwanted marriage to another. She begs him to, "Listen to my cry, and come flying to me!"

Romantic love was not considered a proper basis for a Jewish match or marriage. Only the scholarship of the proposed son-in-law and the lineage and dowry of the proposed bride were part of the equation. Concepts of romantic love were a by-product of "modern ideas" of the late nineteenth century and were also fed by the breakdown of the traditional authority of the parents in selecting spouse(s) for their child(ren). Said children accepting the choices of the parents was another casualty of more modern times. Age at marriage also crept older in the late 19th century as opportunities for education presented themselves. Girls attended both secular gymnasiums and universities as able, while males from religious families remained in Yeshivot and were less exposed to modern European literature and its ideas.

The famous Russian and German writers were dismissed as not having *yichus* (a good lineage), like the Torah scholars. Writers of the non-religious communities and reading the literature of the Enlightenment were considered suspect by many observant Jewish people.

The Watching Heart

If I hold my watch against my ear, I can hear it ticking. I don't know if the rhythm is anything like my heart, but the steadiness reassures me. I was kind of folded against myself, sitting up against the back of the loveseat with my left arm thrown up over my head. That position put my watch (on my left wrist), I think, right up against my ear. I sat that way for a long time, listening. It must have seemed such a miracle to the first wristwatch wearers. It goes. It is still going. Listen, it is still going. There is nothing like the present—the gift of life is in the present—that's why we call it: the present.

Act 2

Connectedness

Because He Wept

Because he wept (asking forgiveness?) I was in holy space.

I stood there, one hand resting on the bed and the other, I believe, resting atop the surgeon's shoulder. He had come into the double room, drawn the curtains around my cubicle, and announced his intention of changing my compression bandages. This was, perhaps, the first time since the amputation, though I have nightmare memories of pain, drainage, and menstruation-stained sheeting.

Anyway, by day three perhaps, I could stand, clear-headed, and keep my balance on one foot, with only the light touch—one on the bed and one on his shoulder. He had knelt in front of me so as to be at the right height to wrap me up, and that put a shoulder in reach. He must have told me to hold on to him. But the unusual thing was that he started to weep. He wept all through removing the previous bandage and putting on the new one, and especially when the "drape" would not stay put over my more private parts.

I had been shaved, of course, and my slimness and extreme youth must have looked exquisitely vulnerable to him. Who knows what was in my surgeon's head as he beheld his work—high-above-knee amputation—and his patient, a young girl of fifteen, forever changed?

What happened next was that I let him weep and allowed only a feeling of love to animate my being and to flow through my hands. I felt in those moments not only whole but totally giving, although I did not say anything. It was enough that he wept, that he was sorry, that he knelt before me as if to worship my body, that he felt a need to bind my wound with his own hands, to be somehow the healer and not the destroyer.

The greatest gift, besides possibly my life saved from the sarcoma, was that I experienced this grace, this sense of all-encompassing love and tenderness toward a man I might otherwise have hated. An ability, a tendency even, to love dispassionately, without attachment, Buddha-like, even Madonna-like, has stayed with me my whole life. A gift of healing for me, and I believe, in that case, for the surgeon. What maturity I suddenly found in myself, to let him weep, to create that space, to be so intimate without any sexual touch, to let him bind my wound, passing the elastic bandage around my pelvis, around my remaining bit of leg, and back around my waist.

Love is something you choose.

As American as Apple Pie

Leah took care of me from age three to eight and taught me to make apple pie—just one scant teaspoonful of sugar sprinkled sparingly over each layer of sliced apples and plenty of butter, cut into small slivers. Eat your heart out, former Parisians, when you taste real American cooking at our house.

Marie, our housekeeper from when I was eight to eighteen, had her signature dishes too: pineapple yams (not to mention pineapple hams, all stuck with cloves). To make the yams, mash them (canned or cooked) with butter, brown sugar, and cinnamon. Combine with half a can of crushed pineapple, preserving the juice to drink later. Spoon the yam mixture into a clear Pyrex bowl and top with a geometrically arranged layer of tightly packed marshmallows. Heat about half an hour in the oven until marshmallows puff up and become brown. If possible, serve in a bowl-shaped silver-plated charger so they stay hot through the meal and so the little girl at the table can puzzle over whether we were still rich or not. Were we rich in France?

About the ham: a giant ham was the pièce de résistance in the Marie years, at least before my oldest brother's Bar Mitzvah. Great slits would be made in the outer fat, creating a pattern of parallelograms. This piqued both my interest in solid geometry and pattern and much later in computer graphics. After the slits were made in the ham, a whole clove was inserted in the center of each diamond, and the entire ham covered in closely spaced pineapple rings attached with wooden toothpicks. I have an idea there was a red maraschino cherry or cherries in there, but I may be wrong about that. Certainly, the ham was basted regularly with ginger ale, which may have also been served to us as a party drink, with a cherry on a toothpick, of course.

Back to Marie: can a woman cover a curved ham surface evenly with flat pineapple slices, not to mention succeed at reading the whole of

Anna Karenina really be as dim as her employers thought? Marie was a churchgoing soul, and she was eager to tell me about the apocalypse and to witness her faith. When I asked my mother about all this, she forbade Marie from telling me any more, especially about the resurrection. Some of it stuck anyway and blended with fears of a nuclear holocaust in my lifetime. Both Leah and Marie came from Georgia, so perhaps I turned out more American, or African American, than I usually think.

Order of the Laundresses

"Guess what, Marie? I'm getting married," I told her excitedly, just a few weeks before the event when I was nineteen.

"That's good, baby, that's real good," she said mournfully, seemingly dejected.

Apparently, she had not been able to hold her head up with the protective order of the African American laundresses laboring in the basement of our apartment building.

Marie had a room right near the front door, a tiny room with an adjacent bathroom of its own. Of course, she knew the goings-on in my room on the other side of her bathroom. It was she who reported to her circle of friends in the building that I was "living with" my soon-to-be husband, but without the benefit of marriage.

My parents had allowed that I could share a bedroom and a bed right there in their apartment with my California boyfriend (born in Brooklyn). When they showed us to our room, I had expressed gratitude that they left us together, and my mother said, "There's no point being hypocritical. You're living with him now."

On the other hand, they managed to marry me off, which was not what I had in mind. With a two-to-three-week lead time, one of the things they achieved was to create a suspicion I might be pregnant, which I wasn't. Nor did I want a veil; I don't know where the idea for that came from, probably my friend's mother who made the dress.

There was enough time for one of my college friends to fly in, dressed to the nines, to bewitch a close family member. He was appointed to drive her to the airport after the ceremony, and they did not come back for three days. They got into a lot of trouble.

Sin

On Yom Kippur, recitation of "sins" is communal and made aloud. This was always explained to me as making individual confession possible. Surrounded by others capable of the same, or even worse, mistakes, it was to be easier to state one's own.

In 1983, the cantor had my older son lead a congregation of 400-plus in the *Al Chet* or "Recitation." A stir went through the crowd as the cantor placed a sturdy wooden box in front of the lectern and then stood aside for the diminutive and fairly recent Bar Mitzvah boy. While I knew he was being prepared to take part in the High Holiday service, I had no idea he would be leading this all-important prayer. Even the rabbi protested, in eloquent sign language, that this substitution of voices was not quite appropriate.

And then my son began, confidently, on key, and with feeling. He caught or maybe created the rhythm with the congregation as he named the sins: "envy ... adultery ... disrespect." And they repeated each phrase after him. I wept a little at my sacrificial lamb because this was surely meant to represent my sacrifice and my atonement as this innocent one took on all the sins of an adult.

In college, there was an honor principle meant for handling academic cheating, as well as for honoring other people. I suppose it worked well enough for keeping folks from plagiarizing but did nothing much for the usual hunt for virgin prey among the freshman class. (What dreadful memories I have of attempted seduction and outright assault, even if gently attempted). College was again a place where I was disrespected and discarded, and I had no framework for regaining my individual sense of self.

What are we aiming for? What is the moral compass? If there is nothing dirty about sex, as my father once said, then why do we still refer to them as dirty books? Context matters. In the context of an overheard mother/

daughter conversation, the comment "There is nothing dirty about sex" added a much-needed second parental opinion.

I used to think of some kind of ladder of sins, a sort of hierarchy where if at least no one was getting hurt, there was no real sin. I think I have become more of an absolute morality kind of thinker at this point in life because hurt occurs in many forms. Blunting the ability to love with one's whole heart is also a sin.

Amends

After sinning, it is most important to make amends. The first step is to admit that one is not perfect and that one has regrets. Figuring out how to make amends is difficult but must be done year-round. If one tries to make amends all at once, it becomes like housecleaning—that is, overwhelming. Broken into smaller chunks, making amends—like housework—becomes manageable.

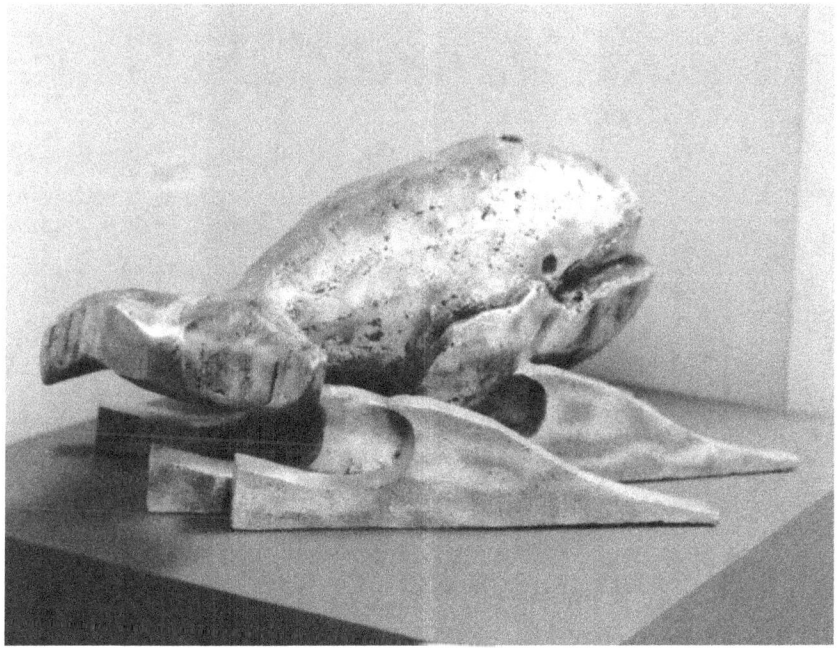

'There Will Still be a Suitor:' A Message of Hope

I was a working single mom, long since divorced, and raising a sixteen-year-old. We were getting by financially, but only just. When I was invited to a Bar Mitzvah ceremony at a small Orthodox *shul* (synagogue), I jumped at the chance of an outing that would include a nice lunch.

Relegated to the women's section upstairs, I was at first outraged at being segregated and then, suddenly, at ease. It didn't matter that I had no husband at my side! It didn't even show! I went back to the Saturday service several times, enjoying the peace of the women's section and the fact that it was the men who set out the kiddush luncheon that followed the service.

At the time of my divorce, I did not think of obtaining a religious divorce as well. When I finally got around to it, I made only a down payment and not the full payment to the court or council of rabbis in Los Angeles who issued it. I just didn't see the point of sending money to a "court" I had never met, and money was tight.

Something about the time I spent in the little Northwest Orthodox *shul* caused me to reconsider my relationship to the "angels." As I told a friend at work, "I think I have to honor my commitment to pay in order to get right with the angels." Of course, I didn't have the money handy, but in reviewing my accounts at the bank, I discovered a small savings account I had completely forgotten existed. It contained, to the dollar, the amount I owed on the religious divorce (which would give me the right to remarry according to religious law).

I also knew I wanted out of the company I worked for, so I sold my stock (which was intended to go toward my retirement) and bought an attractive wardrobe.

People at work assumed I had received a large promotion and treated me accordingly. My self-esteem rose.

I went back to the little *shul* one Saturday dressed in an attractive off-white suit.

At the kiddush luncheon, a tall, white-haired man, also dressed in a white suit, asked me if I was married. I had never seen him before, and he appeared to be in his late 70s. I was in my late 30s at the time, but to honor him, I conversed a bit and said that I was divorced. He drew himself up and pronounced something over me in Yiddish. I did not understand a word. After that, he turned away, and I asked an older friend what had been said.

He had said: "There will still be a suitor!"

Apparently, the gentleman in the white suit had never been to the *shul* before, nor was he ever seen again. Other than identifying himself as being from Los Angeles, no one knew who my "angel of hope" was.

And he was my "angel," because a few weeks later, I met my husband of the last eighteen years at a folk music festival. I was sitting under a tree and embroidering a cloth cover for the braided Sabbath bread (challah) for my future home when he spoke to me. Using my ears alone, I immediately identified the Yiddish melody underlying his tone of voice, even though he was using English words. When he offered to carry my day pack on our way to sample the various ethnic foods from the outdoor food booths at the festival, I knew I had found myself, at last, a "gentleman" from the old school. We were married and, five years later, produced a beautiful son.

How I Met Your Father (Joe: Part 2)

Joe is a year older than my oldest brother. It means that my husband knows what doo-wop is and can appreciate my brother's high school band, "The Explorers." Nick sang bass, and the sound still gives me chills.

"He could be a cantor!" our childhood rabbi opined.

But Nick stuck with college and a music major after his band cut their first album.

Joe loves music too, although mostly folk music over other styles. We independently traveled most years to Vancouver, British Columbia, for its annual summer folk festival held at Jericho Beach. You had to pay to get in, so I suppose it was a primitive form of crowd selection. I was working at the time and could afford the admission, but three nights at a hotel seemed too much. So, my vehicle, a maroon pickup truck, was set up as a camper.

There were bathrooms and a shower at Jericho Beach, and the food booths supplied inexpensive international foods. The festival is always held in July, and the weather was often really quite hot. In 1986, we both attended it in the same year. Still, among ten thousand people, it is amazing that we found each other. I was on my own, but several people from work were there too, and when they ran into me, I was happy to chat.

That, apparently, was when Joe spotted me. He said later that I looked so warm in how I was interacting with my friends. Because of the actual heat, I had scoped out some shade trees near one of the performance stages, and there I stayed for all three days of the festival, as the musical acts rotated among the stages.

A woman friend had offered the advice once that it was important to be at the same place every day at the same time when seeking marriage, so someone who spotted you could ever find you again. I had a book of short stories with me at the Vancouver Festival called *Old Maids* and an embroidery project: the word "Shabbat," with flowers, on a cloth challah bread cover. I had just finished the book, and a pleasant male voice from somewhere behind me said, "Congratulations. You have finished your book." Nice pickup line! He asked if I had tried the booth for Indian foods, as he could recommend the samosas/pakoras. I had not tried them, and he invited me to walk down there and picked up my day pack to carry it. This Boy Scout gesture impressed me more than the interest in foreign food. We still disagree today whether it was the samosas or pakoras that we ate. He says samosas, and she says pakoras and all that.

Periodically, we break tension by spitting out our choice of word. "Samosa!" he'll say. "Pakora!" I'll reply. Bystanders are always dumbfounded.

Anyway, we walked around the site for a bit and came to a puddle. I planted my crutches and swung out over the water, landing neatly on the other side. Joe ran and jumped as best he could, and his rear sneaker went right in the puddle.

"You are superior to me!" he said, and I preened.

Sitting together on a log by the sea, Joe remarked that there might be sharks in this body of water. I had no idea if he was kidding, but I knew he was a biologist. I reached for his hand to hold it for company against the threat, and he eagerly held it back. Before we each left Vancouver, Joe asked for my phone number and suddenly developed a fondness for visiting his sister in Portland and taking me out. Mostly, we went to dinner, but early on, we went to a playground, and Joe hung from a monkey bar to show off. All his loose change fell from his pockets onto the ground. Another playful visit was to an amusement park with the smallest roller coaster either of us had ever seen. It seemed tame enough to both of us. Even so, we were both scared.

I went for advice to the oldest and as it happened, Sephardic, rabbi in Portland. I told him about the religious "get" I had belatedly obtained, freeing me from my first marriage. I told him about my new "suitor," and how I did not know how to think about a possible remarriage. I was not sure about love. The rabbi asked if there was any way to find out about his character. I offered that he had tenure at a university and that I had met his sister, who I liked. "A professional man, a decent man, who loves YOU! WHAT'S TO THINK?"

We courted all the way to Thanksgiving, when I introduced him to my father in late 1986, and we were more or less engaged by Sukkoth 1987. We chose a house in Seattle in September 1987, and I moved north for the wedding in May 1988.

Yahrzeit

The moon is wrong. I know as soon as I step outside that the date is wrong. There is a moon, almost full, brightly illuminating the yard. I cross to the concrete block memorial. A yahrzeit candle is stuffed in the waistband of my pants, and I carry a prayer book in one hand and a small rug plus a pot of daffodils in the other. There are no human footsteps in the snow, only animal and bird tracks. The yard is fenced, but a heavy animal has been in—not a cat, but perhaps a raccoon looking for food.

The date is wrong. It is the English date, not the Hebrew date on the lunar calendar. But every year, I am off sync with the rest of my family on this issue of when to light the candles, and I have decided to do as they do this year—though I will say Kaddish on the "right" Shabbat with my more observant community. I have never been to the actual grave of my father, so I have created a place to remember both my parents and to light these candles. I do this out of doors as the sense of their spirit presence in my house is very disturbing to me.

I am profoundly pissed off at my spouse, so I go out alone. He is inside, bathing his own little Kaddish, our three-year-old son, his one and only, who he has started to describe as already most of the way to a mensch. His Bar Mitzvah is already talked about in hushed voices.

"If I wanted one thing for him by the time he is thirteen," my husband said recently, "it would be that he takes a stand against injustice. And he has already done that, at the bank, when he stood up to the other mother threatening to leave without her dawdling child!"

I walk hurriedly across the yard. It is very cold, and I have come out purposely without my coat. I don't want to stay long, sitting on the snow, even on a rug. I did tie a wool scarf around my head. The moon is so bright, I am having trouble focusing on things far and near. Could it be the light from a neighboring house? No, it is the moon. Looking back down, I can scarcely find the memorial. It is concrete blocks arranged in a "V" on a bed of solid capstones. The roof is more capstones, about two inches thick. The opening of the V faces out, and I am surprised that there is no snow inside it. A quick sweep of my hand clunks against the glass of the last yahrzeit candle, lit there on Yom Kippur.

I plop down on the rug, and I light the new candle. I scrape some snow off the top of the memorial with the edge of the pot of daffodils and set it down. The candle burning underneath for twenty-four hours will warm the roots. It will bloom earlier than anything else in the yard.

With the candle, I can read the *El Maleh Rachamim* prayer, the God of Merciful Feelings, literally "The God with a Womb." In Hebrew, the word for compassion comes from the same root: womb. Other parts of the prayer describe the feminine essence of God—Her enfolding wings. It is some prayer—very poorly translated in books but translated verbatim for me by my Israeli neighbor when my father had just died, when I first wanted to know this prayer. It says that there is a Garden of Eden, for example. Here is the prayer, word for word, in English:

God, full of merciful feeling that is part of the sky, find perfect rest underneath the wings of the feminine essence of God and on the steps of the holy and pure, those that give forth light like the brightness of the sky for the soul of Emmanuel, son of Nissim, who went to his world. In the garden of Eden will be his rest.

Please, God of compassion and mercy, hide him in the safe hiding place of your wings for eternity and bind in the knot of life his soul. He will become the possession of God and will rest in peace in the place where he lies down. And let us say, Amen.

I recite it in the original Hebrew, holding the candle up over the edge of the book, aware of the clarity and coldness of the night air. I know where I am much of the time in the prayer without translating it. Another dimension is inside my mind. And then I put the candle into the opening of the memorial against the blackness of the almost closed V-shaped tunnel. Something happens as the enclosure is illuminated and the light dances back and forth in the space. I become small. The flame becomes large. I become the flame. I enter the flame. A sudden expansion of light greets me and is gone. I am outside the flame, looking at the ivy growing around the memorial's base with astonishment. It is beautiful. It is green. It is of this world. The concrete is hard. I touch it. The candlelight makes the air seem soft. There is up, and there is down, and I am in my body—cold, alive.

Photo: Peter Rudd

Ancestor Worship

This morning, I found the other oar and placed it carefully in the oarlock. The toy boat is only about three inches long, and the oars are not really functional, but it had really bothered me to be missing an oar.

In times of great pain and sorrow, it is somehow distracting, even pleasurable, to make up stories. The stories put things back into some semblance of order and coherence.

Each grief seems to bring a new story, but they are all ultimately about my ancestors. Ever since the world began, there have been stories to pass on culture. Mine are no exception. The odd thing is that even I do not entirely believe my own stories, for if I did, I suppose I would be locked away. In our society, it is not permissible to hear voices, to talk with the dead, to predict or change the outcome of events.

Which has more power, then: wishing, action, prayer, or play?

I have come to the end of my strength many times and am always renewed. There is a life force that comes through me and binds me to life even when death beckons. And in eternity, I know now, I will surely become one with my ancestors.

Road Map

The ancestors give the "road map" in formal terms, such as the Torah, and in their ethical will(s)— as well as their stories of bread and hunger and war and dislocation. But how can they give psychological security *when they do not have it themselves*?

"Physician, heal thyself" is what I would tell my physician parents if they were still here.

Mothers Matter Too is the title of an actual book I have. It suggests that you take care of yourself first. (Instructions on an airplane are always to put on the oxygen mask first and then assist the child.)

A Little Something for Nick

It was not the last time I saw him, nor do I have an actual photo of that moment. I do have a clear picture in my mind, though, of my brother Nick walking slowly away from me, going uphill. He was carrying a little something to eat dangling from his hand in its plastic wrapping. Later, when I caught up to him and asked what it was, he told me it was a couple of gluten-free bagels—a treat I knew he would not enjoy. He was carrying them for his wife in case she needed a little something or a sandwich on her special diet bread.

Unencumbered is how I remember him, except for those inedible, love-offering bagels. I was told, however, that when he died, there were two laptops and two cell phones in his bed with him, as well as his wife and older son in attendance.

I was at a small, live classical music concert some weeks later. A new thing happened for me during the music. When the bassoonist began to play, I heard my brother Nick inside the music. He arrived when that instrument started playing, and his presence grew stronger for me as the sound swelled and filled the room. He has entered the room; I thought, he is here, he is in the music. From that time, I developed the idea that his soul was to be found wherever I looked for it—among birds in flight and always in the triumphant music of wind instruments.

When we were little, my two brothers were often awful to me. Nick used to call me a "patsy," but in Yiddish, a *shnook*. I did not know what that meant in either language. I let them blatantly cheat and steal my money when we played Monopoly. Once, they put me in the trunk of our parked car. But there were other moments of great tenderness, especially with Nick, when he would push me on the swings, steady me on my first roller skates, and escort me on foot to birthday parties while posing in his grownup raincoat as my father.

He told our actual father that he had to relent, and I had to be permitted

to go to the Yale Homecoming weekend my senior year in high school with the son of a family friend. If I was not permitted, my parents would be standing in the way of my future social success.

"All right. What do I know about America?" my father replied.

Once I moved West, Nick came to visit me when I was pregnant with my first child in order to encourage me in my Lamaze classes. He came for Bar Mitzvahs and weddings and as a surprise for my fortieth and sixtieth birthdays. I loved him for that. He was the relative to whom I could tell, or write, things that I could not tell the parents. I felt like he understood and got an accurate picture of what he heard or saw.

There was one visit after our mother died, and I was putting my inheritance windfall into two years of sculpting toward a downtown show. I showed him my newly enlarged studio/garage with skylights, my latest half-life-size clay figure, and my backyard hot tub with its bench and arbor. He said: "No, no, no! First, you work, and then you retire."

I replied, "Why wait?"

A few years later, when I was unhappily employed in documentation and print production for a high-tech company, Nick tried to create a plan with me to rise on the corporate ladder. Stopped short by my reply that I was not interested in the corporate hierarchy, he listened as I was instead of the opinion that it seemed to me a good time to gather a load of castoffs, to make a run to the dump with my pickup truck, to plant a garden, and to look for a new boyfriend for the spring. Reluctantly, he replied that I might be right.

Before he died, he said he was sorry he had not spent more time with me over the years. I reminded him that I had always written to him. What I meant was, "You were always in my mind, and I was and will be, always with you."

Graduate Students' Minyan

In a year that contained contemporaneous loss and also Holocaust remembrance, it seemed important to connect with new circles of Yiddish learners and help foster a new minyan.

We volunteered to hold the graduate students' minyan for the Sukkot holiday, and some previously unknown young people showed up. The first five or six came on lighted bicycles down our fogged-in street, up the driveway, to the harvest festival booth (or sukkah) in our backyard. They were of this time, dressed in Lycra and wearing helmets, but their names were old: Yiddish names, Biblical names, Israeli names. *Am Yisrael Chai* (the people of Israel live). Their politics were progressive, egalitarian, post-denominational. Their numbers varied at a Shabbat service and dinner from ten to forty.

The lead cyclist reached into his knapsack and produced a homemade Bundt cake, apple, from his great-grandmother's recipe. I was again speechless. I make the same cake. The minyan-aires continued to be a part of our lives as we hosted the occasional gathering. There is no building, no dues, no mortgage, just shared meals and optional Sabbath/ holiday prayers. They also represent an underground national movement to transport worship and song away from institutions and back toward the home. Most of these recent grads are single, working, some new to local tech companies, or in grad school. It fills the empty nest a bit for us to offer space for them to find each other, and they bring the food and clean it up afterward.

Their tunes are largely Carlebach. The last song traditionally sung each evening is a blessing on our house and table at which they have eaten. I like that. The final words in their homemade books state: "We give thanks for a wise tradition which commands that we set aside time to feel joy."

Japan 2013

"You can go, but I am not going!" was my first response to my husband's invitation to go to Japan to accept a prestigious award. It would entail meeting the emperor and empress of Japan too. "No!" I was really clear for myself. But the invitation, practically a command, was for the eminent scientist and his wife, and G-d help me, that was me!

We were assigned a travel agent attached in some way to the palace, who did not approve of my plan to stay alone in a hotel in Kyoto while my husband attended a meeting at a university in another city. Nor did she want me to bring a mobility scooter, confusing it for a while with some kind of motorcycle. When I went into some detail about my mobility, she took it all the way to the sergeant-at-arms to the emperor, who advised that I wear an artificial leg. That got my dander up!

I lined up my trip clothes on the bunkbed rail until I had suitable outfits for the trip. My husband refused to go shopping for a suit, so I just went out and bought him one at the Burlington Coat Factory. He refused black shoes, too; for just one day's wear, he thought it a waste, but I threatened to buy those without him too. They did need to fit, so he came along. The suit jacket was fine, the pants a little loose. I don't remember what we did about the tie.

We were flown on All Nippon Airways Boeing 787s to and from the annual award ceremony of the Japan Society for the Promotion of Science. That year's topic was evolutionary biology, which is also the exact academic field studied by the current emperor of Japan, his father (Hirohito), and the younger of his two sons. Joe was selected for that year's recognition for his work on statistical methods for inferring phylogenies.

Boarding the flight and flying first class, I was handed the lithium battery from my scooter as if it were dinner. It could have brought the plane down if stored in the cold of the luggage area, and I marveled at being asked to hand carry it personally. I was, at that point, fatalistic about the whole journey. When the stewardess tucked me in tightly with a plaid, invalid-type blanket, I knew it was going to be an uphill trip all the way. I was going to rebel somehow. One sees very few wheelchairs out and about in Japan, and their occupants always were tucked in with plaid blankets underneath their dispirited faces.

Despite flying in a horizontal "bed," we arrived jetlagged out of our minds after the eleven-hour journey. We had a plan to meet a colleague and his family for a meal. They were so very disappointed that all I wanted was a large bowl of soba and miso soup. Joe had fried this and fancy that and was awake, writhing with indigestion, while I slept the deep sleep of the carbo-loaded. The following day was our meeting, and I had rehearsed my simple hairdo and simpler makeup. The car sent for us was an enormous, accessible van, like for multiple wheelchairs. When we drew up at the auditorium entrance, there were paparazzi, which was terrifying.

Indoors, we were led to a waiting room, and I was interrogated over the two gift-wrapped paperback children's books I had brought as gifts for the empress. This was apparently not in the protocol, and I had to unwrap them and explain to the unfriendly agents why I thought she might like a volume called *Kibitzers and Fools* and another called *The Adventures of Hershel of Ostropol*. I had researched her interests, chief among which were folk stories for children, and I thought she would like them. Indeed, before we left Japan, she had two Japanese children's books, in English, sent to me.

There was a bathroom just across the way, and we were given time for one last nervous trip there before being marched away individually to actually meet the emperor and empress. This marching involved being surrounded by men standing close and stepping in unison, so there was literally no escape. We could have been being escorted to our execution, that is how it felt. As a warm-up, we were both shown into a room, me first, entirely filled with men in black suits, with no guidance as to where we were to go. I stopped and swiveled slowly in place. I knew we were to meet the minister of education first, and I simply picked the most photogenic man on my far left and advanced toward him with an outstretched hand.

I got it right, and we were both invited to sit down. We chatted briefly, though I do not remember Joe saying anything.

Joe was then escorted to the emperor, and I was escorted first to the empress. She was a small and gracious lady, and she took my hand(s) to thank me for the paperback books of folk stories. She said they were of great interest to her as she would be meeting with Holocaust survivors on the following day and had no sense of the culture from which they came. She asked me a bit about what I knew of Japanese culture and, prepared, I threw out the name of a contemporary sculptor I admire. It took her a few seconds to recall him, but then she expressed how happy she was that I showed appreciation for Japanese art.

Next, I was shown in to see the emperor, who was standing sternly in front of a cloth backdrop. He asked me for my first impression of Japan, and, unprepared, I blurted "color." He turned slightly as if to hear better, and I qualified my remark by talking about the particular colors of the sea and the sky, the land, and the painted buildings, all different from the USA. He was the one asking the questions, but I don't remember any more of them until later, when we got to the reception.

The Award Ceremony

The whole award format was quite a bit like a Bar Mitzvah ceremony: a raised platform (a *bima*) in an auditorium, a new black suit (for each of us), seated dignitaries and a flag, a call (an *aliyah*) for Joe, the presentation of a medal and certificate, his thank-you speech, a nice little nosh in the downstairs social hall, and, in the evening, an eight-course dinner.

Joe's Pants

Joe's Burlington Coat Factory pants were a bit loose around the waist, though held with a belt. When it was time to shake hands and leave the auditorium, I realized that an aide had taken my two crutches to be stored during the presentation. Fortunately, she handed one back; but, still, if I was going to shake hands with my right, I needed an anchor on my left. I grabbed Joe's belt from the back and held on for dear life, balancing on one high heel and letting the right crutch cuff dangle so I could shake hands, first with the emperor and then the empress. I was overwhelmed with the vision of Joe's pants falling down in front of them and the entire assembly of the Japan Society for the Promotion of Science! This thought caused me extraordinary amusement, and I grinned unabashedly with pleasure. In turn, the E & E's faces relaxed and smiled warmly and broadly back. No one and nothing fell down.

There was even a short clip on Japanese TV evening news showing Their Majesties, a bit of Joe's thank-you speech, and warm handshakes all around.

The nosh in the social hall was mostly *treyf* (not kosher), and I doubt I ate anything, but it was the occasion for more-casual chatting with select scientific colleagues, who were honored to be invited to an occasion featuring the emperor and empress. I had another short chat with each of them, though for lack of a topic, I ended up telling one of the Hershel of Ostropol tales, rather a violent one.

Among other things, the emperor asked me, "Where are you born?" and I said, "New York! My family is like a mini-history of the Jews—from Russia to France (after the Russian Revolution), from France to NYC (running from the Nazis), me from NYC to the West Coast, no doubt my sons continuing on to Japan!"

The evening eight-course dinner was with eleven senior scientists from the society and me. I literally put feathers in my hair for the occasion and wore velveteen. I was riding on my mobility scooter, and this stopped all conversation while it was wondered at. Where was the motor (small, underneath, lithium battery)? Where was it made (Taiwan)? End of discussion. The eldest scientist held forth about the shortcomings of someone who was not present before I shushed him that that was not polite. Perhaps in polite retaliation, he informed me that the next course would be "the testicles of the cod." Whatever it was, I did not eat it, sticking to the recognizable.

I was a tourist in Kyoto while Joe attended the International Biology Symposium. I saw a lot of art and of shrines and paid attention to fabrics and crafts. Among the shrines were some filled with baby things. It took me a long time to get any kind of answer out of anyone regarding what these ubiquitous shrines were all about. It seems that they are for the souls of the unborn babies: miscarried, aborted, stillborn, in order to have a place to pray for their souls. Never had I encountered any formal recognition of this near-universal grief of women. Only recently, I came across a reproduction of a European wood carving of the Virgin Mary, with her full sleeves full of the images of small babies! (She was meant to be ready to carry their souls up to heaven.)

Basically, Japan was like going to another planet. It was useful that I had some very basic vocabulary, but I must say gesture and sign language, in general, is universal. I had no problem with being understood for simple purchases and meals and even got used to all the bowing. I had never seen anyone sincerely praying to wooden idols before (at some of the shrines), and this made a big impression on me. It also put the bowing to people in a certain context, as saluting the divinity within all. Even the news anchor on TV bows to the TV audience before starting his report. There cannot be an expectation to bow back to the TV, can there?

We struggled back to the airport with all our stuff and the folding mobility scooter on the train. Compared to having a cab and driver waiting for me every morning in Kyoto, we were not leaving in style.

Joe and I returned from Japan just before *Thanksgivukkah* (Thanksgiving/Hanukkah), jetlagged but with impressions from the trip. That year, we played the dreidel game with yen coins. Preparations had started with the sartorial improvements for both of us, Pimsleur brand Japanese language CDs from the public library, and the purchase of the Lonely Planet series guidebooks for Japan, Tokyo, and Kyoto.

Look Like a Nun

Staying in the hotel in Kyoto by myself, I had to figure out how to get through dinner. I was tired and wanted a beer—actually two. That is enough to make me visibly tipsy when I walk on crutches. Fortunately, I had the forethought to dress like a nun hoping that no one would accost me in the hotel restaurant. Actually, I don't remember anyone else there besides wait staff, who were overly solicitous except for a leering busboy, who openly laughed at me trying to manage walking in my low-heeled dress shoe. I felt disrespected. Cannot a grown woman have a beer?

An Antisemitic Remark at the Local Post Office Leads to a Major Cultural Exhibit

I was fumbling with closing the flaps on a USPS box filled with (bagged) homemade chocolate chip cookies. I was going to mail them to my younger son, away at university in Chicago for his first year. A rather good-looking man in line kept trying to engage and assist me, and I kept brushing him off. I could do this myself, in my own way, sliding the box along the counter, for example. He took exception to the brushoffs and, perhaps noting the Jewish name on the box or my Semitic nose, suddenly hurled the following epithet: "Oh, why don't you just go back to Israel or wherever you came from!"

I was surprised. Neither of us had lost our places in line; all I did was reject his patronizing and egotistical help.

At around the same time, I went to a quilt exhibit in a hall located a couple of suburbs north of Seattle. There, carved into the wooden split-rail fence around the hall, were the words: "Zionism kills!" I fixed that easily with a pen to read "Zionism skills!" But I was quite shaken up for a second time.

It seemed to me that there was a deep ignorance in my area about Jewish people and Israel. When I was subsequently invited to a meeting with the Washington State Jewish Historical Society concerning their fall gala preparations, education was still on my mind. The meeting, however, was to explore the idea of an exhibit of Jewish artists to serve as a backdrop and possibly as an auction fundraiser for the one evening. I had experience with how difficult it is to determine what Jewish art is, much less who is a Jewish artist, and also with how unfair and unfeasible it is to ask artists to do an exhibit for a one evening show! By the way, Seattle does not have an actual Jewish museum, although it has an active Holocaust Center, with a speakers' bureau, to educate and inspire. (I also once had an official of the Seattle Arts Commission inform me that they do not give money TO Jews!)

The Jewish artists with whom I was acquainted held a variety of ideas about the relative importance of various issues, and a group meeting, whichever one of us called for it, would be worse than "herding cats." Instead, I decided to form my own non-artist committee of Jewish women, peers in age, to advise on a coherent concept for a temporary, educational Jewish museum. There was an existing city program to match vacant storefronts with conceptual exhibits, and I applied, and my concept was selected. Somewhere during that time, the Board of the Washington State Jewish Historical Society voted not to support my concept as an official activity. Still, the Jewish Federation allowed me to be selected as a program eligible for a Kickstarter campaign under their auspices, and I raised $5,000 toward the photographic installation and for moving costs. The most suitable storefront available was adjacent to the Bellevue City Hall, across Lake Washington from Seattle. The vacant space was a venue intended for social gatherings and was 20' x 80', with both electric power and huge windows, as well as a couple of reflecting pools outside.

What I was trying to do was cultivate understanding by demystifying a culture and defusing stereotypes. What I learned, to my surprise, was that the majority of visitors thought that Jews were a race. Jews are not a "race". It is unclear what "race" even means as a term except as used by the Nazis, who copied how "racism" was used against African-Americans in the USA and applied these same principles.

Jewish people are more of a people, connected by language(s) and customs, and adhering to certain religious practices (or descended from those adherents).

Even college-educated people were unaware of basic Jewish history, including the "sack" of Jerusalem by the Romans in 70 AD, the expulsion from England in 1290, or the Spanish Inquisition in 1492. A map of the Pale of Settlement also had to be explained in the context of the Holocaust. "How could a people go through so much, and still endure!" said someone with a Jewish name as he shared his childhood memories of a Seder at some friends' home. "Where is the cup for Elijah?" he also remembered upon seeing the exhibit's set-up Seder table. He sincerely wanted to know.

The vast majority of visitors were not Jewish, and there were a number of interfaith couples, not all of them young. Visitors who identified as one-quarter Jewish seemed to be the most interested in learning at least something about the Jewish part of their identity, or heritage, or health history. All said that they "knew nothing." Some came as family groups and taught each other as they toured. We had published three scheduled times to consult with someone from the local Jewish Genealogy Society, and there was always a visitor present with questions for her on how to search their own ancestry.

I thought this was largely going to be an art exhibit within a context of Jewish culture (Yiddish titles to the sculpture and "Voices and Visions" posters illustrating great Jewish values). Then, as we added more and more Jewish elements (a Passover table, set up with a box of matzoh and an extra chair for a guest, a hutch filled with holiday objects, a mock-up of a Torah, its mantle stuffed with two bolsters), I thought we had a mini-Jewish museum. As the spring weather improved and we had more people walking in, it became obvious that what we really had on our hands was a diversity exhibit. People on their way to City Hall and those from City Hall on lunch break stopped in, as did passersby. Located across from the Bellevue Transit Center, we were visible to brand new immigrants (Mexico, Ukraine) and less recent immigrants (from the Philippines, India, England) coming through and asking basic questions. The exhibit windows facing the Transit Center had the Hebrew alphabet in both printed and cursive form, as well as a colorful mural of children. The sign read "Pop-Up Cultural Heritage Exhibit: Setting a Place at the Table." The illustrated timeline depicting 1948-2013 stated "65 years of Jewish and general culture", with a separate large display board for each decade.

I did not ask anyone if they were Jewish, though people asked me. Four Latino visitors, three African American visitors, two Filipino visitors, two Indian visitors, two Ukrainian visitors, one English visitor, and one Japanese visitor stopped in. Intermarried family groups of all ages came in together. People in their 80s particularly appreciated the exhibit as a history exhibit, with its photographs of changes in everything from cooking equipment to media, dating from the late 1940s until today.

It would be interesting to have pop-up cultural heritage exhibits from other groups, too. Someone commented that his parents, when they downsize, could do something like this exhibit in terms of a complete set of ritual objects!

One of the Indian visitors, after carefully studying the sculpture of family groups, none of it devotional, commented that there was nothing particularly Jewish about the figurative sculpture. Aha! The unifying and universal theme: some things change over time (like technology), some things do not (the family, the festivals, and the "table"). This holds true for many, many cultures. We get a great deal by appreciating the similarities between groups. We have at least had some similar experiences. And we are largely a nation of immigrants.

"Really cool!" said a 20-something.

"Feels like home!" said a 30 something.

"How can a people go through so much and still endure!" said a 40-something.

"Good job! Feels like a Jewish home," said a 50-something.

"Bringing history to life!" said a 60-something.

"I see my whole life scrolling before me!" said a 70-something.

"I like the whole thing. The concept is fantastic!" said an 80-something.

Two Chinese American ladies came through. One was from Seattle, and the other was visiting her from San Diego. "What is this?" they asked, and I explained.

"I have seen all of Bellevue," the visitor replied, "and this I will remember. I know what this is. I feel it in my heart," she said, motioning toward her heart. "Family is very important."

I replied that: "This is what art is: to take what is inside and put it on the outside."

Benny Goodman
Jack Benny
State of Israel established
antibiotics become available
rayon invented
rotary-dial telephones in use
dip pens give way to fountain pens
upright typewriters in use
hats commonly worn

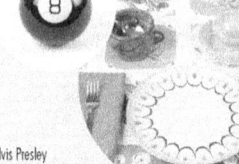

Elvis Presley
Jerry Lewis, Sid Caesar
Marcel Marceau
Allen Ginsberg, the "beat" poets, beatniks
polio vaccine developed, Jonas Salk, 1952
Night of the Murdered Poets (Soviet-Yiddish writers), 19
DNA structure described, 1953
H-bomb developed
Korean War
Boeing jet 707, 1954
Suez Crisis, 1956
Sputnik, 1957
Mouseketeers, Zorro, the Lone Ranger shown on TV
77% of Americans have a TV
Mike Nichols & Elaine May improvisational comedy duo
Barbie dolls
Louise Nevelson shows sculpture at MoMA

SETTING A PLACE AT THE TABLE **FOR JEWISH CULTURE IN THE NORTHWEST**

› GARTERS WORN WITH (OR WITHOUT) A RED RIBBON*

› DEAR ABBY GIVES ADVICE

TIMELINE: THE WORLD KEEPS CI

› DR. RUTH, SEX THERAPIST AND CULTURAL ICON

› WOMEN OF THE WALL DECLARED ILLEGAL

Bat Mitzvah becomes common
Simchat Bat ritual reintroduced
space shuttle Columbia
klezmer fusion develops
Campaign for Soviet Jewry in DC
Reagan/Gorbachev summit, perestroika, glasnost
Berlin Wall comes down, 1989
the Internet
Disney-fication of childhood
first Conservative woman rabbi ordained, 1985
Gilda Radner, comic genius, dies of ovarian cancer
Itzhak Perlman tours with Israel Philharmonic
Orchestra in Eastern Bloc and Soviet Union
global warming and climate change concept spreads
Mothers Against Drunk Driving organizes
Joan Rivers named "Queen of Comedy"
American Girl dolls
Supreme Court Justice Sandra Day O'Connor appointed
John Lennon, Anwar Sadat, Indira Gandhi assassinated
Mount St. Helens erupts
yuppies

portable phones and personal computers take over
War in Iraq
increased interest in vegetarianism
O. J. Simpson murder trial
last decade of Victor Borge, the Clown Prince of America
Lewinsky scandal leads to impeachment
George Burns's career spans vaudeville, film, radio, TV
Dolly the sheep is first mammal to be cloned
multiculturalism
hip-hop
genocide in Rwanda and Bosnia
Mandela elected President of South Africa
Supreme Court Justice Ruth Bader Ginsburg appointed
World Wide Web
Opening of Benaroya Hall, Seattle, 1998
National Yiddish Book Center opens
interest in genealogy increases

*The red ribbon was a superstition, a talisman to
protect against the evil eye and any other danger.

doo-wop
Allan Sherman ("Hello Muddah, Hello Fadduh")
Pete Seeger, the Weavers, Woody Guthrie, the Limeliters
Bob Dylan, original songwriter/poet
hootenanny parties and open-mic folksinging
Fiddler on the Roof with Zero Mostel
Theodore Bikel sings Yiddish folk songs
Berlin Wall constructed, 1961
Cuban Missile Crisis, 1962
the Beatles
Seattle World's Fair, 1962
March on Washington, 1963
President Kennedy assassinated, 1963
Civil Rights movement
Free Speech movement, 1964–1965, Berkeley
Six-Day War, 1967
Martin Luther King assassinated, 1968
Neil Armstrong lands on the moon, 1969
Timothy Leary promotes LSD, 1969
subatomic particles described
Princess phone in use
Human Potential Movement describes self-actualization
portable and electric typewriters in use
Whole Earth Catalog published
birth control pills widely available by prescription

Roe v. Wade
girls wear pants to school
women wear pants to work
Earth Day established
first Reform woman rabbi ordained, 1972
Title IX
New Games, based on cooperation
Watergate scandal
klezmer music revival
Yom Kippur War, 1973
refuseniks in Soviet Union
Vietnam war protests erupt
Boeing jet 747, 1970
Microsoft software, 1976
gene sequencing first developed, 1977
Our Bodies, Ourselves published (Boston Collective)
Jewish Catalog published (Michael & Sharon Strassfeld)
the "Me" decade
macrobiotic diets in vogue
Roots: The Saga of an American Family

» PANTYHOSE INVENTED

» WOMEN'S MARCH ON FIFTH AVENUE

GING AROUND US 1948—PRESENT

» MADELEINE ALBRIGHT BECOMES SECRETARY OF STATE

» FIRST MODERN ORTHODOX WOMAN RABBI ORDAINED

911 hits NYC and the world is changed
iPod portable media players
Macklemore starts to release mixtapes
Obama, an African American, becomes US President
Skype (Sky Peer-to-Peer) released
rise of the Tea Party
financial downswing hits hard
iPhone is released, 2007
China becomes major economic power
War in Afghanistan
The Daily Show with Jon Stewart
Kindle launched
Supreme Court Justice Sonia Sotomayor appointed
Polartec fabric common for casual wear
veganism in vogue
locavores
Facebook

Arab Spring uprisings in Mideast
increased interest in gluten-free products
legalization of gay marriage spreads
Snowden reveals secret data
Google Hangout for classes and homework
performance fabrics for fitness clothes:
Supplex nylon, polyester, Lycra spandex
Ariel Sharon dies
threats from Iran, North Korea, and elsewhere
Nelson Mandela dies
Supreme Court Justice Elena Kagan appointed
Tablet computers become ubiquitous
Mark Bittman advocates "flexitarianism"
1 in 8 Americans go hungry, 50% more children do so too
peak of stock offerings for cupcake shops
Chinglish opens on Broadway
moves for legalization of marijuana
foodies take on cultural status

We celebrate
70+
YEARS
of NW Jewish Life
in the Diaspora

Setting a Place at the Table for Jewish Culture

I just spent six weeks gallery sitting a Jewish pop up cultural heritage exhibit, for the most part by myself, in an area of Greater Seattle called Bellevue, next to Bellevue's City Hall. I designed and created the exhibit over a three-year period in collaboration with a cohort of boomers, a professional photographer, graphic artist, and printer.

I had completed docent training through the Henry Gallery at the University of Washington in 2007 and was comfortable with speaking with the public. For this exhibit, I led more than 125 individuals on docent tours. The exhibit, (see Facebook Pop Up Cultural Heritage Exhibit "To cultivate understanding of cultural heritage through art"), also had a social media presence on Facebook, with more than 3,932 views.

A photo of "gone gefilte fishing" on Facebook, of me sitting with line and pole by one of the reflecting pools and fishing for a glass jar of commercially made gefilte fish, received much attention.

This gag photo I had taken of myself just before Passover illustrates the reach of the "table," or food customs, and also that *"laughter is heard further than weeping"* (Yiddish proverb). Viewing this photo also led people to see other photos and activities from the exhibit on FB. For example, one of the most popular activities at the exhibit was to trace one's own family's journey to Seattle on a large world map.

The New Yorker had published an article detailing a radical exhibit at the Berlin Jewish Museum where visitors could ask questions of a Jewish person (sitting in, and protected by, a plexiglass box, the "Jew in a box").

In my exhibit, I was not sitting in a Plexiglass box. I was there and available four afternoons per week for a four-hour shift, giving tours and answering questions, starting with "are you Jew?" not "are you a Jew?" and not "are you a Jewish person?" Nothing bad happened.

There were zero unpleasant incidents. I was never scared.

The Double Brain

When I first heard about the concept of drawing being a "right brain" activity, I decided to test it. I was teaching a class and drew an example of something on the whiteboard. I was going to continue to speak, but much to my surprise, I could not. I simply could not engage both my hand to draw and my tongue to speak.

So what unites the two hemispheres? Or what is a double-brained person? They say that making music is the only activity that truly utilizes the whole brain and teaches it to make use of both the intuitive and the linear, but there are people who are like that most or all of the time. They are engaged with the scattering of details while also pulling them into some sort of system or whole. Like the chocolate/butter mixture cementing the flour mixture to make a cake, the brain also requires milk and eggs—thin and thick, translucent and opaque—to join the two hemispheres. What is the connecting fluid? Music.

Wrong Husband

It was my older son Ben's thirtieth birthday, and I invited his father (and second wife) to join us. Ben and his wife, me, and my second husband, and our first grader (Zach) were all to meet for a birthday Sunday brunch of waffles. All went well and was even jolly, though as we each ordered our favorite flavor, I endeavored to correct my husband. He had just ordered coconut waffles, and I knew he did not care for coconut. I reminded him that he did not like coconut. He looked at me a bit wildly and assured me that he did. Ben's father piped up quietly that it was he who did not like coconut.

"WRONG husband," said my second husband kind of loudly, and most all of us laughed heartily. The next day in school, Zach's class was to write up their activities from the weekend. Zach apparently wrote a credible enough account of the morning, the coconut waffles, and the wrong husband, that his composition was passed among all the teachers of the pre-k through lower school, and I was teased gently about it by several among them in the following weeks.

Resilience

George Washington and the Balloon

The first ones to reach me were the clowns. The exaggerated expression painted on his face was easy to read as compassion. "Are you OK?" he asked, tilting his face winningly while holding on to the windowsill of the passenger side of my car. I nodded yes, although I was in shock and pain. The other car had hit me with a strong glancing blow on the driver's side door, right where I sat. The accident was my fault. There had been only the smallest road sign that my lane was ending at the turning point.

I don't remember a police car or being towed. There was no hospital visit. I was shaken by the impact but actually, even more so, by the clowns. There was a circus at the nearby mall, and the off-duty clowns were the closest pedestrians. My reaction to seeing clowns on a city street, out of place, goes way back to George Washington. Since seeing visions might turn out to be reality, one must be able to trust that visions arrive to be helpful.

George Washington himself came to visit me in the pediatric ward when I was fifteen. Just out from various pain killers, I assumed I was hallucinating or something. He had the face of a clown but the costume and white wig of our nation's founder. He also had balloons. He sat comfortably and silently in the chair beside me and demonstrated how to blow up a balloon. His clown makeup and red nose belied the seriousness of his instruction. Then he gave me a balloon. I had a little trouble getting started but marshaled my resources to give it a good blow. Then I blew up the balloon all the way full.

"Very good," he said, or something like it, attracting the attention of a nurse who chased him out away from me.

"Not her! She's just post-op."

By the following day, feeling bored, I swung down to the chair and then into a nearby wheelchair. I rolled to the closet, extracted my guitar, and proceeded into the hallway. Launching into my hootenanny repertoire

(*Michael, Row the Boat Ashore, Swing Low, Sweet Chariot*, etc.) I effectively drew most of the other patients out of their rooms as I led song after song.

The elevator doors opened onto the hallway, and it took my parents a few seconds to take in the scene. Their tense, anxious faces softened as they realized who the song leader was among the wheelchairs. Still, that did not stop them from scolding me and bundling me off to my semiprivate room and my bed, and firmly rehousing my guitar.

"You have to rest!" my mother said.

A few weeks later, when I refused yet another physical exam from yet another expert, simply refused to sit on the exam table, my father said proudly, "it shows character."

French Language and Culture

Both sets of my sons' maternal grandparents were born in Russia: Grandpa's in St. Petersburg (in the north) and Grandma's in Odessa (in the south). Both families fled during and shortly after the Russian Revolution of 1917. Grandpa's family went to Finland by sled, and Grandma's family went to France by boat across the Black Sea and via Istanbul. My earliest memories of geography come from my mother recounting these trips, illustrated with a spinning globe of the world.

Both of the fathers of these two families were imprisoned and threatened with death, literally walked out in front of firing squads, prior to their escapes. One was released because he knew the judge and the other by offering a bribe. In any case, the families remained intact at that time.

In Finland, my father's family consisted of six brothers and sisters, of whom he was the youngest. So far as I know, he was the only one to receive formal religious instruction and to celebrate a Bar Mitzvah. His own Yiddish-speaking maternal grandparents lived with them in Finland during his early years, and they are buried there in Mustamaki. Jews were not allowed to attend high school in Finland, so after Bar Mitzvah, my father (their grandfather) was sent to Paris in the care of two older sisters already studying there. He was deposited in the courtyard of the local school and left. He spoke Russian, German, Yiddish, Swedish, Finnish, and not one word of French. He did not succeed in gaining admittance, and his sisters tried another school the next day. By the age of sixteen, he became wholly independent of his sisters, living on his own throughout his student days in Paris. He did not see his father again until he was eighteen.

He retained a lifelong love of country vacations from his time in his early years on the farm in Finland. As a medical student, he organized a group to rent a house outside of Paris for weekends and holidays. Chaperoned by her brother, Joan's mother was one of the medical students involved in the communal "La Folie Douce" rental, which means Sweet Craziness.

Joan's mother's family had traveled more or less directly to Paris from Russia, and by pawning jewelry and silver had reconstructed the family business: the manufacture of noodles. Ten years later, tired of the noodle business, Grandpa Weinberg invested all his capital into molds to create cast-stone likenesses of Edward VIII, soon to be crowned king of England. Edward abdicated to marry Wallace Simpson, and the family went back to manufacturing noodles. Joan's mother described shelves upon shelves of the rows of completed portrait heads in small, medium, and large. The molds themselves were quite valuable, being made of metal, bronze actually, and were the source of capital when the family fled France ahead of the Nazis...

One week ahead of the fall of Paris, having completed her course requirements, Lucie and her parents left Paris and went to Marseilles. There, Grandma Weinberg bought huge sacks of macaroni and settled in to await transportation. When Joan's mother questioned the large quantity of pasta, Grandma Weinberg apparently replied, "I have lived through a revolution. People will be hungry, and we will feed them." And so she did. The family was on one of the last boats to America from Marseilles, most likely obtaining passage again by paying bribes.

The Night of the Long Knives 1972 (Still Mastering Knives)

Now I cut clay almost daily: big linoleum knife slices, more delicate morsels with wooden and with wire tools. I need to cut clay to make stuff, and coincidentally, it lets the pain out. How does one cut bread? Hug the loaf and turn it as you cut? Or put it down and saw it? And how does one drink schnapps? With thumb and first finger, or tipped up with thumb and second finger on the bottom of the glass?

Cutting used to be part of daily life, and most if not all men carried knives. I have two pocketknives, four paring knives for sculpting clay, the previously mentioned linoleum cutter, and small pointy knives I use on my clay "reliefs." Slicing while changing depth levels is the best: the depth, the control, the lightness. Cutting through firm clay is nothing like paper or cardboard, with its accidental "paper cuts" to the skin of the fingers.

I could say I love knives now, though they have, in the past, occasioned terror with the kind of damage they can cause.

Our first "married" car was a brand new, forest-green Volvo sedan with a butter-soft, pale beige interior. We got an infant car seat to match when Ben was born in 1970.

One night near the Fourth of July, at the land in the Lewis River valley, a vandal or vandals broke into the car and sliced up the interior: the headliner or ceiling, all the seats, and yet more slices through the back and seat of the child car seat. The nearby (but vacant) canvas teepee got the same treatment: slashed to ribbons. If it was one vandal, he must have tired his arm. The thing is, my first husband and I were already separated, and I was sleeping alone on a mattress near Benjy's crib, in a lean-to without a West wall, much less a door or a lock. The Volvo was unlocked and quite close to us, but I heard nothing, although I did stroll out in the moonlight, naked in fact, in the middle of the night, to pee in the bushes somewhere. Thankfully,

I personally was not attacked, nor the baby. The repair person at the auto upholstery shop was visibly upset by all the damage, said he had never seen anything so sick like it.

The general area had a history of utopian communes, and so we were folded into myth, I suppose, as Hippies? Commies? Jews? to be chased off.

Picker and Pickee

I used to pray while riding on the chairlift. Meditate. Focus. My young son, who learned to ski at the same time, asked why he never could talk to me on the chairlift.

"Because I am praying," I answered.

Over time, I observed that I skied better if I took an aspirin first. In fact, relaxation was an important part of not falling, or falling gently if it was unavoidable. I also noticed how women seemed to use their hips in shifting weight more effectively, and that grace was part of staying upright. Staying in control, by contrast, was an aggressive, masculine-type feeling of power. After skiing, I discovered how a hot tub would remove the pain of overused muscles and also that the most mobile amps (or gimps, as we called ourselves) strapped on simple peg legs.

I wanted one, too, and had to overcome the objections of the prosthetist(s) forever after, who categorically said that they would not fit a woman with a peg leg. I insisted, and I danced about when I first put one on. I was never going back. Three pounds instead of thirteen! I could go three times as far and three times as fast. I could pivot on it at my workbench or on the disco dance floor. I was freer than I had been in over fifteen years. Yes, some people hated how it looked, and I was once invited to supper by a band of homeless people, but I mostly did not mind being treated like a third-world person. I could get it on or off easily, so I could sit in comfort for dinner. "Take off your legs," I once announced to dinner guests. "Dinner is ready, and we are about to sit down."

I drove to Seattle a couple of times in those years, once for a gallery opening where I was exhibiting a sculpture and once to try yet another prosthetist looking for a more comfortable cast socket to wear.

For the gallery visit, I left my fourteen-year-old overnight for the first time. He was with another young teen, and I warned them repeatedly about the house rules (my anxieties). They were not to cook, and I had prepared a roast chicken for them. They were not to answer the door to any stranger. They were not to snack on any weird foods that might cause stomach ache. My anxieties were so strong, I actually produced all three disasters myself while the kids were perfectly fine until noon the next day.

First, I removed that roast chicken from the oven before turning it off, setting fire to the dishtowel, and then charring the linoleum when I dropped the burning towel. Then, at a rest stop in nowhere Washington, a dirty-faced and unkempt-looking man raced to my car as I got in and tried to open my door. I got the door locked in the nick of time and saw his scary face close up at the window. Then, at the art opening, having skipped my own dinner to get there, I ate lots of weird crackers and deli meats, and cheese besides. I had a royal stomach ache all night and did not have any nostrums with me. I was staying with the friends described below and did not want to wake anyone stumbling around for an antacid. So, I suffered from all my fears!

When I came up to Seattle from Portland to have a new socket made for my prosthesis, I asked if I could stay with Rabbi J and his wife. They said sure. I went out in the morning to go to the supermarket to get a little something for them. Probably Danishes. And there was this very young woman sitting on a bench weeping. So I sat next to her and asked her what was wrong. She said she'd locked her keys in the car. She'd come all the way up from Oregon, driving by herself, and was supposed to start at the University of Washington. She was to have stayed with friends of the family, but they were away in Europe for a month, and she had nowhere to go. She missed her boyfriend, she wanted her parents, and her keys were locked in the car.

I stayed with her until she calmed down. Then we went, and we got a phone book and a phone, and she called a locksmith. While she waited for the locksmith, I went back to J and J's with the pastries, and I told them all about this woman.

"Well, let's go get her," he said.

And so we went back, and she was still there. The locksmith opened her car. And then J and J put her up for several days until she got settled. She wrote me later that she didn't know what she would have done without my help and that she didn't know people could be kind. It was very lovely what she wrote. But, again, like ministering to depressed students when in college, we had cooperated on something from some sort of shared Jewish tradition that's not Reed. Or I certainly don't think of it as Reed culture.

At some point, I went to an all-day workshop on relationships. One of the exercises was to change from whichever stance one usually held onto, whether "pickee" or "picker". Well, I had decided for some time that I was going to be the "picker" henceforth rather than the "pickee" in choosing relationships. Spending a day at that workshop as the "pickee" felt terrible; no control at all! I then felt free to pursue pleasure as a "picker" when it presented itself. If I made sure that I picked a friend, because it was someone I liked, I was much less likely to be victimized in any way. I still had lots of heartaches as I learned how to navigate. And I was always chastened by remembering the Yiddish proverb: "Live like a bum and you will die a lunatic!" *Lebn vi a brumen un ir vet shtarbn a meshugener!*

I was also somewhat protected by my use of the arts to manage my emotions. Some people of the era had a pill or a drink for every circumstance. I tried to make a chart:

If I was sad, I played the guitar.

If I was mad, I would clean house.

If I was lonely, I would sing.

If I was happy, I would paint.

If I felt frustrated, I would sculpt.

If I was agitated, I would sew or knit.

If I was anxious, I would play on the recorder.

I had a good mind, a good body, and a good spirit.

Where There is Nothing and No One, There is Still Love

Situational crises are not an inborn imbalance. But how did I react to external circumstances and stressors?

Alone, cold, in a locked, steel cell, with a steel bench and one thin white blanket made of woven cotton stitches, I shivered with terror and anxiety. Images came and went as I compared myself to various historical figures who had been incarcerated for their beliefs. I had no "beliefs," only that an employer had pulled a gun on me while paying me only half of what he owed me. He threatened to take away even that money (small bills in a paper sack) if I did not leave immediately.

I exited his "office" in the back of the trade center and looked around the vast, empty commercial space. There was a bar area alongside one wall and burly-looking men drinking beer. I approached two buddies who were talking animatedly to each other. I said that there was someone bothering me and that I was afraid. Would they please walk me to my car? They exchanged a glance and did what I asked.

Still clutching the $750 in its paper bag, I drove myself home. Then I sat for eleven days, growing ever more disconnected from reality until my ex-husband drove me to the hospital. There, another two burly guys walked me down a corridor and jumped me, pushing me onto a bed, one laying on top of me the better for the second one to plunge a needle into me.

In my experience, nothing good comes out of being pinned down against my will. I woke up in a room that appeared to be coed, alone on a vinyl mattress. I protested and was escorted down the hall again and thrust into a steel cage. I was very cold, but I took that little blanket and folded and rolled it into the shape of a baby (my baby, me), and I held it close and rocked it and sang to the bundle in my arms until I was calm. Where there is nothing and no one, there is still love.

It was almost Christmas, and then Christmas. A nurse had on a new, pastel fuzzy sweater when she brought me milk and cookies.

"Will you stay while I eat them?" I asked. "I am lonely."

She did stay a minute or two, and I made conversation about her new Christmas sweater. She must have reported that I was neither violent nor out of my head, and they let me out of lockup.

Another nurse, someone I was acquainted with in the community, came by with a basin of warm water and a washcloth. She confirmed that I remembered her and that I knew her by name. She bathed my face and hands tenderly and told me I would see my doctor soon and go home on his recommendation.

Beat the Jews and Save Mother Russia: Genetic Memories

The scythe is the worst. Whenever I am overtired, the scythe looks menacing and sharp. It is, in fact, quite dull. Nearly useless if I recall from my two summers "homesteading" in rural Washington in the '70s.

Periodically, we would try to trim some of the meadow grass to make paths. We were mostly incompetent farmers, except for one, who actually grew edible vegetables. I made the log "seats," each made of a log with a board nailed on top and arranged the communal eating area around the firepit. We all went naked quite a lot and grew tough, brown skin. It was always a treat to read the latest New Yorker, with its glossy ads, while hanging my bare rear end over a horizontal pole, suspended over the latrine's trench.

So many of my real memories have smell, odor, taste. Perhaps it is no surprise that I carry memories that are not my own—like the sharpened scythe, the brute pickaxe, the shovel to bury the dead.

But I did use a shovel to scoop earth into my mother's grave, as did my father and brothers. But I broke then, in a way that has never been mended. Just handling a shovel reminds me of death, not planting. But that, too, is another story.

The rake and hoe. Well, it could be I have to cultivate my crop: remove weeds, make the pathways smooth. And the oil is for maintenance. Tonight, I painted oil on all the thirsty handles of those outdoor tools. The Destroyers: wrecking crowbar, pickaxe, scythe; and The Creators: shovel, hoe, and rake. To destroy or to cultivate. Winner take all.

But one must prepare the ground for planting: dig, loosen, chop, smooth, flatten. Was that what I wanted to say about the tools? And I forgot the logging saws: one here and one in my other basement. Two houses, two husbands, two homes, two sons, two breaks, two cedar trees.

How I Got My Smile Back

"Above all, I see a great joy in all that s(he) does."

The greatest thing my older son ever said to me, and not in a Mother's Day card or anything, but just so, was:

"You gave me joy."

By this, I understand that my own young curiosity and energy was something he could identify with, emulate. When joy is valued, gratitude cannot be so far behind. I did let him roller skate in the house, even carrying grape juice. I did install a chinning bar in the doorway to the kitchen and pair it with a small trampoline. He would jump on this circular exerciser, leap for the bar, and swing into the kitchen like a healthy young ape. I never minded the movement or the noise. We were alive.

There were some memorable parties, some elsewhere, with drummers and dancing, some at our home with costumes and Frisbees. Throwing a ball back and forth seemed to be the best way to talk. I was obsessed that my father-free home might cause my boy never to know how to throw or catch a ball. So we practiced this daily. And he went to college and then graduate school and became—a juggler.

My smile muscles had simply gone away after twelve years without normal contact with him. Last week, after he called, my cheeks literally rearranged themselves, both inside and out. The continual mourning and grief were greatly diminished by this call. My joy is still inside me, ready to burble and smile. The lips of my mouth regained their more generous, cupid shape. My appetite for food, for life, returned. I could not bear his disappearance. To me, it was like the death of a much-wanted child.

Photo: Eleanor Price

Take Care of Your Health

"Take care of your health, you can always hang yourself later". *Nemen keyer fun dayn gezunt, ir kenen shtendik hengen zikh shpeter.* Yiddish Proverb

I am starting to bounce back from the weariness and sadness over the destruction of my murals in the last two weeks as reported in the *Seattle Times* news story. METRO maintenance crews determined that my four Yiddish language bus shelter murals were weathered and ready to be destroyed. I was not given any notice or opportunity to collect them. At the health club, at the movies, at shul, I am running into folks who empathize over the loss and who generally remark on the lack of order in the local bureaucracies.

Using familiar principles of recovering from trauma, I am focusing on the autonomy of my own body, as well as depending on the safety of my surroundings, recognizing that there is order to the world (sunrise, sunset) and that I am indeed connected to a community.

So, not minimizing the loss (as the bureaucrats did) helped me a lot. I think my original idea of having a third party (music or youth directors of a large temple) negotiate for the same sites as the destroyed murals and working with me and area youth to recreate something (humorous proverbs?) on a Yiddish cultural theme would at least secure the sense of "belongingness" not just to me, but to the Jewish community. Now about those other three destroyed folk song murals—American, French, Scottish—I don't know. I guess I would like to have those images archived beyond my personal website, alongside the Yiddish ones, in the city archives perhaps, whose website features a hideous bronze portrait of Chief Sealth, after whom Seattle is named. I successfully collected the central panels of the eighth mural and a few ancillary panels of some of the other ones. The "maintenance" claim was false. They were not rotted.

"An artist's professional and personal identity is embodied in each work created by that artist. Each work is a part of his or her reputation. Each work is a form of personal expression (oftentimes painstakingly and earnestly recorded). It is a rebuke to the dignity of the visual artist ... outright permanent destruction of such efforts." — Berne Convention

Photo: Eleanor Price

I Still Have the Songs

Yesterday, when I saw that a sixth bus shelter mural I had painted had vanished, I did not react beyond a "hmm," even when the *Times* reporter put some of the leftover nuts and bolts in my hand. I simply put those remnants into the car's ashtray.

Then, today, home on my own, I suddenly knew I had to let out my grief over all this destruction of my work. How to do it? I grouped all the leftover birthday balloons from my younger son's birthday and my own recent birthday. I had purple, orange, white, blue, pink, red, and green. Instinctively I assigned one of my iconic songs to each color, based on the mural colors I had painted. I began to sing, I thought, in no particular order, of all the tunes I had illustrated for METRO.

I sang in English first, *Sweet Betsy from Pike*, an American folk song we sang in elementary school. Midway, I gently pierced the purple balloon with a paring knife. I did not stab. I opened the balloon, and the air went out. I still had the song, and I was still singing, and now I was crying too.

I went next to the Scottish lullaby, *Bonnie at Morn*, that my husband sang to me as a courting song, and I wept harder after I pierced the white balloon.

I moved on to a children's nonsense song, *Ro-de ro-de ra-ne*, whose mural is still up but on borrowed time (pink). Then another children's song, *Patshe patshe kikhelekh* (green), destroyed.

At this point, I began to keen and to rock, but stayed with it as the images I had painted, including a myriad of baby shoes and the interior of my old home's kitchen, flashed past. I wish I could say it got easier through *A la claire fontaine* (blue) or *Oy vunder iber vunder!* (orange), or the resistance song of *Minutn fun bitokhn* (red). I painted that one twice so as not to disappoint the neighborhood children when the first version was destroyed.

The colors of the popped balloons sitting on my table are also now

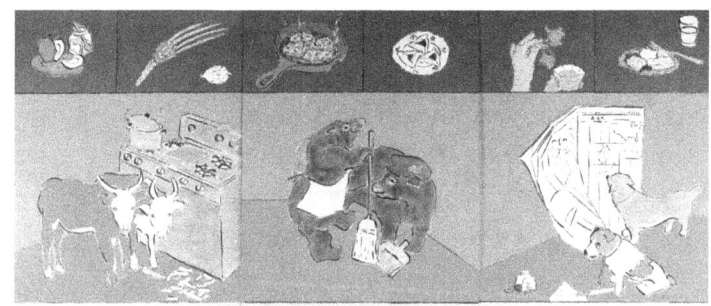

 טאָפּל טאָפּל דיגאַל דיגאַל
אָ! װונדער איבער װונדער,
װי די דיגאַל טאָפּל דיגאַל!
דאָס איז מיר אַ װונדער!

Hob ikh a por oksn, oksn,
Dos zey brokn lokshn, lokshn!
Oy! vunder iber vunder,
Vi di oksn brokn lokshn–
Dos iz mir a vunder,
Dos iz mir a vunder!

Hob ikh a por bern, bern,
Vos zey sheiber kern, kern!
Oy! vunder iber vunder,
Vi di bern shtiber kern,
Vi di oksn brokn lokshn–
Dos iz mir a vunder!

Hob ikh a por hint, hint,
Vos zey makhn tine, tine!
Oy! vunder iber vunder,
Vi di hint makhn tine,
Vi di bern shtiber kern,
Vi di oksn brokn lokshn–

Kinder kert zikh um!

a great comfort, as were painting the mural panels in the colors of my feelings, happy colors at times of great deep sadness. The songs are still there, and I can still sing them, alone or with others. Where there is nothing and no one, there is still love. This has always been the lesson of loss and the drive toward belonging again.

Online comments to the newspaper description of the destruction:

"I looked at your website. Utterly charming!"

"The column is a wonderful cap to the whole episode. You and your art come off very humanly, very well. What a blessing that you had such good documentation."

"Way to go, Joan !!!!!!!!!!!!!"

"I like to see it when people stick up for themselves."

"Not a nice thing to happen. ... When art suffers we all suffer."

"People are going to learn from this."

"Go-o-o Joan!"

"They did what? This is an East coast/West coast kind of thing when they don't even know what they have."

"Congratulations, you got mentioned."

"I read your article and I cried. I really loved those things."

"Hey, we saw you in the paper. You're famous NOW..."

"I heard that they destroyed some of your artwork. That's terrible! How could they do that? Isn't that illegal?"

"I saw the article in the paper. I thought it was very good."

"They can notify you."

"Seattle is not treating its artists right."

"I think it is awful what they did."

"I read about you in the paper. So what is going to happen? I want to know how this story ends."

My Hands Upon My Cheek

I have learned a new way to soothe myself to sleep. I form the backs of my hands into the letter "L" and nestle my cheek into this corner room. The feel of skin contact on my face, specifically on the cheek of my face, brings extraordinary comfort.

Playing With a Full Deck

So now we mix fortune-telling into it—the comfort of the well-worn cards her hands touched. I remember the patterns on the backs and have made them—quite literally—in concrete. Flamingos. Florida flamingos with their necks just so. I had no idea I was making concrete flamingos in memory of my mother. Why is the grief still there? Was fifteen too young to lose her? Did I lose her earlier in fear and rage? I rebelled against her control all my life, and then when I lost her, I missed her. Now I find her answers in her things: manicure tools, playing cards, scarves, mailbags. "Yes, my darling, you were loved."

The Battle Between the Catholics and the Jews

The Battle Between the Catholics and the Jews (my older son, his wife, and me) seems like it is a Battle for Power and Control just as with any other partner. If there was marriage counseling for new in-laws it might look something like the following:

"When I see, or I hear... I feel... because I need/value... would you be willing to..."

(Some ideas from "Getting Past the Pain Between Us", a transcript of a workshop on non-violent communication given by Dr. Marshall B. Rosenberg.)

Or consulting Dr. Google on "how to make a friend out of an enemy?"

- Reach out
- Invite
- Give a reason to see you as a friend
- Look for Common ground
- Apologize for actions that may have hurt them
- Not carry around the weight of that pain anymore
- Look for the best in them
- Ascribe positive motives to them
- Listen
- Open up
- Invite
- Set boundaries
- Don't gossip

Neither of these approaches has worked yet, but the last two on this list are very important.

It cannot hurt to continue to make donations to charities in their names either.

Resistance

Resurrection

I wanted to know what they had done with it. My amputated limb. My right leg.

"It should be buried in a Jewish cemetery," I insisted. "Ask the rabbi."

Dumbfounded, grief-stricken herself, my mother did phone the rabbi, who told her I was right.

"How did she know such a thing?" my mother was said to have asked. And the rabbi shrugged, "*Ver veyst*?" ("Who knows?")

When I was informed that my leg had been disposed of, with hospital waste, in an incinerator, I did not react. It was not until forty-seven years later that I grew appalled at the insensitivity. To literally throw me away, never to return (and no chance at the resurrection).

I did try to figure out how to say "goodbye" to my leg, remarking that it was the one free of scars. My left one somehow took the brunt of falls when I was roller skating, and the huge scabs left big scars. I hugged my leg. I stroked it. I could not believe it would be gone.

They introduced me to a woman prosthetist, herself wearing an artificial leg. She was powdered and perfumed, and I rejected her out of hand as a role model. Her plastic leg seemed ugly to me, especially in stockings held by one of those infernal garter belts. I had no intention of being a lady, much less a grownup.

I fought my mother to the mat to avoid being anesthetized, but it was done, and I woke up cursing at the night nurse, who turned me over frequently to change the blood-soaked pad. Not what you think; I had my period. I was, even then, turning to life, to the tides of the moon, to the rhythm of my own procreative body.

"They will be more interested in you because of the difference, not less," predicted my aunt's friend, GeoGeo. And so he set the stage. It was a wise thing to tell me. And he admired me, with my new dress and new hairdo. He was key in my recovery. In later years he would volunteer to drive me downtown to Sculpture House, to browse their collection of tools. No one else thought of that.

The Ethical Culture Society

The Ethical Culture Society building was literally across the street from our apartment building. My parents had long since made the decision to send us to religious school three blocks in the other direction—to the Stephen Wise Free Synagogue. Still, the allure of a "religion" without religion was there, along with the mystique of never having been inside the building.

Something age-appropriate was advertised: a hootenanny or an evening of folk dancing, and my best friend and I went. That evening was when I met Carlos, who was to chase me for much of a year. I was the willing participant in his wet and generous kisses, clandestinely offered in the mailroom off my apartment lobby.

One time, when we went to take the subway to go to the Village for yet more folk music, he grabbed me up, wooden crutches and all, and carried me lightly, running down the steps. A New York policeman followed, alarmed by my shrieks and seeing a young white girl being carried off down to the underworld by a roguish brown man (mixed Puerto Rican heritage). Fortunately, the policeman was colorblind enough to hear my giggles for that they were, and he stopped his pursuit. My parents grew concerned over the friendship and made sure to let me know of their fear of a little brown baby in the spring. I was outraged at their lack of confidence! Had I not just returned intact from Yale's homecoming weekend?

Recently, I came across an ancient postcard from Carlos postmarked New Paltz, NY. He wrote, simply: "Tell your Mother I miss her." Had my parents actually packed him off, got him out of town? I vaguely remember him waiting for me after school every day my senior year, and then not.

I did have an amazing seventeenth birthday party with or without him, though, because it was also Hermione's birthday, and she brought all her friends to a dance at my apartment. We opened the sliding doors between the living room and dining room. The doorman was alerted that twenty to thirty young African American kids would be visiting. Beautifully dressed, each couple went first to the kitchen to pay their respects to the "sistah" and then joined the party. I moved from group to group, introducing people, and I danced too, in a closely packed crowd of happy bodies moving to the music. I don't remember what we ate; there was no alcohol, and no mess was made! What a contrast to the year before, when I waited all day for a youth group buddy to call for my birthday (he didn't). My oldest brother and one of his college roommates stopped by and offered to fix me a double scotch.

"You shall NOT teach her to drink!" my mother swooped in and insisted. And that was that.

Combining Work and Motherhood

I was still riding a bicycle from Lair Hill to downtown in my seventh month, with my thirteen-pound fiberglass and metal leg, when I finally simply fell off the bike. I was somehow unhurt but stopped riding it. In the absence of any direct bus, I started hitchhiking down Second Avenue to my general office job. That stopped when one of my former Portland State University professors gave me a ride, horrified that I was hitching with my husband's knowledge, "when anything could have happened to me."

In retrospect, I really did not understand that, among other things, Second Avenue has a wretched reputation. I should have been alerted by the frequent presence of "diamond" rings in the cash register, collateral for short-term loans given out to streetwalkers of my boss Clarence's acquaintance. Working reception, filing, and billing in the office of an artificial limb shop gave me an awareness of some of the cost of the Vietnam War.

When the document came in from the federal government stating, in advance, how much they would pay this "contractor" for the manufacture of arms and legs for young men who would be losing their own in the coming year, I joined in the protest marches. There I was, heavily pregnant now and no longer able to sport my own plastic limb, marching on crutches with other protesters, as far as I could walk.

Earlier, when I was at PSU, still with my hair in long braids, zero makeup, and often sporting a tailored, khaki shirt (from Abercrombie & Fitch) with epaulets no less, the rumor got started that I had lost that leg in one of the wars against Israel. I enjoyed the respect until one day, I was asked to stand in a political science class and defend Israel's position in the 1967 war against a hostile professor. This was actually my first experience of antisemitism in the Pacific Northwest, though not dissimilar to my last recent one, of being told to "go back to Israel, or wherever I came from." This was hurled at me by a perfect stranger in the Lake City Post Office, where I had just rejected his help to get an awkward package containing homemade cookies for my son in college in Chicago up to the front of the line.

The Culvert Ran Pink

The gutter leading downhill from the culvert ran pink with camellia petals. I recognized these blossoms from a distance because my own driveway is normally littered with them during and after the springtime holiday of Passover. This morning, though, when I first spotted the pink trail coursing down the hill opposite me, I had a moment of terror—of, again, blood. Pogroms. My imagination is good, I will admit, but there are historical facts to back my intimations of horror. Yet life prevails. Roses bloom. A new leaf is forming on the otherwise moribund houseplant in my studio. At this season, too, I vanquished one of the scariest people in my life with a crayon sketch of a tulip on the side of an Easter egg.

The Painted Easter Egg

As usual, I had prepared four bowls of hot water, each with a few drops of food coloring: green, yellow, pink, blue. To get purple or orange, I would dip the blown-out egg more than once. Blowing out the eggs meant piercing holes in each end, one large and one small, and literally blowing the contents out the larger hole by puffing into the small one. The egg stuff could be collected in a clean bowl and made into scrambled eggs to sustain the young artists. We were all young artists with this project. I was at most twenty-four, and my son two. It involved the suspension of perfection and the promise of freedom, color, and experimentation.

The older, grizzled painter who dropped in on us that day was totally frustrated by this project. He handled the colored crayons like the oaf that he was—clumsy and rough. I tranquilly drew an equator line on my egg, then a second band. I drew my tulips above and below, right side up and upside down, as I had always drawn them since I was four or five. I dipped the bottom half in one color, the top in another. The wax of the crayoned tulips resisted the color of the dye and turned out bright against the pastel background.

"Yours is better than mine," he said angrily. "I cannot do this." And he stomped off and out. I never heard from him again, although it being a small town, I did see him around a few times. But there was no longer any kind of hold on me. He was vanquished.

Cooperative Preschool

Now there was a time when I was impeded by child-care needs from doing any artwork at all, yet my toddler was too young for any kind of "school." I started striking up conversations with other young mothers at the neighborhood laundromat, added them to the one or two mothers I was already acquainted with, and voila, we had a co-op.

We hired a young unemployed "teacher" to work every morning 9-12, and we each took a day of the week to "work" with her, simultaneously hosting the co-op at each of our homes. Split five ways, her paycheck was not onerous, and each one had four free mornings to pursue our own artwork. The children became really good friends, though I do not know what became of any of them now.

Some seven or eight years later, one of these moms ran off with my date, and we were not any kind of friends after that.

I was in NYC visiting at the time of the National Organization for Women's march down Fifth Avenue in 1972 (Women Strike for Equality). We chanted "out of the kitchens, out of the houses, out of the jails!" I was carrying my toddler in a backpack while I marched, though friends took turns carrying him too. I felt more important when I was the one carrying him.

Back in the Portland playgroup, one toddler named Freddy, who wore a voluminous pink overcoat and matching bonnet, his mother's nod to feminism, was our only near accident. He one day climbed out a window onto an unprotected balcony and was fortunately snatched back inside by our paid helper. The prospect of sudden death of an overly adventurous toddler scared us all.

The Car Was a Runaway

It started off downhill slowly, picking up speed. My two-year-old was just visible, standing up in the front seat. He had climbed into our unlocked car (at the land) and either knocked it down into neutral or released the parking brake, maybe both. The car was headed full tilt for a stand of trees at the base of the hill. No one else was around. Only me. I chased the car through the tall meadow grass aiming for the back door closest to me. I was going too slowly to make it. The car continued on its trajectory. I flung down my crutches and hopped, great hops, with arms going out for balance, and grabbed for the handle of the door. It opened; I catapulted myself inside and flung myself face forward between the two front bucket seats. From there, my hand found the brake pedal, and I slowed and stopped the car.

Safely in "Park," with the parking brake on, I embraced my child. The crutches lying at some distance gave credence to my story. The great hops were never repeated, and I would not wish the terror on any parent. Children must never be allowed to play in parked cars. They think they can drive.

The Size of Paper

Scarcity was part of my parents' and grandparents' lives. It led to a sort of thrifty-ness with simple things like string, heavy brown wrapping paper, rubber bands, and aluminum foil. My mother used to stroke the wrinkles out of a used piece of aluminum foil, saying it was such "beautiful" material, a shame to throw it away. So we would reuse it as long as possible. Throwing out bread was also next to impossible because my mother would repeat tearfully what her father had always said: that he had "seen men ready to kill for a crust of bread." Years later, at art school, I had to be encouraged to draw to the edges of the large sheets of paper, as opposed to thriftily in the middle or off to the right, to make room for more drawings on the same page.

Thrift, the Great Depression, the Second World War, these were all reasons to save string, brown paper, odds, and ends of different sorts. Art school in the 1970s encouraged the use of large 18x24 sheets of paper, as well as drawing right to the edges, even clear off the paper altogether. Personal poverty meant that I saved pencil stubs as though I might never again have a proper tool to mark with. Now, I have oh so many art supplies. There is a specialness to travel with the stubs, with a miniature watercolor set and brush, and small pads of paper—tight and tighter to compose in such a small rectangle, an entire view, a reclining figure, or a sprawling abstract form.

I get a little panicky when I start to run out of paper.

Art-School Antisemitism

It was unusual for me to be trimming pottery in a long dress. The ceramics department was holding its Christmas party, and our teacher had gathered most of the students around him so he could hold forth in the manner of professors everywhere. This time, perhaps after a holiday beer, he got started on the iniquity of Jews and their widespread influence on world economics.

I was sitting at a small distance, working on my hand-thrown pots before they would become too dry to trim their bottoms or "feet." I stopped my wheel and picked up the metal stool I had been sitting on. Holding it as a shield in front of my chest with two hands and with its legs pointed forward, I walked slowly toward the group. I don't think I was limping, or not much, as I was a pretty good walker at that time. I aimed my trajectory right toward the teacher as the other students peeled away. I kept my face blank and continued to advance. He started to blabber: "I didn't mean anything" and "take it easy" as I continued forward. When he was finally alone, abandoned by his enablers and clearly frightened, I stopped in front of his cowering posture.

Convinced I had done enough, I returned to my pottery wheel with my stool. He never made antisemitic remarks in class again. I did not report him, though someone else might have. (I had said nothing and not touched him with my "weapon.") By the next school year, he had left, for a variety of reasons, among them that he did not care for teaching.

The Stalker Carrying a Rose

He showed up in my basement, rapidly descending the outside stairs and into the open door. I was not, at first, particularly frightened, although I did not know him. He claimed to be an old classmate of mine from university and tracked me down through the artificial limb shop where I worked. My place of employment later gave me a different story; they had revealed to him where I had gone to university, a large and urban one with thousands of students.

What he wanted was to renew old bonds, which were, in fact, nonexistent. The other thing he wanted was to rape me. This became apparent as he followed me around, always herding me, trying to cut off escape. Prattling cheerfully and nonstop, I distracted him enough to make my escape outside into the fenced backyard. Only marginally safer, I made my way out the open gate toward the kitchen door and the phone.

He followed me.

When he began to encircle me against a wall, one palm on either side of my head, I slid down against the wall and away from his potential embrace.

Continuing to prattle and mindful of my seven-year-old playing calmly nearby on the floor, I ventured the opinion that while I would love to go out with him, I simply must have a chance to fix myself up and to get a babysitter for the evening ahead.

He accepted this idea and fixed a time for his return, adding that he had a gun.

First, I called my boyfriend, who did not believe any of it. And then I called the police. They advised that I could ask them to send an officer at the stated time of the "date" so I could tell the stranger in front of an officer that I did not know him, did not wish to date him, and if he appeared on my property again, I would have him arrested.

The man showed up as he had said he would, and so did the police. Standing there in his snug, white duck trousers and carrying a single red rose, the man tossed down the rose and stomped off, and was not heard from again.

Temptation of Beruriah

For my younger son, I had started knitting when the fifth pregnancy held. The fine needles and narrow yellow wool poked out of my knapsack in plain view. This was a clue that my would-be seducer should knock it off. It worked. Protection.

I got the front and back of the sweater done before the slightly preterm birth at thirty-six weeks. I have never made the little sleeves. When he started kindergarten, I found a light blue sweater vest at a thrift store. It could have been made by my mother or grandmother; the pattern was exactly the same. He wore it for all the dress-up occasions until it was way too small, completing his outfit of shirt and tie.

My mother was still alive to knit for my older son, really complicated patterns (to me). I remember one with buttons at the shoulder and one with a shawl collar against the wind. He wore that one for years. I still have it.

Knitting Needles in the Backpack

The knitting needles were clearly visible in the open backpack. They were slender, with fine, pale-yellow yarn cast on. I cannot remember which came first, actually: the charged hug from another sculptor along with the comment that I was growing fat or the glance into the backpack. In either order, the two facts—getting fatter, knitting in fine wool—suddenly added up.

His facial expression turned to horror, a sort of dumbfounded, deep horror he could not conceal as he broke the hug. Zipping the knapsack, I took it up and left him there. Left him with his imaginary scenarios. I knew where I had to go. I had to get home to my husband. Still, some upset remained and manifested itself as false labor shortly after the car ride home. Not another miscarriage! So close to viability.

The physical pains were quieted with some new and startling medication. My husband sat with me at the hospital, trying and even succeeding at being amusing. He set out imaginary cards for solitaire on the screen of his new laptop in order to demonstrate its wonders. The huge belly laugh I produced when he could not figure out how to actually move the cards was the rest of my cure.

The false labor stopped. We went home. Three months later, we had our healthy baby, indisputably our baby. I never saw the Lothario again, and he passed away some years ago now. Of course, it helped that at the time, I had him evicted from the rental.

If not for the insurance provided by carrying the knitting needles and baby sweater project, he might indeed have simply thought me fat and continued his attempt at seduction, or whatever was implied. However, one does not tell a woman she is getting fat as a part of "smooth" talking.

A Feminist/Traditional Bris for New Parents Over Forty

About fourteen women friends gathered quietly in the living room after instinctively taking off their shoes in the front hall. Actually, there was also a handmade sign that read, "Please remove your shoes," which had been calligraphed by my older son for the occasion. The few men, four I think, went into the kitchen with my husband. This was to be a reversal of a bris, where the new mother cowers alone in a bedroom. I was to be surrounded with loving attention from women. My husband would have a friend or two to keep him company.

My older son had a circumcision with the pediatrician two weeks after birth. It was awful. I was alone. I couldn't go to him. There was nothing spiritual about it. Although an amniocentesis had told us we would have a normal baby from this new pregnancy, we had requested not to know the sex. We were unprepared for a bris when the baby arrived a month early, and I felt that I had to create part of the ceremony to feel it included me.

We had been married with a huppah, a minyan, witnesses, and a ketubah, but without a rabbi, and I wanted a homespun event again. I usually take direct action against potentially stressful situations by having an "alternative" type plan. In my mind, there is no place for men to act as enforcers of things that are disrespectful to women, to their needs or feelings, or to what they want, and patriarchal Jewish customs sometimes do just that.

My labor had reminded me of the physical strength and intuitive knowledge of women, and I wanted my women friends to share in these most intimate memories and in sanctifying my son. Many of them knew that I had undergone three miscarriages before producing this baby. I had struggled with a tremendous sense of being punished by heaven, of feeling at fault. The days following this live birth were a profoundly emotional time for me, and I knew that I needed much support.

I was stunned by the ignorance of my doctors about the psychological effects of multiple miscarriages and other stress. I needed to tell the story of a difficult pregnancy and labor to people who would listen. A song by Ginny Reilly written to her own unborn child, *don't be afraid, don't be afraid, don't be afraid to come out and play... there will be happy endings, warm woolen gloves, and someone new to love*, was playing on the tape deck as I emerged from the bedroom to loud applause. "Can we clap?" someone had asked as I appeared. And I said, "Yes!"

Taking in the layout of the room, I realized it had been my intent that the men be able to hear but not see us from their post in the kitchen. I said as much aloud and felt so frightened by my audacity in creating a women's prayer space that I asked everyone to breathe with me a minute to regain my composure. I then asked the oldest woman to light a single candle to acknowledge the new soul I had brought into the world.

I reminded the group that "the soul Thou has created came pure from Thee." We were to name the baby "Zach," from the Hebrew for "pure" or "clean." I was rejecting the superstitious notion that I had been punished for my "sins" through my miscarriages.

I went on to describe that I must really like my grown son to do it all again twenty-three years later! I was a single parent for sixteen years and had not remarried until some years after I obtained a Jewish religious divorce: a "get." The essence of that ceremony, that I was free to marry again, helped me to finally let go of the rancor of the past.

Sometime later, I had written: "Where there is nothing and no one, there is still love... In this love, we are connected to all things... the body... is nothing as compared to the capacity to connect with love and to generate love. To stop this flow is the only tragedy in life. To open it was the greatest thing one can do for another."

My present husband, a geneticist with no previous children, had informed me that we each contributed some three billion bits of DNA to make the three million base pairs of DNA that went into our baby. I told the group that we had discussed our desire for a child from our earliest dates and that we had met only after I embroidered the pillowcases and was finishing up the challah cover for my future home and marriage. I bought and installed a mezuzah on the future baby's door as soon as I was pregnant. Someone was coming. I had to get ready.

At thirty-six weeks, I made a pot of chicken soup. I went to the park and sat and meditated in front of the lake and prayed to gather strength. I went to the swimming pool to reduce my edema, went home and packed my bag, and went to bed early. At midnight, my water broke. Later, I wrote: "The armor cracked in childbirth. Hold me against your open heart. Take my pain. Take it. Take it. Breathe with me, count with me, watch the clock become painless. Capable and anxious, focused visually, and lost in lavender smells."

The mohel who, believe it or not, worked at Microsoft, had asked that a chair be reserved for the prophet Elijah, who comes not only to every Passover seder but to every bris.

As long as we were inviting the departed, I had one chair devoted to the handiwork of my grandmother, one for my mother, and one for me. Busy professionals all, we had still sewed and knitted for our much-wanted children and grandchildren.

My mother's mother was a midwife, and my mother was a pediatrician. I had a strong sense of their presence in the delivery room and had felt safer as a result. It seems to me that I have repeatedly experienced some sort of "veil" between this and some other world as being transparent at times of birth and of death. Some would attribute this type of perception to grief or stress. To some edge of madness. There are, however, many modes of knowledge, and they are not all rational. An artist might well use romantic, even magical thinking to try to make things come out right through creative visualization.

Some women friends have asked me why I would put myself through so-called "natural" childbirth, unmedicated childbirth. I have never felt more capable than when giving birth, and it is thrilling to feel that strength. Just as it takes the right woman to make a mensch of a man, it takes the right man to allow a woman to be powerful. Joe and I were knocked out to see Zach emerge from my body, that a woman's body can "take this bit of sperm and make it into a person. I mean, if that isn't worthy of respect ..." said Joe. "And then her body starts making milk. I mean, it's just completely amazing."

Blessings for a Feminist Bris

New Blessings On the Birth of a Son

You will learn how to be a man from other men, but you will also learn how to be a man from the women in your life.

A loving voice, a willingness to help, a loving touch, and most of all, a loving heart is what I wish for the new man in my life.

A man learns from his parents, friends, and teachers, but also one day, G-d willing, from his wife.

New Blessings For Parents

To include your man in labor is to include him in the mysteries of women,

to gain forever his respect for the power of women and your respect for the softness of men.

May the bonds we made during our labor nourish and sustain our marriage for many years to come.

Yiddish Proverb For Parents

"It is an art to buy merchandise and to bear children. It is an even greater art to sell off merchandise and to rear children."

A kunts iz tsu koyfn skhoyre un tsu hobn kinder. Noch a gresere kunts iz skhoyre tsu farkoyfn un kinder megadl zayn.

I Take the Elevator By Myself (Part 2)

I was sitting in a wheelchair, my crutches having been taken away as "weapons," when a TV program about stalking came on. I asked, then demanded that the channel be changed as it was not under my control to do so. When my request was denied, I had to maneuver my wheelchair among a forest of dining room chairs and tables. Impatient to get out and growing angry, I shoved chairs out of the way.

Quickly surrounded by five or six men bent on controlling me, no one asked me what on earth was the matter. After the national amputee ski races—when all the female names, addresses, and phone numbers were published in a guide—"weirdos," as we called these predators, from all over the country, started stalking the women. I had my share of uninvited late-night phone calls and unexpected, unwelcome visits from such stalkers.

The more I was manhandled, the more I fought. I was angry, but I was also frightened. When I peed myself, they took off all my clothes, and my transformation into madness was complete as I snarled and pretended to prepare to bite them.

Placed in seclusion with a peephole for any passerby to view me, I grew increasingly cold and disoriented. I felt so cold that I had to imagine a way out. I entered into my imagination to create companions who could warm me. I "became" the teens huddling in their snow cave in the tragic Mount Hood school expedition where only two survived, and I "became" a Resistance fighter, thanking my mother for rescuing him. "Merci, Lucie," I repeated louder and louder until it became simply "Mercy! Mercy!" and two women nurses burst in to rescue me.

I knew my name. "Joan, have you just had a baby?"

I knew that I had just had a baby. They sat me up and took me to the showers, and then installed me in a normal room with a bed and with blankets. I returned to myself. "Can't I even take a couple of days off without something like this happening?!" one woman complained to the other nurse. "What were these guys even thinking?"

The facility was clearly segregated (Seattle, 1993), with all the black clients on one side of the quadrangle. I wandered over there a few times because people were more friendly and sociable. At least they would say "hi!"

One time, I started singing and "Miss Nellie" took it up right away, with a wonderful rendition of *Amazing Grace*. Many others joined in and then "staff" chased me back to the white side, forbidding me to return where I "did not belong."

Such respect for white people did not extend to Jewish ones, and I was given many pork-based meals, which I would not eat. "No special treatment" was the answer when I explained what I needed.

My short yoga workouts were charted as "bizarre repetitive movements." The guards were truly ignorant. At one point, I got ahold of a small plastic water pitcher so I could fill it at the water fountain (which was not accessible to someone in a wheelchair) and then pour into a cup. Challenged over this special privilege, I appealed to an actual doctor who came over to ask what was the matter. When I explained, he gazed at me, aghast, and said, "But you are completely rational!"

The second time I got off the elevator by myself (like in elementary school) was some forty years later, when I was released from a privately run county evaluation facility. This place, like my first school, was housed on several floors in a high-rise building, albeit with barred windows and locked doors. The elevator had been called for me and would, for a change, stop at our floor. As the doors opened, the occupants shrank back, and I felt again small and short and younger, sitting in my wheelchair. They seemed so tall to me. I was weighed down and encumbered with both crutches in one hand and my peg leg in the other.

As the doors began to close again, one of my tormentors on staff challenged me, "You've missed it!" he said with finality.

Not me, I thought to myself. *I am getting out of here and fast.*

I thrust out my right arm, bearing my peg leg aloft, and wedged the fiberglass socket into the closing elevator doors, forcing them open. I do not remember ever moving so quickly or decisively in my life. At that moment, I was unstoppable and invincible. I took the elevator down to the ground floor, was wheeled to our car, the wheelchair taken away, and finally driven home to my waiting baby.

After the baby was safely born, I was very tired and a long list of duties awaited, from writing thank-you notes to preparing for a trip to Japan in a mere five weeks. I begged my obstetrician, and also my physician father, to inform my husband that he had to cancel the trip. Surely there would be other invitations. Certainly, I could not be left with a newborn for the projected month-long visit.

The OB said my husband would get it when he saw what a newborn is, and my father said I could not stop him if he wanted to go. I would have to hire help. I felt utterly abandoned. I was nursing. I was only sleeping an hour at a time. I was anxious. I was hypervigilant. I was starting a slide into postpartum depression.

The household help in the mornings only woke me with her kitchen noises of dishes clanking and cabinets shut firmly. The noise of anyone's hairdryer in the nearby bathroom was a torment.

When a visitor told Joe I might possibly hurt the baby (if I was indeed depressed), he called the police and had me taken to an ER and then an evaluation facility. Like the children's story of the farmer and his wife who argue over whose job was the more difficult (and so they trade), Joe was now going to be the primary parent with significant help from my older son and from the hired help in the mornings. He canceled the trip to Japan. He learned formula prep and round-the-clock bottle feeding and changing. Our helper did the baths, and so did I—locked up but allowed to visit with the baby when he was brought to me (almost daily).

I bought a package of sewing thread in many different colors to remind myself that I could still identify and process emotion through color, and also a bar of pure castile soap. I could then hold the back of my baby's sweet little head under the sink faucet to shampoo his hair so he would know my touch and also not get cradle cap.

I played medieval tunes on my recorder once it was declassified as a "weapon."

Joe pleaded with them to release me after two weeks so I could take care of the baby. He was exhausted! I was told I was lucky my husband would take me back. After I returned home, I studied infant massage videos so I could continue to comfort and connect with my baby through touch. And I bathed and dressed him endlessly for the same reason. I had never stopped wanting to take care of the baby. I wanted this baby, though I never finished the thank-you notes for the presents.

Postpartum depression is complex and how it is treated is a feminist issue. Charlotte Perkins Gilman wrote about this in the short story, *The Yellow Wallpaper*, published in 1892. She, however, had no interest in caring for her newborn and was locked in the attic by her husband due to her "nervous" condition.

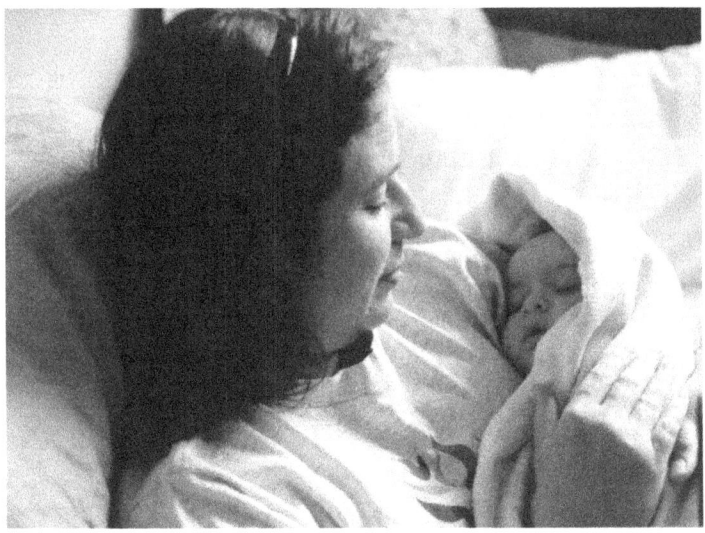

How Did This Happen?

I prayed at the Western Wall in Jerusalem for a healthy baby between miscarriages, and I had another miscarriage after that. I had felt something electrical pass from one hand to another as I leaned on the Wall with arms outspread against it. I was strengthened by the visit to the Wall. I decided I would try what the doctor wanted to do, which was to support a pregnancy with progesterone. *Hof oyf nissim nor farloz zikh nit oyf a nes.* (Hope for miracles but don't rely on one.) That tinkering with Nature may have been part of the hormonal storm following birth.

The nurse at the Swedish hospital suggested I stay another day as one night was not much rest for an older mother after a birth. I was not comfortable there as most of the nurses were not nice, and I wanted to go on home. The hospital nurse's follow-up was scheduled for the eighth day after birth, and I asked to reschedule because of the bris or ritual circumcision. I never heard from them again about the regulation postpartum visit. Later they argued that they assumed "my people" would take care of me. But it was negligence on their part. Meantime, I had photos to send, and congratulations and many presents to acknowledge with thank-you notes. One of the Japanese scientists offered Joe congratulations on the continuation of his "Y" chromosome...

I felt some censure and fear of "punishment" about breaking patriarchal norms with my "feminist" bris ceremony. I became afraid.

Even unwrapping the traditional spiraling bris bandage became "seeing" a newsreel of Jewish history to my eyes and mind. In historical context, a bris could mean identification as a Jew. This could be dangerous! Lighting the Sabbath candles, I also time traveled briefly, seeing many detailed scenes, one after the other, of candle lighting in other places and in other times. I was part of this whole vision, this whole tableau of history! Pattern(s) on wrapping paper and fabric began to take on meaning(s) to me, some positive and some not. Our backyard suddenly seemed menacing, with animals (cats? raccoons?) with glowing eyes. I think that maybe my husband got really scared.

I was lying on a pencil for making more to-do lists, I suppose, but when I got up to be taken away, I glanced back at the pencil and promised myself that one day I would write about this.

I put my engagement and wedding rings on the mantlepiece before I was escorted out of my home. I had made my husband cry, yet I knew that I would be the one labeled and punished.

Knitting Needles (Part 2)

The sweater vests go way back—before central heating, probably. Anyway, my grandmother made them for all the males in her family, and so did my mother. The design was a basic V-neck. Flat, smooth knit on one side, purl on the other, with one or two braided "cables" up the center or at the sides by way of embellishment. I was happily surprised when I found a pleasant, deep-sky-blue, brand new sweater in about size 3 in a second-hand store when I was pregnant with my second son way across the country from New York—in Seattle.

After my son outgrew it, I started on a bigger one in his favorite color, green, following the blue one as a guide. Alas, he grew faster than I could finish it (it was way too wide at first, and I had to redo a lot.) Still, the thought was there: protection. From what? From cold, from starvation, from lack of color and fire and passion in life.

The knitting of sweater vests—a form of protection, really—has a very long history for my mother and grandmother and probably for many other people. They were always V-necked to allow for a clean shirt collar to emerge and had two cables—twists in the design—running one on each side of the front and sometimes of the back. It turns out that the cables are actually quite easy to make. You collect three stitches on a small, extra knitting needle and hold it off to one side while knitting three more stitches. Coming back to these reserved stitches, the twist is made. The length between twists is determined by how many rows you knit before repeating the above procedure.

My mother brought me wool and fairly large needles as part of my recovery at age 15. The color was a seafoam green. She actually researched which color would have the most soothing quality. I finished that sweater to fit me, but when she asked me what I wanted to do with it, I told her to give it away. Perhaps giving that sweater to charity was what saved me. Anyway, I never had to look at it again. It was 5 knit, 1 pearl, so it had a pattern of grooves and a boat neck.

Last Christmas time, I bought myself an acrylic cable-knit sweater at a department store. All those alternative piles of color. I chose and bought seafoam green.

In college, I survived lectures and lovesickness by knitting my intended a pea green sweater. He was a redhead and helped choose the heather wool. I think he said once that he still has this sweater. Anyway, it was straight knit, no grooves nor cables and a plain crew neck. I don't actually know how to do necks or join in sleeves, and I cannot read knitting directions to save my life. I follow my mother's example: I knit a sample couple of inches, I measure the circumference of the person, I multiply.

My current husband never got a sweater from me. I did make him a nice scarf early on, but he lost it on like the first or second wearing, so that was it. I made a couple of hat-and-scarf sets for my older son. He wore the one in elementary school, but I doubt he wore the set I gave him for college. It had stripes for design and for protection, as they all did.

The Vests for Protection

My father's companion had laid out all the clothes for the burial, all in variations of brown. I knew something was missing in the bunch. My father had asked me, he left instructions-that is, he told me privately, in person—it must have been six months before he died—to please be sure he was buried in a certain blue vest my mother had knitted for him. It was the last such project she had made for him before she died.

My father said to me, an adult of forty-six, that he somehow had an idea he would be cold there. Where? Did he picture himself inside the box?

"I have this idea," he said while miming a shiver, "that I might be cold." (This after fourteen years with another woman following my mother's death.)

I promised. I was not there when the funeral director called at the apartment for clothes for the casket. My father's partner had carefully laid out a complete matching outfit of trousers, shirt, and jacket and objected that the sweater vest spoiled the "look" and did not "go" in terms of color. My brothers, themselves wearers of sweater vests for many of their formative years, intervened. At least they gave the sweater to the funeral director along with the other burial clothes. I assume my father was buried in it as requested. I hope so.

A shroud would indeed have been simpler. Imagine an argument over the clothes to be buried in. Who, exactly, was going to see?

For me, though, the idea that my father wanted to be buried with something of my mother's love on his very body was meaningful and wiped away some of the sting of his replacement—another woman in the house. Recently, she sent me a lot of photos of him. Is she downsizing? Does she want to forget him? It has been now sixteen years since he died. She is eighty-one.

I'm Not Broken

"I'm not broken, I work perfectly fine!" is what I say when children point and stare at me.

"I have two ears, even if I only have one leg," I say.

It is rude to say loud things about people right in front of them. It hurts their feelings to talk about them as though they are not even there. It makes them feel invisible and as though they are not important. No one likes to feel that they don't even count.

I always like to say my name if someone forgets I am a person and not an exhibit in a zoo.

My name is "Joan," I say, and I am a "people" just like you.

What makes people be people anyway? Some people have brown eyes, and some have blue or green ones. They are all people. Some have light skin, and some have dark skin, and they are all people too. Some people have curly hair, and some have straight hair, and they are all people. Some are tall, and some are fat, and some are short, and some are thin, and they are all people. People are different from each other, so it isn't their bodies that make them exactly the same.

Everyone does have feelings, and thoughts, and spirit, and a heart, and a mind, and a soul to store them in. The "containers" or bodies we live in are different. Some of us are girls or women, and some of us are men or boys, but we all have thoughts and feelings, feelings and thoughts. Even people who come from different countries and who speak different languages have feelings and thoughts.

So little details like sizes and shapes, and how many fingers and how many toes you have, are not what makes a person a person.

I like to ski.

And swim.

And have parties.

And grow flowers.

And make sculptures.

And read books.

I have a husband and a son. We are a family. I am not broken. I work perfectly fine.

It's boring to have people stare at my leg or want to talk about it all the time. I live in this body, and it's OK with me. If every time I spoke to you, I said, "Look! One nose! You've only got one nose!" and laughed, I bet you would get mad after you became self-conscious and embarrassed. "Quit staring at my nose!" you would say. "It's on my face! Leave me alone!"

Now that you know how it feels to be pointed at and stared at and talked about out loud as though you had no thoughts and feelings, as though you were invisible, are you going to stop being rude to people who are different than you?

Maybe you would like to think about what I can do that you can't.

I can cross puddles without getting wet.

I can dance with three feet.

I can wear one pair of socks for two days.

I have an empty place near my lap for someone small to sit.

I can fit into very small spaces.

I always have tools with me to reach high places.

No, I can't run. But I can draw. I can't walk, but I can ride a bicycle. I am lucky I have my hands—special hands that can communicate tenderness. Even if I didn't have my hands, I have my brain. Even if, God forbid, I didn't have any brain and thoughts, I would have my heart and feelings. And even if, God forbid, I didn't have my heart and feelings, I would have my soul and my spirit, and I will have those forever until the end of time.

Because we are all part of the same spirit, which does not die.

Where there is nothing and no one, there is still love. In this love, we are connected, all things, and all people, living or dead, and we are whole. The shape of the body, the container of our spirit, is nothing as compared to the capacity to connect with love and to generate love.

To stop this flow is the only tragedy in life. To open it is the greatest thing one can do for another.

If I salute the love within you, I can connect with any human being of any age, gender, shape, or size.

My spirit is whole. The souls of all the "broken" are whole. My body is not a punishment, although it is a lesson.

The limits of the body create the need for pacing. The mind controls the pace. Tapping into infinite spirit confuses the pace because, in infinite spirit, there are not only no boundaries but no limits.

In my work I take things and feelings that have no boundaries and literally try to give them form. The body is the channel for spirit. We are the vehicles. We are the candles, shining. Our love reflects The Love. To love is not personified in a human being but in human doing.

Hay Bales

One summer, when my youngest was about seven, I enrolled him in a "farm" day camp. There, he would be allowed to chase chickens, climb trees, and, best of all, ride horses. He did learn to do all those things and seemed to enjoy it, but my strongest memory is of the hay bales.

A large number of hay bales were arranged near the barn in a single layer—not quite a square, more like a maze. Apparently, there was another boy who was a bully and who would amuse himself during "free time" by chasing my son around these hay bales, threatening him with what would happen if he were caught. For whatever reason, I'm claiming genetic memory here, Zach would run from him until "recess" was over.

One day, when I was there to pick him up at the end of the day, I personally witnessed the "game." It really upset me to see and hear this child-bully, and I ached for my gentle son. At least he was skillful in feinting right and left and seemed to be quite a bit faster than the hollering, rather heavy kid. But it was what happened next that really amazed me. Each child at the camp had to wear a cowboy-style straw hat except when riding horses, when they actually wore bicycle helmets for safety. In any case, I watched in amazement as Zach pretended to hide behind this and that hay bale, crouched down with only the hat visible. Then, as the noisy bully arrived, he would escape, running in the nick of time. And then he placed his hat on a far corner of a bale and crept away from it. On cue, the bully, roaring with triumph, launched himself physically on the immobile hat.

The howl of frustration that followed, and the jubilation of my son, was a proud, proud moment for me as a parent and especially as a Jew. My son had been so clever about that bully, and he was clearly demonstrating his *Yiddishe kop* (Jewish head).

One Foot in Each World: Zach at Age 10, Joan at 55

Because of the "merit of the ancestors" and the strength of the golden oak tree, I will be allowed to live out my days and not know an early death.

My mother's death served as my insurance, as did her mother's before her. I still have the padded mailbag, addressed to me in my mother's hand. It is stamped "insured," in red ink, within a sort of oval, a protective ring.

Rings and stripes, triangles, diamonds, and squares are all magic shapes, conferring protection from evil. Stones and feathers, shells and twigs, leaves and bark are all usable for calling down help from the spirit world.

Answers come in voices, smells, and rearrangements of objects, even in (rearrangements) of smells. For instance, just now, as I approached the clay bin carrying a clean wet towel as a cover, I smelled a strong smell of eucalyptus instead of mold. A fresh, strong, clean scent replaced the musty odor emanating from the clay bin. I sniffed the towel, but it smelled only faintly of soap and chlorine bleach. There were some branches of dried eucalyptus stuck in a jar on top of the bin. Perhaps the damp released a bit of their perfume. But it was gone again so quickly and had been so strong that I can only assume the scent to have been my answer. Work. Sculpt. Create in clay.

And what of words and stories? Let me continue to set down bits of the journey and the reader can decide for themselves.

Quilt Making

Aligning everything in the universe is not possible for mortals but arranging triangles of colored cloth into patterns is within our grasp. Admittedly, I saw a particularly inspiring exhibit of quilts, but I went because I wanted to make one, or really, two. My eldest brother was very ill, and his eldest son was going to be needed. This, in turn, would leave his own young children without their father for a while. I wanted to make them "blankies." I wanted to do something to keep me anchored during the dreadful period of waiting for the shoe to drop. With luck, maybe my brother would make one last trip himself. We would all be together, he would see what I had made in his honor, and best of all, the final stitching and knotting of the quilts could be done during the visit. This would keep all of the women, and some of the men occupied and away from the endless grieving at the side of the patriarch. At least some of the loving presence would go into the quilt projects, would be a tangible reminder for those kids of how many people they still had, how much love surrounds them, how connected is the extended family.

About color—How to: Did you just go to a fabric store? How did you even begin? Actually, at another quilt show, there were sales booths of "fat quarters" and supplies, and I had started to collect. This process is much like finding a blouse to match an outfit: not just contrasting color but fabric and feel, scale, and touch. I did a lot of geometry on paper, trying to figure out how many of these "quarters," which in reality are fixed-size squares of fabric, would be needed.

I watched two or three YouTube videos. Mostly, I looked at the quilts in a couple of exhibits and decided I could figure it out as I went. Mostly true. Color, I am definitely still figuring out. Even seeing color is a challenge. Primaries and orange and purple are easy enough. Forming quilt patterns means finding contrasts, subtleties, and similarities. Colors that at first blush seem to match, or at least "go," suddenly clash.

I like and need color because there is so much gray in my surroundings. The weather, for one, is often gray here. And one feels more alive surrounded by color. I have to be careful what I wear, though, for good or bad. Red makes me overly emphatic, blue is calming, green is healing, black is deadening, brown—except for a strange green turd color—makes me look ill, yellow and orange are unflattering, and at this age, white is too harsh a contrast to aging skin.

In my quilt designs, I can use any colors or combination of colors without concerning myself as to whether they are flattering to my face.

Art, or alcoholism, I suppose, are really the only choices when the weather is dreary.

A quote from Marcel Duchamp:

"Any artist with reasonable work habits can produce more in five years than can be sold in a lifetime."

That is certainly true in my experience. And I have a storage room full of work ready to exhibit to prove it. Quilts however are a welcome gift for new parents.

The Roots of Vilna

My mother hated it when my father hummed his "little tunes." She claimed he only did it when he was anxious and to drive her crazy. This is not true. My father's parents came from an area of many *niggunim* (little tunes). Traditionally sung at the Shabbos table to lift the spirit, they serve to ease the heart. If tunes can calm anxiety at other times, then this is wonderful, not crazy at all.

When I despaired of ever healing the breach with my own son, a curious thing happened. It involved a cedar tree, its roots, and a sculpture set on concrete blocks. Years earlier, when my mother was dying, I sculpted a life-size clay figure, sleeping peacefully in her actual accustomed sleep position. I cast this in concrete and, with helpers, arranged two rows of concrete blocks, set in a rectangle to act as a base, at the foot of a cedar tree in my own backyard. I knew that I would not be traveling with any frequency to her actual burial place near New York City, and I wanted to keep her near. Actually, what I also did was bury an old pair of gardening shoes she had left behind from a visit to me. This was surprisingly meaningful for me.

Over the years, and especially after a particularly hot summer, the roots of the cedar twisted up toward the surface of the earth, dislodging the concrete blocks until they resembled very crooked teeth. Seeing the disturbed block wall, "the ancestors are angry," I told myself. My older son's rebellion against family and faith has stirred them. Beneath the symbolic grave of my mother, they are showing me that roots can dislodge stone and that statues can topple, even break. The roots! The roots are all.

I tried to arrange with the gardener to get a couple of workers together to move the sculpture away from the cedar tree and restack the base of blocks on the concrete patio. I wanted to free the power of those roots to come to my aid. I was disappointed the move did not happen before winter. Over the winter, moving a fragile, half-frozen sculpture was not a good idea. Still, I considered: how to reach the ancestors.

Finally, just after Tu B'Shevat, the new year of the trees, came my father's Yahrzeit (anniversary of his death on the Hebrew calendar). The gardeners moved the sculpture and its block base.

Now I am communicating with trees. I felt it when we had the sculpture lifted off the roots of the tree, and especially as each concrete block came up. The ancestors are happier without the impediment. The roots grow thicker and push up the trunk.

How can I feel a tree? The sense of peace is at its base, the attachment, thickness, stability. It will get more water now. To sit by the "grave" of my mother is a peaceful thing. To dream. Do they look like they are dreaming, these reclining, sleeping sculptures of mine? I feel everything with my heightened senses. The lightness of a tissue crumpled and thrown. It disperses as much energy as a body! Did the studio chair crack? It definitely rocks a bit more, but it held. Oak, and old, and strong.

I contacted my brothers and wrote to my niece and nephews: in memory of their father/grandfather, help me to get back my son. For the self-imposed deadline of this Yahrzeit, and four days before my son's fortieth birthday, I scanned over three hundred images of his life, from cradle to the present, including a fifth-grade report card and a current web "review." My idea was that he would see again where he came from and perhaps decide on his future route: healing from a codependent relationship, a *refuah shlemah* or perfect healing of body and soul.

I phoned the charity line in Brooklyn before the twenty-four-hour Yahrzeit candle could go out. "In the merit of your father on the occasion of his Yahrzeit you are asking that the *nefesh* (soul) of your father watch over your son from *shamayim* (the heavens)," the operator intoned in a soft South African English, mingled with Yiddish, as I wept. As a tight muscle band unsnapped around my breastbone, I felt a sudden peace even as I wept. It was done. I had reached them, the ancestors, the ones from Vilna, who assimilated into their surrounding culture(s) for more than a hundred years, but who still hummed their little tunes. He and they would watch over my son.

The same father who often rejected me ("this is foolishness," "belly on legs," "little cockroach"), whose pet names held the sting of zingers in Yiddish, French, and Russian, this same father would watch over him. I dreamt of my father's final days when I did not go to visit as asked. The guilt was again unbearable, even though our pediatrician said I could not go, and so I dreamt then of one of my alternative father figures, the Israeli movement therapist, his beloved face always creased in smiles. His face had changed, I remember, after the death of his son in an early terrorist explosion. Yet the smile creases were so deep, they could not be erased.

Hiroshima/Nagasaki Days 1983 – the Shadow Project

Portland-area news media mentioned city observances for the anniversaries of the bombing of Hiroshima and Nagasaki but somehow left out the stories of the people involved in creating these observances.

There were a disproportionate number of Jewish names among the organizers, speakers, participants, and attorneys. Not that it matters, except as a source of pride and inspiration. At the Terry Schrunk Plaza gathering, author and activist Norm Solomon emphasized the "Nuremberg obligation to speak out" as applying to every citizen. He also remarked on how strange it was that local police had given out numerous citations the previous night to demonstrators who placed posters and created shadow images, but that no one was arresting leaders planning the genocide of entire peoples through nuclear war.

The Shadow Project itself was a remarkable feat of organized outcry. Originated by Alan Gussow in New York and carried out there the previous year, an entire network of people in Portland formed under the leadership of Donna Slepack. It was kept secret and spread through word-of-mouth only. A hundred-and-eighty volunteer artists were found to carry out the project, as well as the technical support and legal counsel they required.

In Hiroshima, people within three hundred yards of the epicenter were LITERALLY VAPORIZED, leaving only their shadows outlined in the street. The purpose of the Shadow Project was to "help people imagine and comprehend the overwhelming consequences of a nuclear war." About 1,800 shadows were painted through the city of Portland, including some along Capitol Highway, near the Mittleman Jewish Community Center.

Training sessions were conducted for the volunteers about staying off private property, and great precautions were taken to provide everyone with a homogenous "paint" composed mostly of whiting powder, which would disappear easily in a couple of weeks without washing. Whiting is used as a paint additive or for whitewashing walls. (It is basically crushed Tums.)

The real story is how it felt to participate. Radicalizing. There is nothing like action, any kind of action, to remove a feeling of helplessness and numbness. With friends and family, we each took turns standing in front of a bright light, tracing the outlines of each other to make the stencils.

This was the year my older son saw the famous Roman Vishniac photo of the small boy in the Warsaw Ghetto with his hands up over his head. It knocked him temporarily speechless and then: "How could they? I mean, children!" For the Shadow Project, he somehow took a similar pose but crouched and turned away as though from a bigger light.

The teams of adult artist volunteers went out at 2:30 a.m. on August 6, preassigned in their own neighborhoods, to place as many shadows and posters as they could before getting stopped by the police or dawn, whichever came first. The action was planned as a legal one, a nonpermanent substance on public streets. But it was a reasonable assumption that it would not be viewed that way. The secrecy, despite the information given on the posters, resulted in some people responding as though to vandalism. There were many citations and one booking.

But, again, the real story is what it felt like to paint my own death image, and that of my son, on the crosswalks and park entrances that we used in life. It felt deeply necessary and important and strengthened my own commitment to nuclear disarmament as nothing else could. An action taken outside of society, in the middle of the night, with a lookout for the police, made me feel strangely committed to the preservation of that society and tender towards my human ties within it.

On Nagasaki Day, I met my son in front of the Federal Building to join with many others in holding hands around the building in a peaceful and legal gesture. There were almost enough people to go around twice. As one of the speakers said: "We stopped Vietnam!" There were pro-Reagan signs, too. My son asked what and when was the McCarthy Era. This was the same child who was astounded that the Holocaust happened in his grandfather's era.

The single most important event during my first year at Reed College was watching my very own political science professor hauled off in a paddy wagon during a peaceful anti-Vietnam demonstration. The '60s generation was then thirty-five-plus, and some of us had children. At one time, there was a catchy slogan about the family that prays together, and in recent years we've seen the family that plays together. But now it was a time for the family that says together: "We can make a difference."

Lebn Gebliber (Survivors)

There were so many of us, of my Boomer cohort and friends, who did not "remain in life" or survive their 30s.

Death by accident, by suicide, by misadventure. Disregard for the power of the automobile (car accident). Disregard for the power of heights (leaping off the collapsing scaffold). Disregard for the power of too much introspection (transcendental suicide). Disregard for the power of the river (whitewater rafting). Disregard for the power of the ocean (a small trimaran on the vast sea.)

What children would these people have raised? What lives might they have had? All cut short.

When I saw my first husband lying by the side of the road in the Oregon countryside, I first assumed he had been murdered. The skin of his beloved face was a normal color, though, and he got up suddenly and stood there alive. The fright I had felt was like a deep memory of loved ones torn away and trampled. In a world where people had done terrible things to other people, how close and precious were the bonds of love, and how trivial our small marital disagreements suddenly seemed.

Which world shall I, did I, inhabit? Was it always so informed by the past?

I described a WWII-era film to my maternal uncle and aunt, remarking on how clever a pictorial representation of a young girl on a swing was, crying, "Mame, mame!" It was a perfect poetic shortcut for depicting the destruction of her village. My aunt replied that, for them, this was too close.

"It was real for us, you see. We don't need a film."

This shocked me.

There is, of course, the obvious world—namely, the current consensual reality. Then there is "the other world." Or, maybe even considering "the other world" is a taste of "the world to come," as it is referred to in Yiddish.

The historical and sociological worlds add still more layers of worlds: which century, which decade, and why? For example, my father's parents were married in the year 1900, and there are lots of photos of my grandmother to document the change from corsets to less-structured garments for women. My father's attitudes, while mostly modern and up to date (he disliked long skirts and long hair), partook liberally of the attitudes of the late nineteenth century, when his mother's attitudes were formed. I have found evidence of her ideas in the techinas (women's prayers in Yiddish) of the late nineteenth century which I researched after I miscarried. It was, in fact, not until I started studying Yiddish that I began to understand my father at all. Where did his tremendous resilience come from, and how did he find humor in any situation?

My father was frightening, too. His rages were uninterruptible and fearsome. If I was the unfortunate cause of the outburst, I would be sent to my room. There, I would cry and sniffle and wait for my mother to rescue me, to tell me I was OK, to find or provide some tissues. I will never forget the misery of pacing the room, looking for something on which I could wipe my nose.

Serendipity

The Little Players

The Little Players lived in our building. They were a repertory theater of astonishing marionettes who spoke and danced and sang. The characters were both male and female, sometimes at the same time. Years later, one of the company's two people wrote to me that they considered themselves to be my "guardian step-angels."

They took care of my imagination while I was reinventing myself as someone who was going to live out my life. They telephoned upstairs whenever there was a cancelation, and there was going to be a free seat for a performance. I would put on a dress and be effortlessly folded into what was always a packed house. A neighbor read a glowing review about the repertory company of marionettes and their creators/animators in faraway London. It took longer for them to get press in the United States.

Surprisingly, my first dentist (incompetent and painful work) had practiced out of this same ground-floor apartment. It only just occurred to me that a place of dread for me was totally replaced by the magic of creation, imagination, and performance by two partnered men in an atmosphere of expressiveness and joy. I think in many ways that their act of charity in saving me free seats saved my life by turning some of my home values on their heads and encouraging me that the life of the imagination was life squared.

Bill sang, he acted, he did voices and made the marionettes dance. Years later, my homemade clay puppet heads convinced my hard-headed father that perhaps I had enough talent for art school.

How I Met Your Father (Lew: Part 1)

"For our hands are strong, and our hearts are young, and the dreamer keeps a-dreaming." That was the start of the chorus to the song I was teaching high school students at a Jewish camp weekend in California. Only a freshman in college myself, I had been invited down for Thanksgiving weekend from my school in Portland, Oregon, to be the weekend song leader. Gathering everyone's attention after every meal in the dining hall, I was to teach and sing camp songs.

It was too far to go to New York City for a weekend, and I had never been to San Francisco. I had already traveled to Israel and then on to Europe. Upon hearing that I had temporarily abandoned my 13½-pound prosthesis and taken a train from Paris, where I was supposed to remain with friends of my parents, to Geneva where I met a school friend in order to hitchhike to Milan, my mother had stated that "Il y a un Dieu pour les innocents!" (There is a God for the innocent!)

Secure in the knowledge that my busy parents would not be sufficiently "au fait" (with it) to question my exact plans in the USA, I booked my flight to arrive a couple of days before the Friday-Sunday retreat. I checked into the YWCA downtown. Safe. Clean. Cheap. Centrally located. I was still seventeen. From there, I wanted to see City Lights Bookstore as I had read Lawrence Ferlinghetti and some of the Beats. I caught a ride to North Beach with a pleasant guy driving a VW van. The next day, Thanksgiving, I went to Golden Gate Park and happened to strike up a conversation with a young woman my age who took me home to have a turkey dinner with her family. I will admit this was all serendipitous, but I stayed safe, clean, and fed. Back in high school, during the Cuban Missile Crisis of 1962 in late October, events happened just before our midterm exams. I remember my parents insisting that the near hysteria at school was just an attempt to get out of studying and that nothing bad was going to happen. They said this with apparent perfect faith in the future, an attitude that impresses me to this day. Still at the time, 1965, the camp rabbi was horrified.

I met the camp bus downtown with all the other participants, and it was not until later that someone queried how I had gotten there from the airport. "You were wandering around on your own for TWO days in San Francisco?!"

On Sunday, at the end of the weekend's activities, I was placed in the care of the twenty-four-year-old caretaker with strict instructions to deliver me to my flight. We spent a peaceful afternoon first, strolling in the woods, and on our return, he presented me with all his single, mismatched socks.

"I have never known what to do with these," he said, "and I have finally met someone who could use them."

I should add that he kissed me before putting me on the plane and started phoning and then visiting me at college.

The California camp rabbi called the New York City youth rabbi who called me. Did my parents know about my boyfriend? I was still underage, and the camp could get in powerful trouble. I talked the rabbi down. I had never told on *his* improper advances.

This was during Vietnam, and Lew the caretaker was applying for conscientious objector status as a Jewish man. He needed the support of an establishment rabbi to do so. The temporary job at the camp was to give him a safe and paid haven while his draft board thought it over. My job at camp was to be some sort of role model, I suppose, fresh off of being a borough youth group president in Manhattan, a song leader, and a cancer survivor besides. Anyway, I could hold a dining room full of teenagers hostage with my voice and guitar to sing old songs and learn new ones.

By the next year, I had left college properly between semesters, on leave, and moved down to Monterey. Lew and I had both been to Israel and shared the idea that if people knew each other's languages, there could be peace. We enrolled in an intensive Arabic course, the only two students, where we studied and competed happily together. Then we got married on a visit to our parents in New York and moved back to Portland.

Israel

The orientation meeting for the Mitzvah Corps youth trip to Israel had been deadly serious. We were high school students from all over the United States, and the program was relatively new. The meeting focused on cautioning us about dangers we might encounter and was clearly designed to frighten us as well as keep us safe. Cultural differences were real and could get us into trouble. Specifically, if a girl kissed an Israeli it would be interpreted as "consent." It was spelled out to us that there was no such thing as "making out" as we knew it. Beware!

We were to be placed with individual families, work at assigned jobs related to the absorption of immigrants and travel together periodically as a group. "My" family was from Romania, and I spoke French with them. So much for improving my Hebrew exposure. We were all based in Tirat HaCarmel, an area almost without Arabs south of Haifa and near the sea. I worked at a daycare center with four-year-olds and was assigned a shade tree in a field of rocks as well as a group of children.

We had nothing by way of toys or equipment, and the children considered me to be a human jungle gym for climbing. They took turns tumbling into my lap for a quick cuddle, but the one thing we found to do was to sing. The Israeli children's songs had hand motions: slapping, clapping, waving the hands this way and that. The most popular one was "David, Melech Yisrael, Chai, Chai Vekayam" ("David, king of Israel, lives and endures forever"). They never seemed to tire of it. Again, not much was happening to improve my Hebrew! In the afternoons, I "taught" English to older children, but without books or supplies, just mime, repetition, and smiling. On weekends I went to the beach with my host's daughter, age nineteen, and her boyfriend. They towed me out beyond the breakers on a small inflatable raft so I could do some actual swimming while they hovered, and kissed, nearby. I had a crush on one of their friends, a handsome Mizrachi Jewish guy of their age who took me to meet his mother when he left the beach to change. I was horrified by the sheer number of children she had—eight to ten of them— and by his brusque order that he required a clean, pressed white shirt to dress up. On the spot, I resolved, but unfortunately forgot, twice, to never get involved with a "prince," an eldest son.

Our group toured Jerusalem and the Galilee in chartered buses but did not go to the south (Eilat) nor the far north (Safed). We did see the waterfall and natural pools of Ein Gedi, memorable for me partly because it was determined I should be carried on the rough trail.

We were soft North Americans, the children of anxious Reform parents. The constant shepherding became oppressive and I decided to try to leave the trip for a stopover in Europe instead of returning to New York. I got letters and phone calls from home to allow me to fly to Paris to join one of my brothers and stay at the apartment of prewar friends of my parents. Once there, I unloaded my heavy artificial leg. My school friend had been a camp counselor in France for the summer and she had a friend in Geneva. Our plan was to have a look at northern Italy before we had to return. I took the train from Paris to Geneva and we literally fell down laughing at our reunion in the station. Our hostess and other nearby Swiss were horrified at the spectacle.

* * *

The next summer, 1966, my friend and I planned ahead and looked for a kibbutz that would take us both as summer workers. There were always some Americans as well as Europeans anxious to experience true socialism. Indeed, upon arrival, I was issued some necessities: an electric tea kettle, a jar of instant coffee, and a large block of halvah. The candy was meant to be a month's supply, though I could not know that. I had never had access to that quantity of halvah before and made myself sick! I was also issued work clothes, which were washed and pressed, and boots in my size. I was surprised to see that party or special occasion dresses were also rotated as communal property. Then, G_d forbid, I was assigned to work in the laundry, ironing. The assumption was that I could do that sitting down, but after several days of it, listening, largely uncomprehendingly, to the gossip and assorted opinions of the other ladies, I begged to be sent to the fields.

There, I carried a sort of mailbag over my shoulders and walked on soft, plowed earth under the (dwarf) apple trees. We were to pick the apples and deposit them gently in the boxes at the end of each row. At least there were no ladders to climb, and I grew very slim around the waist from all the reaching upwards. We were not hurried or chivvied about; in fact, we were encouraged to sing as we worked, and we did. We started at 5:30 a.m. and stopped for an eggy breakfast cooked outside on a camp stove and served with thick rye bread at about 7:30. After breakfast, we worked until lunch at 1 p.m. held in the communal dining hall. There, we met kibbutzniks from other work details, including a pair of guys who invited us to watch them (artificially) inseminate the sheep in the evening.

The five-to-six-hour day was considered enough for visitors. Kibbutz members worked until about 3:30, cleaned up, and spent the rest of the day with families. The parents among them were so relaxed, free from shopping, cooking, cleaning, doing laundry, ironing, and paying bills and taxes. They were really there for their children and I was so envious. The children lived separately, in children's homes according to age, with trained teachers to look after them. The groups of children were like brothers and sisters from babyhood onward. In fact, the various kibbutz movements had to arrange visits between individual kibbutzim in order for the grown kids to find mates who did not seem like incestuous partners. Grown women seemed exceptionally free of gender stereotypes to me. I watched with interest from an overpass one day as a woman crossed the freeway on foot. She was wearing a dress or skirt, but she never hesitated as she approached the median wall between north and southbound lanes. She simply hiked up her skirt and threw her leg over it.

On days off from the kibbutz near Jerusalem, I would hitchhike in one direction or another until I felt that I had seen the rest of Israel forbidden to us the previous summer. The most daring, and possibly stupid, trip was to see Masada and go on south to Eilat. For this trip, I went with a Dutch girl, age twenty-four, from the kibbutz. She should have been smarter. Anyway, she was larger than me and afforded some protection. After touring Masada, it was growing late and an official stepped out of his office and asked about our plans. Upon hearing we planned to hitch to Eilat, he promptly invited us into his office, stepped outside of it himself and locked us in it.

"I cannot be responsible for what will happen to you," he shouted. "You will be safe here. I will be back in the morning. There is a bathroom."

"Where will we sleep?" we asked

"On the floor," he replied.

And so we did. A version of the same thing happened when we got to Eilat late the next day. A gentleman at the restaurant asked our plans, and when hearing we thought to sleep on the beach, he insisted on lending us his apartment without him in it and locked us in again, stating that he could not be responsible for what would happen to us on the beach.

One of the earlier hitchhiking trips had led me to meet a foremost Israeli movement therapist and his family. My driver had simply decided that they could help me somehow. I spent the rest of my Israel stay with them, first recovering from all the overexertion walking in the kibbutz fields with the heavy prosthesis (my remaining calf was now completely rigid and painful), and then training for strength and flexibility.

Before leaving America, in the airport, I had halved the contents of my knapsack so it would be lighter, leaving one skirt, one pair of shorts, etc. When I settled in with a Shabbat-observing family for my last month, my mother took it upon herself to mail me five or six dresses, which mysteriously went "lost" and never arrived. My personal wardrobe did not recover for years. I did fine with my one skirt and a pressed blouse. Not only did my new family light the candles and greet the Sabbath bride with song, but they also always had a freshly made cake. Arye would tell me that he knew his wife loved him because she always made his favorite cake (fruit with a streusel topping) for Shabbat.

Not long after I left Israel, their son Chanan, who was in the army, perished in one of the first terrorist explosions. This one was a school bus with an army guard. It was too horrible to take in, especially in the period before terrorist explosions were commonplace. The family was inconsolable, though also stoic, and I wrote to them for many years. I am still in touch with their eldest, a daughter.

My Israel experiences were like a warm bath followed by an icy rain. People in the streets looked like each other and also like me. I would see my brother's eyebrows here and my father's nose there. I was not quite differentiated from the group, just like I was never quite a separate individual from my family. Everyone wanted to care for me but also to fix me. There was connectedness, affection, camaraderie despite the occasional rudeness—a group of youth once commented "Zeh lo ooga" ("That is not cake") on passing by me in the street—but another one of them elbowed him to shut up, because people were kind.

The IDF Major

"Here it comes," he said he had thought to himself, the tears and the self-pity. "What was I thinking of to bring her here?"

We were at the ruins of a twelfth-century Crusader castle and the only way forward was over a high pile of rock. I measured the distance and height with my eyes, vaulted to the top using my crutches as parallel bars, and stood on top of the stone. This so captured the major's imagination that he and his driver took me next to tour their nearby army camp. I was paraded along with him on his usual tour of inspection, and one by one, we were effectively both saluted by each of the troop leaders. I have no idea now, though, how he explained the impromptu inclusion of me - in Hebrew, with my one long braid of hair, one leg and shorts, swinging along on my sticks.

I held myself well; maybe that was it. And I was alone out in the world, on the road actually, where the major had his driver stop to give me a ride. Later, the major did tell me a little about his WWII history, living with the partisans in the forest from the age of twelve before coming to Israel. This tough dude admired me.

Hepatitis

I must have eaten some unwashed fruit somewhere along the way in my exploration of the land. There was a specific platter of ripe figs offered by a young Bedouin girl somewhere in the Negev. There was not any place to wash them even if I had thought of it. I paid for the figs and ate them. The symptoms of hepatitis B (foodborne) are somewhat diffuse and it took a couple of weeks to develop, but there was pain in the region of my liver—that is, on my right side, and I lost a great deal of weight very quickly. My host family called the doctor, who diagnosed possible hepatitis B and administered gamma globulin shots with a large syringe to both my host and my friend the major, just before I left Israel at the end of that summer. Their last memories of me would have included, quite literally, a sharp pain to the behind.

When I disembarked at JFK, visibly thinner, ill, with pain on the right side, my mother and brother exchanged glances. I was taken around to one specialist after another, and without present-day imaging capabilities, it must have been difficult to rule out metastasis. One parent wanted to keep me home (my father) and the other to let me start my sophomore year on time. I did recover enough to go back to Portland. I had a screaming fit first, accusing my parents of showing more interest in me when they thought I was dying, that they cared more about me in my death than in my life. I went back to school and finally accepted the advances of Lew, the California camp caretaker I had met the previous Thanksgiving. I left school at semester break because I could not live without him. I felt I could not be separated from him. I was done with my parents.

Yad Vashem

At the time of my visit, Yad Vashem memorial in Jerusalem had an exhibit about the young resistance fighters who fought against the British Mandate in the years just before statehood (1945-47). (They were underground members of the Irgun, and this exhibit is now associated with a museum in Haifa.) There were huge photographic blowups of young faces lining a hallway and then an empty room, empty except for a platform and a noose. These young heroes and heroines had all been hanged for their crimes by the British. The British! Those safe, tea-drinking types who loved flowers and sweets! I could hardly believe it. The actual history sunk in, of resistance against British rule, that tried to limit the arrival of some 100,000 survivors from the Displaced Persons camps to Israel. The beautiful portraits of young people who never grew old moved me deeply. I took in this hallway of faces and resolved, on a bodily level, that I *would* live, for them.

At the Holocaust Museum in Paris, which I visited in 2005, there is a whole room of photos on the walls of children from happy times: school portraits, birthday parties, and so on. My great-aunt's name was even listed on the memorial wall outside. While this carnage was also deeply affecting and distressing, it was the fighters of nearly my own age who impressed me so much.

Ein Hod

I think I just happened on Ein Hod, but maybe someone told me about it. It was a small village, somewhat in ruins, south of Haifa, at the foot of Mt. Carmel. There were some archways that led to nowhere, lots of steps and stairs, and many studios and homes already occupied by artists. The village had been deserted for some time previously before the first artist moved in. My visit was before the community was officially organized and developed as an artists' colony and tourist destination. Already, though, there was clear evidence of the conquerors taking over the conquered and expelling them, with the beautiful views of the Mediterranean as the spoils.

I talked to a couple in an open courtyard who were child survivors, now married adults, both artists. The wife confided in me that sculpting was the only way her husband had to deal with his wartime past. They professed ignorance of what had happened to the original inhabitants. "They left," was the most I could get out of anyone. I recognized the charming stonework as Arab designed but it was not until recently that I learned that the original inhabitants had indeed fled in 1948, mostly to the West Bank, with one large family relocating themselves just four kilometers up the hill and starting up a new village that was eventually added to the Israeli power grid. We had Romanian cousins who themselves had fled to Israel for safety post WWII. They were our poor relations, and we sent them care packages all through the 1950s—clothes and food at first and then "luxuries" unobtainable in Israel, such as razor blades and ballpoint pens.

At the time of my visit to Ein Hod, I thought it was a great idea for a commune to be filled entirely with visual artists. When I discussed coming back someday with the staff person at the village "museum," he asked where I lived now. When I said NYC, he looked at me like I was slightly insane and said that I was already there, in the very center of the art world.

I had a similar experience in a New York City gallery while still in art school. I was unwrapping photos of my latest sculpture, a male torso shown chest to thigh, while the gallery person protested that I could not possibly be finding what I needed to be an artist out there in "Orygun." Confronted with the photo of the nude torso, he changed his opinion to, "I see you are finding all the stimulation you need in Oregon."

Adventures with Lew (Lew: Part 2)

The last day, I hiked eight miles—so eager were we to leave the isolation and hardship of the mountains. It was September and the nights were growing colder. Lew washed his socks and in the morning they were frozen solid. He somehow attached them to the outside of his knapsack and they flapped around all day, getting dry. It did not rain on us; the daytime weather was sunny and blue.

I hiked with Maggie and her little daughter, and the men went on ahead. They walked faster, and they wanted to talk. Maggie was very gentle with her little daughter, and I could keep up with them. By the time we would catch up to the guys, they would have set up camp and started the fire with an eye toward supper.

When we met the few other people on the Pacific Trail, tough sporty types, they were always upset that a three-year-old and someone on crutches were sharing their hiking challenge in the High Sierra. We covered fifty-eight miles in ten days from Yosemite to Bishop.

Further Adventures with Lew (Lew: Part 3)

I suppose part of what we shared were happy experiences with traveling. Lew's brother once said that he personally did not have to travel first class, but he certainly would not travel "no class." That seemed to be our specialty. That is actually what we did do, such as the time we drove to Vancouver, BC, with the express goal of staying at the Sikh temple overnight for free. They welcome travelers, Lew assured me, and we would get food too. We were offered a soupy dal of lentils and a spot on the floor in an area reserved for men. We were a married couple, so that was the arrangement. At 4 or 4:30 in the morning, the chanting of prayers began and it was impossible to sleep. The volume increased as more voices joined in, lasting all the way to breakfast. It was definitely an experience, although I found the melodies completely unfamiliar. Lew, however, knew to make a "donation" for a "dome" the group aspired to before we left. I felt that Lew knew so much more about the world than I did, a very old feeling stemming, I think, from the older know-it-all brothers I had!

(I found myself in another religious hostel in Boston years later when I booked into the Friends' House, not the Friendly B & B, by mistake, when traveling for a cousin's bar mitzvah. We were welcomed, housed, and when leaving I knew to make a donation—not for their "golden dome" this time like at the Sikhs', but to the work of the American Quakers.)

Early spring and school vacations would put Lew in mind of taking a trip to Mexico. Every couple of years, he liked to replace his "huaraches," leather sandals. He would custom fit these by wetting them and wearing them wet for several days in a warm climate until they molded to his feet and became extra comfortable. On Lew's initial trip to see me at college in Portland, he had visible holes in the toes of his overlarge sneakers from the Goodwill. I was so embarrassed, I insisted on buying him a pair of shoes. This was not a good omen for the relationship, but I did not get that then.

When we were still based in Monterey, California, we hitchhiked to Baja, Mexico, with no particular plan. Our last ride was with a vacationer whose pickup truck was entirely filled with booze. He was headed to a cabin of his own, and when we got there, he offered us the use of it while he stayed with a drinking buddy. I could not fathom that someone would plan a week of drunkenness, much less bring all the supplies. We got free housing out of it, and our driver did not have to drink alone after all. I wondered what his sorrow was to necessitate that much beer and wine.

We had stayed in campgrounds when traveling up the coast in our "Woodie" station wagon from Monterey. We were moving to Portland to start at a new college, and I had a raging toothache. I was pretty sure it was an impacted wisdom tooth as I knew how that felt. Ice was no longer helping, and when we got to San Francisco, we stopped at the Outside/In Clinic in Haight Ashbury so I could get some antibiotics. We were probably quite dirty without regular showers, and I am sure I had nothing on but a Mumu dress.

The much-overworked doctor started taking my history by asking what drugs I was on. When I insisted nothing but birth control pills, he was momentarily diverted but repeated his question. Pulling up my best Manhattan voice and manner, despite what were probably pee streaks on my leg, I informed him that I was the daughter of TWO doctors in Manhattan, that I had an impacted wisdom tooth, which I would be having pulled in Ft. Bragg on our way up the coast, and that I required antibiotics to quiet the tooth until then. He wrote the prescription, but he did shake his head a bit at the disconnect between my appearance and my request. We stayed in San Francisco with a friend of Lew's, again from the circle of youth group administrators (I actually knew her counterpart in New York). She was living in an abandoned church with her partner, a lawyer for the Grateful Dead. I was less impressed when this lawyer opened the front door to us without any pants.

It was good to get cleaned up, and I set about organizing my clothes. There was an iron too. Heading into the bathroom to retrieve my prosthesis, I came upon someone who resembled my husband, who had just left for a walk. I apologized for the intrusion to the stranger, and when he came out, he assured me that finding a spare leg in the bathroom made him feel right at home. His brother-in-law had a similar one left around the house in Oregon. I think he offered me weed, but I refused. I was on a mission to iron my blouses for the trip north. I was not going to be caught in a dirty dress again. The fellow climbed into a basket chair overhead, smoking quietly, and I ironed everything I owned nearly directly below. When Lew returned, he was agitated about whether I had been harmed in any way by the visitor, who turned out to be Ken Kesey, but no, all had been very peaceful, said Kesey, what with the ironing.

When I first went to the Oregon coast, and we had stopped for gas, I was entranced by a mom-and-pop gas station. Each of them had navy garage coveralls on, and the wife also filled tanks and cleaned windshields. Her face was not terribly clean, and her hair was unfussed-with, natural. Actually, she resembled an Israeli kibbutznik. She would have been scorned in Manhattan. I liked the idea that I would live in a place where gender roles were flexible and where women could be powerful.

Once, when I left the Portland art school after dark to go home, I walked to my car in the deserted park blocks. I was in a dirty sweatshirt and jeans and carrying nothing except a hairbrush. I never carried a purse in those days. Approaching me was a gang of interracial youth, young men, and I deployed my best New York skill—I kept walking straight ahead and did not flinch from them. As they passed me, the center guy, clearly the leader, said, "Evening, Sister," and I was through.

When we ordered our wedding rings from an artisan in New York, he had advised plain bands, saying, "You are simple people," implying we did not need anything fancy. We both admired some of his textured work, and that is what we asked for, although I think the texture was on the outer surfaces, with no holes going all the way through. The texture played havoc with both bread dough and clay gathering in all the little crevices. The ring was hard to keep clean. Nevertheless, I still have it and keep it on purpose as a reminder of our marriage. I was distressed that Lew sold his as soon as possible after our separation and divorce. It was pure gold, heavy, and so it was worth something, whatever he thought of the marriage.

The Power of Wool (My Swiss Army Knife Saves The Day on the Rio Napo)

I bought a dozen balls of different-color, highly dyed woolen yarns, as well as a bright purple woven shawl with fringes. The shawl has always been displayed wherever I have lived. I have used it for simple warmth, for comfort, and for prayer at home. I finally acquired a white wool *tallis*, a traditional Jewish prayer shawl, in honor of a bar mitzvah in the family some seventeen years ago. I wear that one in *shul*, a modern Orthodox one where I am only one of two women who don the traditionally male garment. It is just like the purple one, though a much finer weave: warmth, comfort, and a connection to a prayerful state. The blessing to envelop oneself in the shawl glorifies the One who spread out the heavens, and with the shawl, we make ourselves, literally, a "tent".

In the late sixties, opting to miss our formal university graduation ceremony, Lew and I flew to Miami and from there to Quito, Ecuador. He had been there before, traveling and teaching English, so we had a couple of people to look up: a Catholic priest in monk's clothing, sporting a fancy wristwatch, gold cigarette lighter, and accompanied by someone who appeared to be his girlfriend. The second visit was to a Hungarian feudal landowner who rode an enormous horse and lived high in the mountains with a soft-spoken Ecuadorian wife. They maintained an army of serfs and servants to manage the land and house. In addition to visiting them, the plan was to go see the jungle. This involved a short airplane ride, a bus to the end of the line, and a harrowing river crossing made on a simple platform suspended from a giant pulley system like a laundry line. A box was gallantly placed on the platform for me to sit on; I was launched, alone, across a rather large raging river. Of course, I held onto the box for dear life, conveniently forgetting it was in no way attached. I was a bit shaken on the other end, but I was OK. We then traveled by motorized canoe down a tributary along with the weekly delivery of mail and beer. While our guide was telling us that headhunters (real ones!)

had killed missionaries as recently as 5 years ago in this area, the motor died and we drifted to shore. He asked if either of us had a knife and I supplied mine. He fixed the motor with the knife and a bit of string. The jungle was amazing: huge leaves large enough to serve as a raincoat for a child. We ate a diet of giant avocadoes and many plantains and stayed overnight in a house on stilts (because of the snakes!). The ladder up was a single log with footholds carved out.

Just when we thought we were way past civilization we saw another motorized canoe going the other way filled with Anglo devotees and their white robed guru! When we finally arrived at the airstrip for the current Western missionaries we took the first plane out. The cabin door had no functioning lock and was held shut with a bent, rusty nail.

The second time, I got married out of curiosity. I knew about the short term (four years or less) but had never imagined how a forty-year liaison (like my parents) would feel like for me. How is it different being married from being prey? Being prey doesn't really change, as long as you still have your body, and even later as long as you still have your smile. At least, I think that is what it is.

I had the most interesting outfit when I was still in my twenties: stretch pants that had a diamond pattern, maybe two inches across each diamond. I felt like I slithered when I moved, even though it was a conservative gray with a navy pattern. There was a navy vest that went with it and a grey cardigan, yet it was the sexiest outfit I ever owned. I just found a spare button and a bit of yarn for it, attached to the original tag. On the original tag is written "AristoKat, made in Hong Kong, one hundred percent acrylic, size twelve." At the moment, I cannot remember if this was a pre- or post-pregnancy outfit; maybe both. But I remember being whistled at by my welding teacher and asked, "where I had gotten this body and why I had been hiding it." I guess he knew me only in maternity clothes previously, as that is when I took his welding class.

Post-divorce, I went to see him and his family to acquire a puppy from their lovely dog's litter. She was a very protective shepherd mix, who I took home without an idea how to care for a dog. She would not let me roughhouse with my son without interfering, and she would not let us swim without jumping in to "save" us. I loved that dog, but I mistreated her by leaving her alone all day while I worked or went to school. In compensation, she destroyed our beautiful oriental rug, which was mostly red and handed down from my grandmother. I thought the dog could run at the beach with my little son and give him a playmate. Certainly, the dog was big enough for either of us to wrap both arms around.

Stories From the Buttons

I have no idea where the set of eight brass coat buttons comes from (as well as one small one meant, no doubt, for a collar). They were in my mother's sewing box and in a plastic holder. Among her buttons and mine, there are many anonymous white ones meant for men's shirts, but the treasure is in the odd-cloth-covered one. There, a square olive-green suede one from a coat I had in 1971, which I wore on my escape to San Miguel de Allende. The customs people were puzzled by the artificial leg and the expensive coat, not to mention the brick of sculpting wax and small, sharp knives. That was the one, and only time I had to remove my prosthesis in airport security. I guess it looked like a brick of hashish I was bringing into Mexico.

Then there is a lilac crepe-y cloth-covered button from the dress I went back to Manhattan in after camping all summer on the previously mentioned half of a quarter section (eighty acres) of land in rural Washington state. Getting ready (for that trip) involved washing in a bucket of very cold spring water and, more challenging, giving the same treatment to a very grubby two-and-a-half-year-old. Later, I asked my parents how they knew I was OK, especially after all the trauma of the preceding year (marital separation, assault, and vandalism of car interior and infant car seat.) My mother replied: "Because you came home in a dress."

Now that I think of it, this was the same dress I wore when I stood up in court for my "no-fault" divorce and demanded my maiden name back. The judge denied it "for the sake of the child," he said, and I defiantly changed my driver's license and took my name back.

The dress was one of two I bought at Sears Roebuck—one lilac and one pink, or maybe light blue. I only really liked the lilac one. It had a collar and buttoned cuffs, buttons down the front like a coat, and a little tucking around the waist and bosom to give it shape. At the time, I had a pretty good shape, and I felt grown-up and attractive. Even the judge had said so: "You are reasonably attractive, and so you will probably marry again." This, of course, was enough to keep me from marrying for another sixteen years.

There were several early offers of marriage I barely remember now. There were fellows who were interested in me and others who I was interested in. These were however seldom the same folks!

So who did I want to get together with? There was a pacifist, as well as a sociopath with danger written all over his charm. They were neither the marrying kind, though a more amenable fellow with children from his previous marriage meant weekend playmates for my own child and the excuse for overnight playdates. And so, I lurched from one relationship to another and eventually stopped wearing clothes with buttons in favor of T-shirts. I think buttons went out of style anyway.

Birthday Cupcakes

I kept the cupcake baking tins when I re-married and moved to Seattle.

My son was going off to college, and I am not a muffin maker. What was I going to do with all those clanging baking tins?

Still, I stocked the little paper cups that go in them for liners, and I waited, sometimes more patiently than other times. In due course, I had another son, and sure enough, had the paper liners to start baking birthday cupcakes again.

Then came the day when he asked for cookies instead. "Nobody has cupcakes anymore," he said, all of age nine or so. Suddenly, this year, at seventeen, he asked for cupcakes again. At this age, he left the flavors to me. I chose a rich chocolate with a vanilla frosting decorated sparingly with spicy red cinnamon dots.

They were delicious, seriously delicious, better than the two competing bakeries at $3. Each. I got special paper napkins, too—yellow ones with red letters spelling "happy happy happy." And square, turquoise paper plates with yellow letters spelling "happy happy happy."

But he didn't want plates or even napkins. The cupcakes held their crumbs when held between thumb and finger. There was enough butter in there to cement the chocolate and the eggs and flour.

First, you melt the butter with the chocolate and then beat the eggs with milk. Alternating pouring ⅓ of each liquid mixture with ⅓ of the powdery flour, baking powder and salt, you unite the dough into one batch of extreme caloric value. The smell while baking these birthday cupcakes is heavenly and lasts a couple of days if you don't air out the kitchen. And I licked the bowl, raw egg and all.

1991 Adventures With Joe Before Zach (Part 1)

My laundry was clean and dry when my underwear fell off the balcony onto the patio below, where we had been welcomed the evening before. Fortunately, the meeting was taking place indoors somewhere, and there was no one to see me nip down to the patio and retrieve my things.

We were at the Weizmann Institute of Science in Rehovot, Israel. Joe made good on his promise of a trip to Israel, where he did not think he ever wanted to go, if I would just accompany him on an earlier trip to Germany. In Israel, I still had enough rudimentary Hebrew to go about by myself and friends to visit from my earlier trips.

After Joe's meeting ended, we still had several days to explore with a rental car. We went through the Galilee region on our route to Tzfat. Passing through an Arab Israeli village, I was struck by how healthy and well-fed the people looked, especially the children. The contrast with the Arabs of East Jerusalem was cruel. There, I had observed a great variety of Third World health problems accompanied by implacable hatred during a prolonged strike every noon.

In Tzfat, we saw the famed Sephardic synagogue from centuries ago, but with bright, lurid blue paint inside. The ancient streets were somehow familiar in scale, a human scale intended for pedestrians. At an artists' co-op gallery, I saw small sculpture bronzes of human figures by Moshe Ziffer. His figures were the most beautiful I had ever seen anywhere, as they depicted a quality of lovingkindness, somehow made visible. This was a new standard for me to try to achieve.

From Israel, we visited the island of Crete, and the Palace of Knossos, with its wall paintings, some of which we saw later in Athens. The earth colors of sepia, ochre, black, and dull red were very strong and explained why we had seen such "classic" colors in Denmark at the Thorvaldsen Museum. In Crete, we saw the largest thrown ceramic containers I had ever imagined. I inquired and was told that the raw clay itself was heavily invested with sand, and later made sure to always purchase clay with a good percentage of "grog" so as to extend its strength.

We also visited a number of sites of tombs on Crete, even more impressive than what we had seen in Jerusalem. There were stairs with steep slopes going down, down into the earth, narrowing and becoming steeper all the while. I am sensitive to noting a change in the rise of stair steps, and these proportions were clearly intended to induce dread. "What purpose if I go down to the tomb? Can the dust praise You?"

On Crete, early one morning, we were awakened to the sound of a ram's horn, a shofar. Was it the end of days? Villagers were filing towards the main square, where the mayor was making some sort of announcement. So we saw a shofar in actual use to "gather the people."

On our car rides around the island, we saw occasional donkeys still in use as work animals. Real donkeys. Not like the ones who posed for tourists. We also got ourselves turned around and inadvertently took off across a field off the main road. There was a sort of a track that branched through the olive trees. We stopped to ask a startled farmer for help. If not for Joe's understanding of the terms "anode" and "cathode" from the Greek, we would still be there, midway between the upper and lower village.

We had picked one Greek island in particular to visit: Santorini. It had magnificent views and the blue skies and white buildings still seen in the postcards. Other than those, I mostly remember how many tourists there were and that the donkeys were not "real." That is, they were just for the tourists who could ride the poor things up the steep hillsides.

By the time we got to Greece, we were somewhat done with antiquities. Still, it was Athens, and we went off to the extraordinary National Museum. We saw more sculptures and more pottery with figures dancing around the curves. After lunch, we were going to go see the Acropolis, only to discover that it closes daily at 2 p.m., and we had missed it. Flying out of Athens the next morning, we agreed to gloss over the fact that we went to Athens to see the Acropolis.

Further Adventures With Joe Before Zach (Part 2)

I noticed the sign for a music hall almost immediately on my arrival in Leeds, a smallish city but the home of the Henry Moore Study Center and Library. There was also a university with a sculpture department, and I had written to them in advance. I was assigned to a woman sculptor who took me around to see her work and that of a few peers. These were all installation-type works, interesting in their own way, but not particularly to me. I spent several days in the Moore Library while my husband went to Germany yet again.

In the library, I was grazing among the vast number of books and reproductions. One of my finds was a small volume in French titled *Erotiques de Cimitiere* (*Erotics of the Cemetery*), whose photos depicted graceful, languid, stone carvings of women in repose, possibly in eternal sleep, but tied to earthly beauty, fresh and young. I Xeroxed the whole book and understood my own connection to sculpting female figures depicted in attitudes of repose and pleasure as my own battle against the forces of premature death.

I never did get to the music hall, even though Leeds had a long-standing tradition of Vaudeville theater, which I really enjoyed back in Oregon. The Leeds Hall was up a tall flight of exterior stairs with no easy escape from fire nor unwanted attentions. I am still sorry I missed the performance, whatever it was.

After Joe returned, we rented a car and went around looking for Moore sculptures in the area, and then on to the famous Lake District, beautiful though not as memorable as expected. There were some oddities like John Ruskin's house and pond, where in olden times the staff would chuck the dinner dishes after breakage or after use! There was also a visit to the pencil factory in Kendall, which included traversing a quaint bridge whose image is reproduced on every box of my actual drawing pencils. We also saw a lovely concrete cherub in someone's garden and inquired after it. It was not for sale. The lady had brought it home from a trip to Italy years ago and seemed terrified that we might be planning to "nick" it.

Around that time, we locked ourselves out of our rental car with its electronic locks and had to climb in the back seats to reach the front seats. We could still do climbing like that.

Physical bravery/foolishness was demonstrated again when I planned a visit to an outdoor sculpture garden. I must have seen a brochure for it somewhere, either in Leeds or more likely at a London museum, where we saw an exhibit of large Chagall sets for the theater. There was an address in Surrey on the brochure, and we consulted train schedules, took up our day packs, and headed out. When we arrived at the village, not only was there no taxi stand, there was no building at all, and no people. We had to hitchhike to even get away from the train station. Deposited at a gas station, we called the gallery where the director was flabbergasted that we had simply come out to Surrey from London on the train. She came to fetch us in her car and gave us a tour. It was even more wonderful than the brochure, or than I had imagined.

The gardens, themselves, were lovely and, with surprise focal points of sculpture popping into view, it was positively magical. I gravitated toward the figurative work, of course, but the abstracts were also beautifully sited among foliage, which suited them. My own concept of outdoor sculpture morphed into one of the joys of creating a garden for sculpture. My subsequent projects in Seattle included creating a large outdoor installation for the yearly art festival Bumbershoot. I invited landscape designers as well as sculptors and paired them. Each sculptor had their own immediate landscape designed to feature the sculpture as the focal point. A passing art critic told me that I had created something "that looked like the Garden of Eden."

Adventures With Joe and Zach (Part 1)
(Oxford, Wales, Cherbourg)

I began to study Yiddish to honor my father when it became apparent that he was dying. I applied for a summer intensive program in Oxford, England. Joe and Zach came too, and we rented out our house in Seattle to a traveling scholar for ten weeks. Likewise, we rented from an academic in Oxford. There were children next door, and I sent Zach outside on the sidewalk with a radio-controlled car to attract the children so he could meet them.

The first night, out for a walk, we located the closest small grocery store, which had a sign in the window for summer camp/daycare at the College of Further Education. The dates squared with my Yiddish program, and the daycare was within walking distance from our apartment. Zach had a wonderful time there, and he was made much of by the staff. Meanwhile, our neighbors were horrified that we would send him to the equivalent of Community College as he might pick up "the wrong kind of accent."

Joe had a colleague who offered him office space while we were to be in Oxford, which led to the interesting and widespread rumor that Joe had been offered a "Chair at Oxford." It took some time to squash that one as it was literally a chair he was offered—a place to sit.

I thoroughly enjoyed the Yiddish program and especially the teaching style of Peysakh Fiszman (z"l), a gifted storyteller and mime as well as a Yiddishist. I adapted the use of gesture in conversational practice, and he told me, "You murder the language, but you make yourself understood." He also complimented me as an artist when he told me "You are an artist. You leave everything out and I still know exactly what you mean!"

We took several we took side trips: to Legoland, the prospect of which made Zach as happy as I have ever seen him, and to Laugharne, where I admired the view Dylan Thomas had from the boathouse where he worked. It seems that smooth, tranquil water is ideal for soothing the artistic temperament. In recent years, I myself have enjoyed monthlong residencies in the San Juan Islands near Seattle. A water view does rest and recharge the brain. I can attest to that.

At the end of the intensive program, we took a ferry to Cherbourg and spent time on the small roads, not motorways, of that corner of France. There was astonishingly good wood-fired pizza available everywhere, and the owner of our hotel would give Zach a bonbon if he would say "bonjour" to her in French. However, she would not give us more jam beyond the single spoonful on our breakfast plate. "It is hard to make," she said, "and expensive." In Paris, on our way home, I encountered a similar thrift when I found myself in a pitch-black basement toilet room when the timer on the lights suddenly went off.

It was in Oxford, during the summer of 1998, that I bought myself a glorious Indonesian print dress in autumn colors to wear for the wedding of my older son and his girl friend. They had been living together for six months and said they planned to marry. I had advised him to wait a full year but did not expect them to take my advice. They didn't and attempted a courthouse wedding in mid-year. Without an appointment to be married, they did not succeed. Instead, they married on the Oregon beach in the spring, with two witnesses and no one's parents. A month later, we gave them a dinner and a pie with little figures on top since they didn't want a party nor a cake.

Some months later, we hosted the two of them and her visiting mother and grandmother for a couple of days. We celebrated with a large buttercream & whipped cream bakery cake, the remainder of which the ladies gleefully slid into their portable cooler (in hot summer weather) to take back home with them. La Comédie humaine is something my father used to say about those inexplicable acts for which we must have tolerance. It has taken me a long time to understand his perspective of enjoying manifestations of the human comedy instead of being so upset by them.

The first two to three years in a separate town from the newlyweds were more or less normal, but communications steadily deteriorated from there until there weren't any. At this point, my beloved older son has not been home for more than twenty years, a source of great sadness to me.

Adventures with Joe and Zach (Part 2)

These were sweet years for me, as it became clear that my younger son, Zach, would also do beautifully in a small private school, as had my older son, Ben. In his interview for preschool, Zach had already drawn a large, even, letter "C" with the tip of a glue bottle before the teacher had even finished with directions for the test! She said to us: "He will do very well here," and she was right.

My days were freed up during school hours for my various projects. My early cultural projects for the preservation of Yiddish involved a great deal of time on the telephone. For Halloween that year, Zach wanted to dress as a telephone. We created the homemade costume out of cardboard with a painted "dial." When he was dressed and admired, Zach said quite definitively, "Now you'll have to pay attention to me because I am a telephone!"

Many Halloweens, Jewish holidays, and birthday parties followed. The most interesting birthdays featured Zach's early interest in cooking and cooking shows. I had gone into his school in pre-K to do the soup demonstration accompanying the story *Stone Soup*. The kids used carrot peelers, some for the first time, and some claiming they had only seen grandmothers use such a tool. We constructed a passable borscht out of ordinary vegetables the children were actually willing to eat. The teacher remarked that in all the years she had done this project, it was the first time the children were willing to eat their soup.

Once we started the cooking-based birthday parties, we could not seem to stop. I think the first *Iron Chef*-themed party involved two teams and a huge quantity of mashed potatoes as the base ingredient. From these potatoes, each team had to fashion a (no-cook) appetizer, main dish, and vegetable. They used condiments and spices to their hearts' content as they shaped the potatoes into dishes that were "plated" for a formal presentation. There was an actual meal, too, probably hot dogs.

For dessert, we brought out a plain sheet cake, and they went to work with strawberry and chocolate syrups, etc., and then they got to eat it.

Another year, we made pizza from scratch, and everyone who wanted to had a chance to knead the dough. Zach regularly made such pizzas with his father, so he was only sharing a bonding experience with his friends.

Then there was the year of the three sauces: one vast bowl of pasta (made by yours truly) and a choice of white, red, and green (pesto) pasta sauces to serve themselves. Baguettes accompanied the meal, and one young sophisticate, all boys by that age, called for olive oil and balsamic vinegar for dipping. So, they were already aping restaurant manners as well as cooking.

All About My Clothes

I normally line up my dress-up clothes from all the ceremonial milestones of my younger son's life.

1) The Yiddish programs' ivory silk, V-neck, blouse with fabric-covered buttons and fine black wool slacks.

2) His Bar Mitzvah: velveteen patchwork jacket with mandarin collar and crazy quilt embroidery, with a pistachio silk blouse with a yoke in the back, and charcoal grey cuffed slacks. (It was just too cold in January for the swishy autumn print long skirt meant to go with the pistachio blouse.) I was no longer accustomed to wearing a skirt, in any case. Women in trousers in synagogue was another step toward emancipation. I already owned a white stripe on white wool prayer shawl, or tallit, purchased originally for a cousin's son's Bar Mitzvah some seven years before.

3) Eighth-grade graduation: black straight-leg pants with a blue, black, and silver brocade jacket and a turquoise tank top underneath.

4) New York cousin's wedding: black jersey leggings with a long multicolored velour jacket with a purple V-neck underneath.

5) High school graduation: black bell-bottom cotton trousers with a short lilac jacket, a scarf with iris print, and an olive tank top underneath.

Zach was not home for summers once he started college but worked in local internships there, culminating in full-time employment when he graduated. We made visits to Chicago, and he still visited seasonally, and we took trips to the beaches in the Northwest.

6) College graduation: a grey jersey wrap top with important Turkish jewelry, faux silver and garnets, with black slacks.

I don't remember what I wore for each of my own events (sculpture openings) during that same period. When there was a chance to plan or prepare the refreshments for an opening, that always took precedence over my outfit. It was always a scramble not to look like "someone's mom," as I was once referred to, nor like an arty fashionista all in black. What I do remember was that I always wore a necklace to remind me of the power in my own chest.

This is How it All Ends

Wallet-sized pictures of the grandchildren—on a shelf near packages of Fleet enemas. Filthy glassware, enough for scads of company in this tiny house—a round table with two leaves—a locked liquor cabinet with glass bottles labeled "scotch," "bourbon," "vodka," "gin."

Dishes, enough for parties of ten—Wedgwood with flowers from England, too old to say microwave- or even dishwasher-safe. One crazed bowl hinting that dishwashers are out. A whole other set in Japanese Mikasa with gold rim, and let us not forget the Franciscan Apple set. Three sets of company dishes. I have four. Rotten steps at the back porch. An ancient canoe. Older yet, a chaise and armchairs meant to go under a curious gazebo, which had a full-sized brick fireplace. No fireplace indoors. There was almost certainly a Christmas room somewhere, but I did not make it upstairs or down.

I like to go to neighborhood estate sales. This is how I practice my religion: a clear sense of my own mortality. A chance to live now and not hoard my dishes or let my glassware grow so dim.

I want to be in control of my own things and not have strangers pawing over my collections. What about that guitar with scratch marks? I practice my religion this way because it is a holy thing to see how people lived their whole life in expectation of fellowship and friendship, and perhaps only after being widowed, stopped noticing the filth and disrepair. German? Scandinavian? Who collected small plaster casts of the Market Woman and the Tinker Man as well as a candle surrounded by two doves?

And so, I have my windows washed yearly, and I am going to rotate "in" all the glassware in the house. Perhaps a sister came to live with her in the end. There was a lot of glassware in that house for one person or even a couple.

Yiddish

Yiddish has allowed me to start over in the language department, and I feel the glee of a three-year-old about using language instead of tantrum. The sound of the Russian of my grandparents still makes me feel torn between their differences of opinion with my parents. French is OK for rational discourse, and it has some flavor, but neither Russian nor French compares with the nuance in the classic Leo Rosten sentence: "Two tickets I had to buy for his concert," which, depending on which word in the sentence is emphasized, could represent several kinds of a "dig." Recently, I have rediscovered modern Israeli Hebrew, which has enough Yiddish "snark," about 30 percent of the language, to satisfy.

Yiddish and Songs of Guilt and Blame

One January, we attended part of the annual Seattle Folklore Society retreat. There were concurrent sessions on song topics such as "Sea Chanteys," "Songs of the Soldier," etc. We were attracted to one titled "Songs of Guilt and Blame" and found no fewer than six or seven landsmen gathered around in a circle. The idea immediately formed to create a separate Yiddish song group, which met for the first time that day during an afternoon break. We have continued to hold an open-house Yiddish song circle monthly at our home and have thereby collected various Ashkenazi landsleit from across the denominational and neighborhood boundaries.

If I were a Christian

If I were a Christian, I would have a better chance of thinking through forgiveness and, yes, gratitude. I could think about the good years I had with my first son before he and his wife cut off all contact and enforced it with a "harassment warning" from the police. But I am not a Christian. My God is still one of anger and of vengeance who permits hatred and bitterness to take root and thereby sentences the "sinner" to become unlovable. If I were a Christian, I could perhaps count my blessings instead of criticizing the ones I have got.

Actually, I have never stopped working these last years on reimagining (both myself) and the God of my childhood as merciful and "seated on the throne of compassion and mercy", rather than seated 24/365 on some kind of "throne of judgment". I would be happy to see my older son if he or they turned up one day.

Act 3

Perspective

The Rabbis Swiveled Like Penguins, in Perfect Synchronicity

When we emerged from the hotel elevator, I spotted a rabbi I knew from my borough youth group activities. He was standing with another rabbi. Now, how did I know that? Bearing? Clothing? Hair? Yarmulkes (probably not)? The one I recognized began to rotate using only his feet, heels, and toes, swiveling exactly like a penguin. In perfect synchronicity, without interrupting their dialogue, the other rabbi swiveled with him until their backs were facing me.

Not to be ignored, I hastened over to call out to say hello and introduce my husband. When I did so, there was a certain thaw as they inquired who had performed the ceremony. They recognized his name, of course, and offered congratulations. I was nineteen, and the ceremony had been in the afternoon just the day before. I wore a dress handmade by my best friend's mother. The dress was a simple knee-length V-neck, with a standup Nehru-style color and angel sleeves (like a bat, my friend said). I had a veil, too, down to my chest. It flattened my carefully puffed hair, and I was most unhappy about that for the reception.

My going-away dress was powder-blue linen, and I have a memory of pearls, though I think that was not a true detail. More likely, I wore my grandmother's amulet locket, an oval of gold with tiny photos of my grandparents and of the ten commandments engraved inside. The inscription on the outside was in Russian "...from Mama and Papa". The amulet had been blessed by a wonder rabbi and given to my mother (for protection) when she was three years old. My mother had apparently intended to give it to me when I turned eighteen, but the cancer at fifteen had frightened her, the big scientist, and she gave it to me then. I hate to admit that I have now lost this locket, or perhaps it was stolen by a Russian-speaking cleaning person, who quit shortly after its disappearance. I still hope it will turn up in some crevice when we move one day.

For our one-night honeymoon in this downtown hotel, I think it was

The Pierre, I wore a white knee-length nightgown with light blue ribbons threaded through the eyelet. It was a direct reference to Disney's original Cinderella and her ball dress beribboned by enchanted mice. I had not wanted a trousseau. When my mother took me to a department store, I selected one slip and one nightgown and refused anything else. She was so disappointed. Of course, these were the days when we limited our possessions to two boxes and could fit everything we owned into a car.

What I remember about our wedding night was my husband removing envelopes from every pocket of his brand-new suit, extracting the cash and the checks, making a pile on the bed, and then throwing them all in the air, crying out, "We're rich! We're rich!" There was about $3,000 in the pile, and as soon as we got back West, we banked it and started looking for land.

Considering how stupid we really were at the time, it is remarkable that we invested all our wedding money in a half share of a quarter section of previously homesteaded land in Washington state. The property had a gravel access road, named after the original Swedish pioneers, Alfred and Myrtle Lund. There were a total of eighty acres of meadow, Douglas fir and cedar trees, a tumble-down cabin constructed with only one nail per board's end, so it leaned and listed, a grown apple orchard, and the foundation to what was meant to be a larger dwelling. Two streams ran across the property, one on each end of the rectangle. We began with it undivided, as tenants in common with another couple, and eventually other shareholders.

After divorcing, we had had it surveyed and subdivided, and deeded over to each partner. I came out with 20.5 acres, some on each side of the access road, which was the most likely buildable spot. The property just sits there now, but at the time of our marriage and our son's first couple of years, we would camp there in a lean-to, and utilize a homemade hole out in the woods.

But I started with the dresses, and the rabbis, and the fact that I was nineteen years old and had been married off to my first lover, in a hopeless attempt to keep me from "being hurt." Whenever I called my parents from a phone booth at a gas station, which was every time as we did not have a phone, they would panic that I had been abandoned. Married, they somehow felt more content, especially when they paid for airline tickets back West and essentially confiscated our car, turned lovingly into a camper by yours truly. To make a camper out of a sedan, remove the back seats. Insert a piece of plywood extending back into the trunk, add a mattress. If desired, and I did, install curtain rods, handmade curtains, and colorful sheets and blankets. Now you have a tiny home, in a car.

The thing about throwing the wedding money into the air was repeated years later, actually, when my first son, Ben, and his wife would count their festival earnings, literally grubby dollar bills, in his old back bedroom. The door would be closed, but I could hear them cackling. Worshiping money; now that is sin.

The Land

With the $3,000 or thereabouts in cash that we received when we got married, my first husband, Lew, and I bought land within forty-five minutes of Portland. This was north into the state of Washington, near Woodland, and along the Lewis River Valley. The property was on a hillside above this valley, with a fabulous view of Mount St. Helens from the access road.

We were pretty sure that somewhere on the actual eighty acres (half of a "quarter section" of the 160 acres originally homesteaded by the previous owners in the early part of the twentieth century), there would be the view through the trees. The central meadow was flanked with trees, mostly young alder, but venerable cedars had been spared, and the whole had been unoccupied for more than fifty years.

The scents and sights of forest, meadow, and wildflowers were fragrant and pristine. A rough track led from the top of the access road, across the meadow, and toward the original cabin, orchard, and chicken coop. The remains of a newer and larger foundation for a more substantial house, never built, were clearly visible.

We never knew why Alfred and Myrtle Lund pulled up stakes and moved to Moses Lake, Washington, but we gave them a down payment and then monthly payments until the eighty acres was ours. We took in business partners until we were eight individuals in all and held the land as "tenants in common." Our stated goal was to save some pristine land from "developers."

Eventually, we subdivided into parcels, though, and I still hold 20.5 acres. It would make a dandy ecology camp, or a blueberry farm, or a Christmas tree lot. There are two streams, each one striping across a short end of the nearly perfect rectangle. One of the first summers, one of the group fashioned a collection box near a spring feeding the stream closest to the old cabin. From there, we simply ran a garden hose to a kitchen sink framed into a sort of counter, and we could wash the dishes from our communal suppers. We made a fire pit to cook over, and I fashioned enough rough benches out of sections of cut logs for us to all sit together for these meals.

I remember a thin but tasty soup made of dried seaweed (from a co-op in town) and filled with tender young beet tops and tiny baby carrots from our garden. We kept a cooler in the stream, too, filled with butter and eggs, cheese and milk. We were all vegetarians at the time (1972), so there was no problem with meat storage. We had a bountiful vegetable garden ourselves, and there were farm stands nearby for corn and berries. We went swimming almost every day near a former mill, with a swimming hole of deep water. My dog, most anxious herself, would leap in to "save me" every time.

When it was time to go see my parents in New York near the end of the summer, I washed in a bucket of cold water and did the same to my two-year-old (who had recently finger-painted himself). I put on a long-sleeved lilac mini dress from Sears Roebuck, dressed my son in clean shorts and T-shirt, and gamely flew to Manhattan. There, we discovered that he did not remember indoor plumbing, and my mother quipped that we would simply have to walk him in the park. This was all fixed with the loan of a kiddie seat with a friendly-looking plastic duck on it.

The next summer, we built the geodesic dome as a central indoor meeting place, near the "running water" and communal eating spot. Other people set the pier blocks and built a deck to receive the structure, but I designed, cut, and color-coded all the framing to be assembled in the dome-raising. I worked at the woodshop at Adams High School in northeast Portland, with some assistance from the shop teacher, and ripped all the 2x4s at a certain angle on a table saw, cut them to length(s) with yet another angle on a radial arm saw, drilled three holes in each with a jig set up on the drill press, and kept them all color-coded with crayon marks.

When it was time to assemble this 24-foot-diameter structure, each intersection took three wing nuts and required no tools to nestle each completed triangle one against the other until the whole formed a dome. All the accumulated errors should have collected at this final top triangle, and we were prepared to hand carve it to fit. There was a moment of absolute silence as the final triangle fit neatly into the void where it was to go, neither too big nor too small, but just right. It was literally a peak experience!

I never got to live in the dome, though it was finished with plywood triangles and "feathered" with roofing shingles. At my suggestion, a cross contour strip of triangles was left covered with heavy plastic to admit light. A door was framed in, and an indoor "kitchen" created.

One of the couples lived there as caretakers for a season, but eventually, with the subdivision of the whole property, it did not sit on my portion at all. I believe it has fallen into disrepair and possibly vanished. I made a smaller one in my yard in Seattle, with a smaller but similar thrill. Tinker toy skills to build one's own house have always been a dream of mine. I started to build my first cabin when I was nine years old, collecting a substantial number of rocks and laying out the dimensions and the first couple of layers.

There is also a photo of me, even younger at five or six, sitting in a large box, though that one may have been a pretend Sukkah. Well, there you are, if you teach children that they can build their own hut or home, they just may do so.

To See Him an Israelite

Lew and I rented a farmhouse with several acres and a barn near Sherwood, Oregon. Since the house was already built, we needed more to do, so we bought a mama goat and her young kid from a nearby farmer and got food for them at the nearby feed store. We had no problem learning to play with the kid; it was just like playing with a dog. We would stroll up there and hand feed them both treats like raw carrots. As the kid grew bigger and very strong, the charging, butting, and handfeeding came to an end. Worse, we had not succeeded in learning to milk the mama goat before she weaned him. In short, we were fools with two goats, a barn, and a feed bill. Someone in the community, perhaps at church, must have spread the word that the renters at the farm, the buyers of the goats, were "of the Hebrew persuasion."

Ominously, every night a large car would slow dramatically as it passed by our home on a short stretch of gravel road. We never understood why that stretch remained unpaved, and it didn't bother our little Nash Rambler. I learned to drive on that old shift car because it had a throttle (I could give it a little gas while releasing the clutch while keeping my foot on the effing brake).

Anyway, one weekend day, a local stopped by to look us over. He had heard we were of the Hebrew persuasion and wanted to meet us, as he had never seen one before. He was particularly taken with Lew's bright, curly red hair, fair and freckled face, and I suppose the prominent nose. Lew stayed very calm and still, though hands on hips, and let himself be looked over. They shook hands, and Lew's large thick workman's hands surely passed muster there, if not with my more intellectual relatives. Our visitor was delighted to "have seen him, an Israelite, a real Israelite," looking just as he had imagined they looked.

We took the opportunity to ask about the large car trolling past our home at dusk every night.

"Oh, that!" he replied. "That must be Hiram and his new Chrysler. He doesn't want the finish damaged by the gravel."

We then asked about managing the lack of goat's milk. But it was too late to learn how to milk. The one and only lesson in milking when we bought the goats from the farmer that sold them had made it look so easy. "Pull down and out on the teat. Aim towards the bucket." No one said anything about how to keep mama still or how to ask her to put up with such a procedure.

The Yoga Society and our 'City' Commune

I started the whole business with the The Yoga Society. I had seen a sign for "Learn to Meditate—Free!" so I went to look. Gradually, the other housemates in our "city" commune, including my husband, started attending regular sessions. I think we were already doing hatha yoga poses together (Iyengar's, from Lew's trip to India a few years before we met). We did this practice together daily in the living room in front of large windows. There was one amusing visit from the local pot dealer who took a long time to grasp that we were not potential customers.

It was a commune, right? Check. Six to eight unrelated people lived there? Check. (Actually. three to four couples, depending on the season). And we didn't smoke pot? Of course not. "We are devotees!" said one of our group standing there midwinter, bare-chested, in shorts. His club foot may have hindered his walking, but it did not matter for these exercises. One time, however, I thought I saw him hanging dead in the basement where we dried our clothes on clotheslines. I got as far as calling the police. The officer slowly walked through the clothes until he saw the same swaying shadow that I had seen outlined against the wall. There were a pair of pant leg bottoms with what appeared to be a twisted foot extended below. It proved to simply be a pair of folded-over pants, and everyone was so relieved.

When Lew left me, it was to take a vow of celibacy and join the (coed, celibate) ashram full time. My mother, visiting, marveled at the similarity to the therapeutic community she was starting for young heroin addicts in NYC, especially the posted rotation of household chores.

I was offended because "if you wanted to live a more religious life we could be more Jewish!" In any case, he picked a fight with me, opened a closet door and revealed two boxes, packed to go, and with which he moved into the ashram. On visits with our two-year-old, Ben, the inhabitants would marvel over the child that he must be the reincarnation of one of the masters. Little Ben could identify the Hindu gods in their loud color photo representations of paintings of them.

"Krishna!" he would point, and the devotees would go "ahhh, o-ohh."

Of course, Lew had previously paraded him around and taught him the names associated with the various paintings. I decided these people were fools.

I did enjoy my new name, bestowed by the visiting yogi from India. I was to be called "Jayadevi" (Victorious Goddess), and though the yogi meditated on fixing our marriage, we parted permanently. I had still done the cooking during the yogi's few days in Portland. I was acknowledged as the best vegetarian cook of our group. It was not that hard, just to put the long cooking vegetables in first. I had a strong enough foundation to know that one does not worship people, though he was a pleasant enough leader.

Within weeks Lew had moved out of the ashram, and into his brother's apartment, along with a teenage girlfriend. I was enraged.

Where is love?

I came to myself when I realized I was scraping the nails of my hands on a raw, jagged brick, half buried in packed and frozen soil. My intent was to scoop up the brick and hurl it through the window of the ground-floor apartment where my husband was staying with his teenage girlfriend. After I became conscious of the fact that I would more likely hurt my hands than succeed in prizing up the brick I stayed squatting there a bit and cried. Then I took myself off to a supermarket and bought a six-pack of beer and a small block of Tillamook cheddar cheese and threw in some salty/sweet peanuts. With these primitive medicaments I soothed my broken heart for a time.

I could not figure out where the love was now located. I was not in his heart, which I accused of having turned to stone, incapable of any feeling. Mine was now blocked, diverted, silenced. I was sure something so powerful, my whole heart, must still exist somewhere, obeying some law of physics that matter could not be destroyed. So I invented a theory for myself, that love still existed. It was around me, and over me, and through me, and like an unblocked stream would simply run along a new pathway.

Lost at Sea

I don't think they even had a radio—or, if so, not a very powerful or complex one, not enough to get help. I do not know if they were even able to call for help. Their wedding had been in the backyard of their rented home, featuring the handmade trimaran boat the groom had built himself. The honeymoon was to be its maiden voyage, a trip across the Pacific to Hawaii. A memorable feature of the wedding were the long faces of the parents of the beautiful twentysomething bride. The parents must have been romantics, as she was named after a tragic Shakespearean character. She was also the beloved of my own boyfriend, who had inadvertently introduced her to his best friend, losing them both to the instant attraction his two friends felt for each other.

I was present at the wedding only as a prop to support my boyfriend as his two friends married. Afterward, the newly married people gave away the rest of their possessions before their honeymoon trip.

"Please store it for us for when we return." I got a heavy oak rocking chair, an oak dining chair, and an old sweater of the groom's. I still have the chairs. I regifted the sweater to my boyfriend some months later (to hold his friend close) after the boat disappeared without a trace. For months, and then years, he imagined that they had perhaps found shelter on some deserted island and that they had not, of a certainty, drowned mid-Pacific.

The groom knew materials. He knew an oak chair was a thing of permanency. But perhaps he could not imagine the ocean or his homemade boat foundering. And why did she join him in essentially a suicide trip? Perhaps it was to prove her foolish, foolish love, her confidence in a man who liked to make things with tools but did not have enough humility to see himself as only human in the face of God's creation: the Pacific Ocean.

Insurance

Years after my mother's death, I found I was still saving a padded mailing envelope addressed to me in her handwriting. I no longer remember what she had sent me in it, but it was toward the end of her life and toward the end of her separation from me. It turns out that when people you love actually die, they become closer, and more with you and in you, than when they were alive. I had moved clear across the country at age seventeen to escape the daily scrutiny of my parents, and now that she was gone, she was truly with me always.

The packaging was stamped "insured," with the letters neatly arranged inside an oval of red ink. I gained a great deal of security from those letters, that message—that my mother valued me and I would be protected from harm on some heavenly level. I guess it felt kind of like a signature of kashrut between the heavenly hosts and me. The merit of the ancestors would once again pave my own way, or at least remove small stones from my pathway.

At one time, I had been considered uninsurable, and my home's fire insurance was canceled. This followed a surprise inspection where the lady found my living room cluttered. I lived a great deal on the floor, like Japanese people, and scooted around my amassed papers, books, etc. There was no trash. I was clean around the kitchen and food. I was just disorganized at that time, a kind of intellectual ferment and inability to put things away. The lack of furniture was a problem for orderliness. When I finally acquired a desk and a filing cabinet, my mess slowly resolved itself. Anyway, this lady from the insurance company canceled my coverage, and I had to beg my original insurance agent for reinstatement. He assured me that I was certainly not crazy and that obviously, the lady had no conception of how creative people lived.

Early Birthday Parties (Ben)

This is perhaps the most important love story in my life, and it is so hard to begin. I had not thought of many of these memories in years, yet it is remembering, it is the good things, that make it worthwhile to revisit memories.

We were a team. I just wrote that in "The Beach", but also I had someone to cherish, and love, and admire for those years of his childhood. Part of how I tried to show my regard was his birthday parties. I was a single parent from when he was 1 ½, and also alone in town with him until he was six and his father returned. Those visits were then every other weekend and every Tuesday evening.

I was concerned that without a man in the house, there would not be a role model. I went to the Goodwill and bought a couple of suit jackets, ties and hats, and the most beautiful pair of highly polished brown brogues. My son was going to have shoes, even for dress up from a costume box. I also added some girls' hats and handbags and added a few of my own feminine Halloween costumes from my art school days. These included a half-slip with hearts on it, a hot pink nylon jumpsuit with spaghetti straps, and an A-line dress with iridescent diagonal silver stripes and batwing sleeves.

These early birthday parties were highly orchestrated: never more children in number than the age of the birthday boy. We would start with my old birthday games: memorizing ten objects off a tray, identifying substances just by fragrance. We also always did a drawing game where everyone drew first shoulders and head at the top of their pages and folded the top down. The next person added chest and arms, down to the waist, folded and passed it on. When these were each unfolded there was agreeable hilarity and usually a clear winner by acclamation (of course the winning drawing was itself made by several people so no hard feelings). Sometimes there was a treasure hunt with clues, but always there was a parade, with Ben in the lead, and several kazoos or things to bang on like drums. The most favorite activity though was always the raid on the costume box, well past the pre-school years...cowboy hats and crocheted floppy hats, handbags and fake cigars, and boys (all boys after about age 7) chasing each other around the room.

There was also the year I built "Nordyland" on a table out in the garage/studio. Nordyland was an imaginary place invented by Ben, inhabited by Nordys. Nordys were stuffed shmoo-type dolls given out by Nordstrom's with the purchase of a new pair of children's shoes. In Nordyland people were always nice and there was an abundance of candy as well as a mountain of marshmallows. I fashioned paper replicas of the images in Ben's drawing of Nordyland, sprinkled candy on top, and made it the prize of that year's treasure hunt. Ben was charmed and delighted. My mother told me on the phone that the other mothers were going to hate me.

At early ages for each he learned to ride a tricycle, to roller skate, to ride a bicycle. He soon learned the buses and could travel independently to school. He played soccer and participated in chess. There was one ultraorthodox family in his secular school whose son was on the chess team. We hosted him a couple of times so he could get to nearby Saturday chess tournaments. Unfortunately, the Dad there decided to try to turn Ben into an acceptable playmate by inviting him for Shabbat and picking him up from our home early in the morning for an orthodox prayer minyan. I had to threaten that he could speak to my attorney if he tried to transport my son against my wishes even one more time. Orthodoxy and this particular family made Ben uncomfortable, and the nerve of that Hasid stating that since Ben's own father did not take an interest in Ben's religious education that he would serve as his father!

Around that point in high school Ben's volunteer job with a cable TV show branched out into a show for him and the friend he volunteered with at the station. The boys were so personable and voluble. They played music like DJs and Ben juggled various objects. "The Rubber Chicken Show" ran on cable for almost two years and was the cause of a dust up with Ben's English teacher about an unwritten essay for class. Look, I told the teacher, he has written and produced a half hour TV show in

the same time frame he was given for the essay. "He is not following directions" was the sort of reply I got. On the whole Ben did very well in school, especially math, and when he got the highest SAT scores in his class the other somewhat snooty parents were more polite to me, the hippie artist who lived on the wrong side of town.

At age three, when we were going downtown to see the Rose Festival parade, Ben wanted to wear a clip-on bowtie, because, you know, we were going downtown. After some time, after college and a master's in math, Ben was running a juggling supply store and had become an ace unicyclist. I heard from friends in Portland that he was integral to leading the same annual parade!

Roller Skating in the House

Maybe I never should have let him roller skate in the house while carrying grape juice, but I had perfect confidence in him then that he would not spill. Years later, I had the same confidence that he would not drop an egg even when juggling multiple raw eggs over the kitchen carpet. He did this to annoy me, to test me, I suppose. Most of all, to be admired.

Years later still, in Portland, walking near the bus station, a panhandler accosted me. He was wearing a winter overcoat, a little oversized. It made him look young, vulnerable. There was a woman with him. She was even wearing a Goodwill hat. And they both beseeched me that they needed money "to go home," only just to "go home." I had stopped walking to listen to them, and my own little family party split up in different directions. My husband took our young son by the hand and walked swiftly away. My older son's wife took off in a different direction. My older son stayed with me, standing at a slight angle between the panhandler and me, guarding me from him.

The rhetoric, his story, was embroidered, and its intensity increased. I suddenly realized that what was in front of me was a gifted actor in a churchgoing costume from the Goodwill. I began to bargain. I actually was carrying very little money, so my tale was true. My purse was in full view and easy for him to reach.

"I will give you three dollars, and that is all," I said.

Avoiding the credit cards and ID, I pried three singles out of my wallet inside my hanging purse and handed it to him under the watchful eyes of my older son. There was to be no grabbing, no shoving, no violence. I now knew I was being hustled for drug money, but my safety was worth the three dollars. We all knew that.

He flashed a grin of triumph, exchanged a similar look with the woman, and thanked me.

My son and I walked away whole and found the others a couple of blocks away. It felt, and was, prophetic that the others had abandoned me to get out of the fix I had put myself in. But my older son stayed to protect me.

The Last Present

Who knows what the last gift will be from a grown child? What word of praise ("You gave me joy!") or illustrated book of children's stories (*Melisande*), or a ceramic eggshell, or seeds of lavender? In any case, grown children continue to grow in unknown directions, to places a mother cannot follow and experiences she will never share. What remains? A memory of the shape of the head, the curve of the back of the neck, of the hips in a squat? Who but a mother can distinguish a squat between one child and another?

When I hired a klezmer band for Ben's Bar Mitzvah party, I first had to get permission to have instruments played in the synagogue social hall while it was still Shabbat. The conservative rabbi did finally agree, in the spirit of joy, and there was wonderful dancing. I had a friend from college who played in the band, and we even got a special rate. Klezmer at parties was still fairly new in 1983, and there were only two such bands in the whole Northwest. When I first heard this kind of music, I recognized it as my own. I felt it in my body, and I knew I was a man, that I had two legs, and that I knew the sort of dance steps to go with this music. It was my strongest experience of some sort of genetic memory to date, and it felt so good to have a body again, complete and strong, and with a culturally identifiable "dance" that I knew how to perform.

Remembrances of Manuel

Manuel Izquierdo is no longer with us, but some of his characteristics as an artist, a teacher, and a father are still with his grown students. In 1973, I was a traumatized single parent raising a three-year-old. My subsequent four years at art school reordered my entire life and gave it a focused and stable sense of purpose. When I graduated in sculpture, with Manuel as my thesis advisor, his final "blessing" was to admire me in my new dress. This was done with a single wordless gesture of his that I should twirl once around in it. Only a man with daughters could have understood the importance of this final stamp of parental and adult approval.

My own parents would not be attending the art school graduation, although they had largely paid my way. Basically, they thought I was "just fooling around" with art. It was not until they visited me a year later and saw "how I kept my tools" that they got the idea I was a serious student of sculpture. After graduation, it was Manuel who then sold me a wheeled sculpting stand, who offered the reminder that it was more important to finish a sculpture than to start another, and who called to congratulate me on my first gallery show. I never wanted to be the kind of woman who would do artwork only when her kids were grown.

Recently, I was asked about my most influential teacher, and I named Lloyd Reynolds of Reed College. It was indeed Reynolds who gave me back a sense of "movement" in art at the same time he taught us calligraphic line. Later, I studied with Fred Littman at Portland State. Littman transmitted all the rituals of European sculpture with a finesse that included working plaster while dressed in a pristine business suit. But it was Manuel who created actual order for his students and urged workmanlike habits such as scraping hardening plaster off the floor right away and not letting it accumulate ever. I still use my art-school-era tools, and my garage floor is free of debris despite years of work in plaster and concrete.

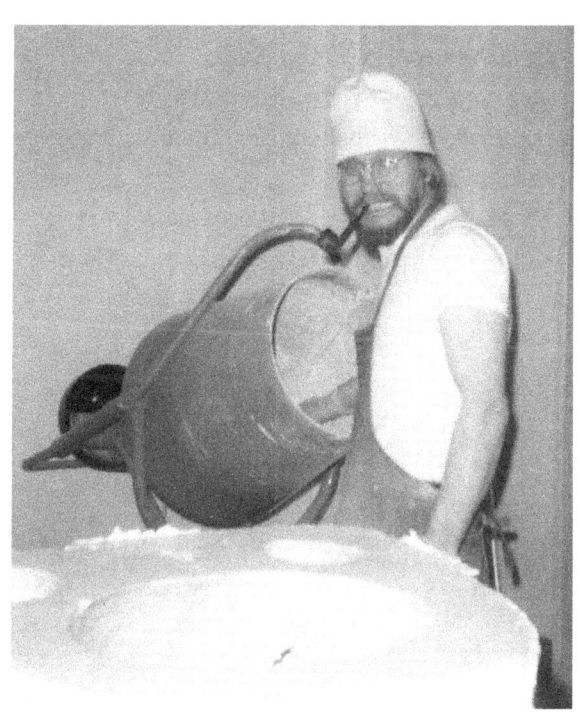

The following tips, applicable to all sorts of project management, are excerpted from my notebooks of the time:

Pedagogy and "systems" of Manuel Izquierdo

- Consider the base and challenges of installation before beginning.
- Take breaks on a fixed schedule.
- Think always about safety and do not work when fatigued.
- Take the measure with your eyes, use calipers just to check.
- Craftsmanship counts. Carry a tape measure and a pocketknife everywhere.
- Take care of your tools, and they will last for your whole life.
- Put it in your will to donate your tools to the school (now Pacific NW College of Art).
- When you don't know what to do next, sweep.
- Leave the studio as clean as you would want it when you next come back.

Darning Patches

It took me a while, several meetings actually, to notice the beautifully patched and darned holes in his jeans. Small stitches outlined each hole, and the void was filled in with a perfect basket weave of long horizontal and vertical stitches. Once I had noticed his pants, I no longer felt justified in dating someone who clearly belonged to another.

I never learned what had made so many small holes in the thighs of his blue jeans. The patching was apparently done during long quiet sessions of fishing. He would fish, and she repaired his clothes. Maybe fish hooks and other bits of tackle would start these holes just like a chance run-in as acquaintances began our meetings. Once hooked, it is hard not to try to reel in the catch.

Still, around this time, they actually got married at her insistence and with an ultimatum. This was also the first time I heard of an ultimatum having any efficacy in a personal relationship. He told me he could not face dividing their collection of music (vinyl records in those times), so he acceded to making their relationship legal. He did not want to give me up as some sort of "payback", but I gave him up.

Could I find as much thrill in the context of my own (one day in the future) committed relationship? I did not know. What I did know was that her sewing declared him as hers more certainly than any ring, promise, or agreement. I can still see the patches in my mind's eye. How she must have taken his pants and character as they were—full of holes—and stitched and wove new thread over every opening until they were healed.

Outside the Camp

I was at an intercity conference of some kind, at synagogue years ago, listening to speakers, and gathering in small groups, when the meeting broke up toward suppertime. A man I did not know planted himself in front of me and said something like, "How about it?" or perhaps something only slightly less crude, such as whether I would like to leave with him. Or maybe he even said "Dinner?"

Amazed, I said nothing at all at first. Then he expanded his limited vocabulary with, "I asked around. They said ..."

Said what? I wondered. That I was "single?" Or perhaps, as I later heard myself once described as 'divorced'."

I finally responded with, "So you're married, right?"

"Yeah, so?"

"And you have kids?"

A nod.

"No," I said clearly and walked away alone in full view of the departing congregants. I had just been identified by the patriarchy as "outside the camp", an unmarried woman free to anyone and therefore not constituting adultery on the part of a married man.

For shame! The shame was on him and on whoever set him on me.

Years later, remarried at age forty, after sixteen years being single (that was in the '70s and '80s), I still could not shake the lingering sense of stain. The "stain" went back to an assault at age twenty-three, when I was old enough to think I knew the score. Knowing the score as a nice young woman means nothing in the face of a socio/psychopath.

Finally pregnant at forty-four and having essentially an unattended birth in Seattle's foremost hospital, I was surprised by the birth of a boy. I somehow expected and wanted a girl. I was sent home after one night in the hospital after a first night spent awake, in labor. I was wiped out, and now I had to plan a bris, or circumcision. At that time, the recommended mohel worked at Microsoft and fit his ritual duties in between staff meetings. Therefore, the time could not be firm. Anyway, I wanted my women friends around me.

The mohel then filled out a certificate welcoming a son named "Zach" ("Pure" in Hebrew).

The father's name was left blank.

My husband is not ritually Jewish because his one Jewish parent is his father. Therefore, he is not counted by the Orthodox sect, and my child does not have a named, Jewish father. I think I filled my husband's name in on the certificate myself...Still...

My tenuous grip on reality postpartum started to unravel badly from that point: a consecrated marriage with a huppah (canopy), three miscarriages, a healthy (male even) baby at almost forty-five, and I was still judged "outside the camp" by some.

Preparations for The Tomb

The rabbi threw out a challenge. If anyone could explain to him why the greatest tests to our faith (the martyrs and, more recently, the Holocaust) should be considered on the most important holy day of the year (Yom Kippur), they would earn the right to give the sermon.

Well, I didn't want to give a sermon, but I was challenged to explain the seeming paradox, which is no paradox at all.

Of course, we are asked to proclaim our faith in the face of challenges to it, for what else could be more meaningful? It is the story of Job all over again. It is perhaps easy to thank God when our families are healthy, and our storehouses are full. But what of misfortune, illness, calamity, evil?

Our faith in God, in life itself, is challenged whenever we face loss of any kind or even the threat of loss. The central message of Yom Kippur is to make choices that reflect our intention to choose life. And yet, the liturgy is full of stories of those for whom death was chosen. What is the lesson?

We cannot ordinarily choose the cause or the moment of our deaths, but we must be ready for death at any time *by the way we choose to live*—not only by making active choices for life but also by being spiritually and emotionally prepared for death.

We can prepare for death by:
- having faced death
- understanding death
- living with the certain knowledge of our mortality
- being ready for death
- welcoming death

The knowledge of our certain death is the single greatest teacher for facing life. It teaches us to live in the moment, to cherish our loved ones, to guard our health, to work for peace and justice in the world, to guard the earth for future generations.

But how do we "face death?" Some of us have had no choice but to face life-threatening illnesses or the death of loved ones. Others reach adulthood with limited experience of losses. Yom Kippur offers the opportunity for all of us to "face death" as we review, in our community, the deaths of other individuals and communities.

But how do we understand death? Death is a mystery, but many people over countless generations have had similar near-death experiences of approaching a great light. Whatever you choose to believe about the soul after death, it is possible to learn about the soul during life.

The soul is the part of a person that is separate from the body and which remains intact and sensate even when the body is hurt.

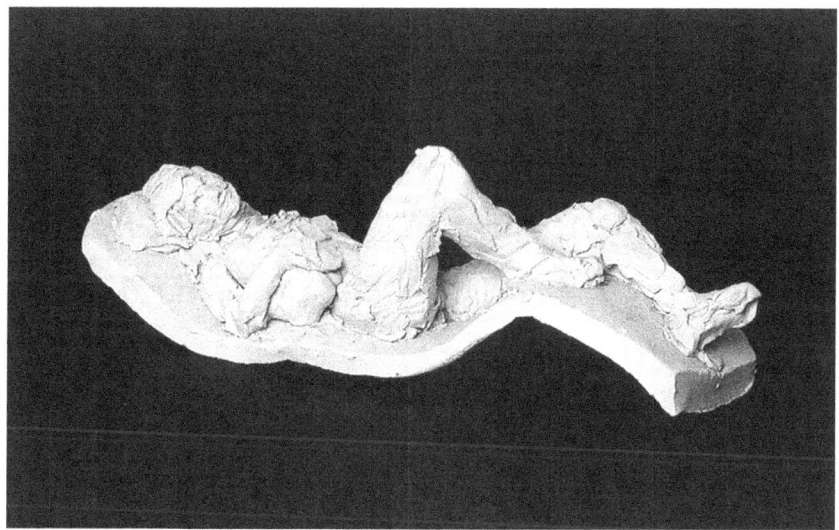

Sculpting Professionally

The drawback to our contemporary idiom, the Internet, is that it has no smell and nothing tactile at all. When I sat at a computer full-time as a tech illustrator/graphic designer for a Portland-area software company, I kept an open box of sixty-four Crayola crayons at my desk. I could not bear the absence of smell at my workstation.

I have been back to clay, green soap, plaster, etc., for many years now, attempting to unify "form" while still leaving some of the crudeness of tool marks on the surfaces. At art school, I was told that my job was to "keep on describing form," even though this comment was offered in a drawing class. It turns out that the actual medium does not really matter. Some years, I can draw more accurately than I can sculpt, and some years it's the reverse. It seems to be a process of intellectual growth to find new ways to describe form and not to produce a consistent "product."

For a gallery show or a specific body of work, a consistent plan and related execution might be necessary. In my opinion, though, once you've got a "product," you risk a manufacturing approach to making it instead of creating each artwork anew.

For me, the title I assign to a sculpture, usually before I even start it, gives me a thought, almost a mantra and sometimes a tune, to hang on to. The process of finishing a clay sculpture, and any further stages, such as mold-making and casting, can be tedious. I get lonely in the studio, the length of time per sculpture working on it without "face time," for example. This phenomenon also helps me understand why figurative work is universal: dolls, deities, even figures without an identifiable narrative (story, memory, meaning) are ubiquitous. Existential loneliness is eased by the presence of these substitute people or faces without the clamor of actual people. Any face instead of no faces will do. Having a title attached to a work of sculpture opens it up to a variety of interpretations for the viewer.

The elegant works of Elie Nadelman (Polish/Jewish/American, died 1946) have always fascinated me. There is a tremendous exuberance in his carved, fluid figures. They represent images of grace and freedom to me. They are also a tremendous bridge between the abstraction inherent in Cubism and a more modern form of expression still rooted in the sculpture traditions of the past. They bridge the stiffness of any carved work with the fluency of clay. I sometimes see some of my work as a continuation of his vision of grace.

Salmon on Skis

My father was visiting our home, and I wanted to show him around Seattle. Parking downtown was hard to get, so we took the bus to the museum. It started to snow while we were inside, and in a very short time, the wind picked up, and the snow began blowing and drifting enough to cause the return bus to change its route. After we got safely home, my father expressed disappointment that we would not be able to go out to a nice restaurant for dinner.

Joe volunteered to go to the store on his cross-country skis and brought back a fine, fresh salmon, head and all. My father was extremely skeptical of us being able to eat it, and he and I both wondered who was going to remove the head! The butcher had thankfully cleaned the entrails out of the fish, and Joe took the salmon out of sight and removed the head. I stuffed the cavity with slices of fresh lemon, and we simply baked it.

After the first bite, my father had to admit it was, in fact, delicious, and we all made a good meal of that salmon and its accompaniments. My father spoke about it in awe for several years too. Ever since, when there is snow, Joe threatens to strap on his skis and go the half-mile for dinner supplies.

My memorable meals in the Northwest have always been salmon, and in Europe, fresh trout. I don't, as a rule, like fish, so this is surprising.

The Story of You (a Book for Baby Zach)

On a fine spring day in May, when roses bloom in time to decorate for Shavuos, your Mom and Dad rode their bicycles together alongside the lake.

During the summer, you started to grow inside Mommy—from two cells into a tiny, complete embryo.

By Rosh Hashanah, the New Year in the autumn, you turned summersaults at the sound of the shofar: *Tek-i-ah!*

Mom had an easy fast for Yom Kippur that year. She had to eat to feed you!

For Sukkot, you sat in the sukkah with us and listened to all the singing.

At Hanukkah time in the winter, our friends played you music on the cimbalom, flute, fiddle, and drum. You already liked music!

When you came along to Yiddish class, and we all sang a Yiddish song, you got excited and punched so hard at the sac of water containing you that it soon broke open.

Headfirst, you slid out into the world, and we promised to take care

of you. We welcomed you into the Covenant, and we blessed you that you would have a long life of learning, of marriage, and of good deeds.

You came with us to shul for Purim. We gave money for tzedakah. Now that you were on the outside of Mommy, you could hear things better. The groggers were too loud for you, and so you sensibly went to sleep in the middle of all the tumult.

For Pesach, in the spring, you looked for chametz everywhere and later, when you were older, liked to fold the starched cloth napkins into shapes. When you opened the door for Elijah, his wine disappeared!

Every week for Shabbos, you watch us light the candles, bless the wine, wash our hands, and bless and eat the bread.

For Havdalah, you hold the spices while we light the braided candle and bless the light, the fragrant spices, and the fruit of the vine.

We sang Yiddish lullabies as zemirot every Erev Shabbos for two years before you came to us. We are still singing them.

Boxes

Yesterday, looking for boxes outside the liquor store in order to pack all our books to move them aside to have the new carpeting installed, a woman stopped and asked to help Zach and me. She was heavy, a little older, but a trooper about bending and removing the insides of the boxes and nesting them to pack in the back of the van.

"We live in Renton," she said, and my son called and said, "Why don't you come up for dinner? And could you stop and bring Chinese food with you?"

"How old is this son?" I inquired.

"Thirty," she said. "They never grow up," and she ruffled Zach's hair, which he did not particularly like.

But I got it, that there are other mothers, other sons. She probably thought I was newly single, and Zach and I were moving on.

Sex Education Through French Folk Song

We used to sing in the car—in French. Led by my mother, who drove half the distance going to and coming back from our weekend country house, we kids would sing out loud with her. Now that I think about it, the singing might have started as a ploy to keep us from squabbling with each other in the back seat. But my mother clearly loved to sing, to belt out smutty drinking songs with gusto and a little glee, the meanings somewhat disguised from us since they were in French.

I aim to sing like that these days: open chest and full volume. The French syllables roll out of the mouth like grains spilling out of a jar, smoothly and relentlessly. My mother lived in France from age three to twenty-five and attended French schools, which were overwhelmingly Catholic in population. She completed medical school, too, still unusual for a woman in the late 1930s. Actually, I remember her fury at my self-assigned duties during my young first marriage in 1967.

"I did not go to medical school in the 1930s, so you could iron your husband's shirts!" she once shouted at me.

Of course, by leaving me in the care of housekeepers as a young girl, I learned exactly what my womanly duties were: to clean, to take care of clothes, and most importantly, to cook— especially delicious apple pies.

But I digress from the bawdy songs in French. It is only recently that I understood them as a form of sex education as well as of French language and culture. They were even offered at age-appropriate levels. First, we learned *Sur Le Ponte, D'Avignon*, a harmless rhythmic ditty about bowing and curtsying. Next, there was *Aupres De Ma Blonde, Qu'il fait Bon Dormir* or *Next To My Blonde, How Good It Is To Sleep*. Sleeping with someone was the contemporary euphemism for making love, so I remember internalizing that blonde was good, like at least three of my aunts, and that sleeping next to someone was also good.

At age six, taken to the big Fifth Avenue FAO Schwarz Toy Store, I wanted to see their famous stuffed animals. Next to a display of horned reindeer was a beautiful, life-size, smooth-faced male doll, dressed in furry Eskimo parka, gloves, trousers, and fur-trimmed boots.

"I want that one!" I said.

"But, darling, what would you do with such a large stuffed doll?"

"I want to sleep with him," I said clearly, loud enough for the sales lady to go into paroxysms of suppressed giggles while exchanging eye glances with my embarrassed mother, who also hid a smile. I don't remember how she got me out of there, but I do remember wanting that man. The next time we went to the store, he had disappeared from the display.

Moving on to a sailors' song, *The 31 of August*, we loved shouting out "Merde pour le roi d'Angeleterre" (shit on the King of England) but also sang along on the chorus of "drink to the health of lovers everywhere." So I learned that lovers were good.

More difficult instructions followed with *Jeanneton*, whose unfortunate meeting with four young men—the intrepid one, the less wise one, etc.—resulted in a gently phrased gang event among the reeds. The sung moral for this one was that men are all pigs. Pretty tough for my age nine or so. A gentler story song in *Sur La Route* depicted a dreamy girl who believes a singing guy that he will stick around after undoing her blouse. Instead, she remains a flower, dying gently by the side of the road.

If all this was not enough to put me off relationships, as well as sex, these songs usually had a drinking component as well.

A La Claire Fontaine was sung to us with the genders alternating, so instead of focusing on the rose (virginity) she wishes was still on the rosebush, "he" mourns "her" rejection based on the roses "he" did not give "her." After all, too much talk of virginity might be unseemly.

Chevalier De La Table Ronde alludes quite openly to the possibility, and even the normalcy, of infidelity, hinting also that the outcome of infidelity might be violence or death.

To round up, the eighth commonly song sung, *Au Claire De La Lune*, is about adult fun, even licentiousness, as being an ordinary part of human nature and of the facts of life, as long as the door is closed.

Why I Like Dots on My Clothes

The first thing I bought with dots was a knee-length British raincoat. I hoped it would make me more visible at crosswalks. People smiled when they saw me out walking, and I felt sort of like something let loose from the circus. Fat lady, elephant, clown. But I like feeling like a character, and next, I got a dotted tank top and then underwear, nonmatching. Last night, I found I was looking online at both a dotted blazer and a dotted blouse, also nonmatching. Then there is this photo of Grandma Weinberg in a dark dress with huge irregular white dots on it. So maybe it is just the cycle of fashion, eighty years past. Or even something fun loving and genetic.

Two Matching Mushroom Hats

As a child, I used to like a Swedish children's book (*Tomtebobarnen* by Elsa Beskow) about a family who wore identical mushroom-shaped and colored hats. It seemed so friendly to me to go about in matching hats—red with white dots. Just before my recent trip to the hospital OR, my apprehensions were stilled when I was given a patterned paper shower cap to put on my head. Observing that the surgeon wore an identical cap, I crowed with delight that we "matched." Suddenly, I found the whole getup amazing: the anesthesiologist and surgeon in light teal scrubs and me in my back-fastening, knee-length gown, sitting upright, cross-legged, I believe, on my gurney. I waved gaily to my husband. "We are all dressed up just like at the spa!" I exclaimed. There was something I found delightful in this otherwise-terrifying scenario. I think this is both inborn and a gift of imagination unique to artists, or it could have been the influence of the pre-med. (There was no cancer found in the lining of the uterus after all.)

Hilda

"Do you know that we lived together in the Bronx? Well, on the same avenue, the one with the drug store on the corner and a bar across the street? Of course, it was during different years ..."

I was sitting listening at a table in the coffee area of the long-term care facility where my friend of more than twenty years lives now. Across from me sat one of her admirers, quite a bit younger but with a beautiful head of snowy white hair.

I did not set out to do some sort of survey on purpose. Still, through visiting this one friend somewhat monthly, as she aged from her early seventies through today, at ninety-six and kicking, I have observed the countless choices of aging in Seattle in no fewer than two independent apartments and three assisted living arrangements. Sociable people, of course, do better in these places, finding new friends, enemies, staff to "*utz*" (make digs) about their own lives. Astonishingly, this latest place includes yoga as well as mindful meditation classes, taught, so far as I can tell, by children. A small sample of many of the issues:

When to sell the house and move to the city where the youngest adult child lives? When to get a larger apartment with two bathrooms, and when to get a smaller one?

When to stop driving altogether and learn the buses while it is still possible to get on them, albeit slowly? When to go into assisted living? What to do when one spouse becomes gaga? Where to be living when you yourself go gaga? And, most importantly, what to do in the next five to ten years before all the above starts happening? The most important things seem to be keeping one's health together and making friends.

Acceptance

In another ten years, perhaps my sons will have a child or children. They would each be wonderful fathers! I hope to be alive to see and feel it. I will be too old to be much help, though I have a wonderful collection of children's books to share. And five suitcases of clothes. Surely I can give some of those away—to shelters, to young friends. It would be nice to be honored at last and to feel the peace that comes with old age. Acceptance perhaps, not resignation exactly, but a letting go of activism would be restful, no longer trying to change anything.

Maybe it is already happening. In my dream last night, I was asked to organize a sales campaign instead of just participate. I would not want to organize anything anymore except my own affairs: what to buy for dinner, which summer shirts to give away. Speaking of which, we have a lot more blankets than we need, but I am somehow still saving the good ones and using the threadbare ones. I hated it that my mother never wore the "good" pajamas that I sent her in her last illness. She insisted she was saving them for when she would be in the hospital. But she died first, and the pajamas went to the housekeeper who became my father's live-in woman friend in fairly short order. I was so shocked to see the pajamas hanging in the bathroom and her long black hairs in the sink. I felt it as a betrayal, but my father professed no guilt. He said he had taken care of my mother until the end and that he needed someone. He found it incredibly tedious to cook for himself!

The Purpose of Looking at Memory is to Revisit the Happy Memories.

"Most people get only one ticket for a ride on life", my friend Marge told me, and I definitely have had at least two! I have been married twice and have a grown son from each marriage. I have lived twenty-five years each in Portland and in Seattle. My art exhibits and art products have intersected with my life, both as a girl born in New York City post-WWII and as a woman who has spent my whole adult life in the Pacific Northwest.

Finishing Things

Finishing things is what counts. Anyone can start a project!

This narrative has become the recital of my days.

Why should I be lost to history?

"One must be of one's own time" (from Honoré Daumier's memoir) in order to make some kind of record of the era. In my life span, I went through the imminent terrible threat of nuclear war, the time of the Vietnam War, the tumult of the civil rights movement, the women's movement, and most recently, the twin traumas of D. Trump and the pandemic.

The Meaning of Life is Life Itself, the First Zoom Seder in the Pandemic: or, Real Life Vanquishes Ghosts

When Joe read The Four Questions in Russian, the two birds showed up. Red-breasted robins, large fat ones, flew screeching, as I remember it (a sound typically given by those defending nests or fledglings) past our kitchen window and on past the dining room. One continued on past, veering to the south but flying somewhat erratically, not straight, calling out all the while.

The other, larger bird, perched on our fence not twelve feet from the glass patio door and fixated on the scene inside with its beady, left eye. What could it see? Candlelight, me, Joe, the laptop open on the table with the images of our Seder friends on the screen, Joe holding a book open with the Cyrillic characters? I had just finished The Four Questions chanted in Yiddish, and before I recite them, Joe's colleague Fred had sung them beautifully in Hebrew.

But the bird stopped to listen, so it appeared, to the Russian version, and perhaps to see us using Grandma Weinberg's damask tablecloth and her Pesadi-ke dishes, bought well after WWII, rimmed in gold, glittering perhaps in the candlelight. Then the bird flew off, confidently, apparently satisfied, in the same direction as the first had fled.

And I thought of my grandparents of the gold-rimmed dishes, who after the pogroms fled the shtetl for the big Russian cities, and after the Russian Revolution fled Odessa for France, and just before the Nazi invasion of Paris fled to New York, and I myself who fled the teeming cities of the East and continued Westward, to the suburban open spaces of Seattle, where a bird is just a bird unless it still longs for its native tongues.

The Thing About Computers

The thing about computers is that there are no people inside them, yet the pull to go check one's email or surf the web is as strong as the desire to speak to a neighbor who calls, "Hello, how are you doing?" from across the street. If there is nothing much new or interesting in email, the compulsion to find someone (or something) of interest on the computer is very great. My favorite example is how a recipe for gefilte (stuffed) fish flew around the Internet among members of my congregation until victory was accorded to our eldest living congregant, who is, in fact, a mean cook of the old Eastern European school. Factoid: she usually serves this stuff commercially bottled in jars, but she can make it from scratch. It is very, very labor-intensive to do it that way, though.

What all this means to me is that my children will have the opportunity to preserve and honor not only their culture's old-time recipes but will be able to find others who share their culture, language, cuisine, and humor with "the click of a mouse." The resurgence of interest in Yiddish language classes worldwide owes a lot to the existence of the Internet!

Superstition and Imagination

For as long as I can remember, the whole family had to "sit for a safe return" before leaving the house for any trip further than a local park. This means putting down the bags and suitcases and sitting quietly until it is clear that everyone is calm, and no one has forgotten anything. We did this instead of going out the door in a rush. It is remarkable how it works and has saved many trips back to the house for a forgotten passport or whatever. I always assumed this was a Jewish superstition, but when I saw it done in a Soviet-era film, I realized it was a Russian custom.

Before women had access to modern ideas, superstition was something in which they had to place most or all of their trust. Once I started looking at "Jewish superstitions," especially around childbirth, I was appalled that they included few weapons against anxiety. Anxiety and fear do not always end with successful childbirth. They can be multiplied with concerns about the ongoing health of the newborn, extending right up until its marriage. In order to protect the child from the "evil eye," for example, a red thread can be tied around the edge of the bassinet, just as a red thread can be tied to a young woman's underclothes. I never understood what protection the red thread on the girdle could provide in terms of deflecting unwanted attention, but I suppose it served as a reminder to the young woman of her mother's watchful eye.

You don't see ghosts; you hear them as you would in dreams, in snippets of conversations.

I could feel the ancestors crowding around my iPad tablet as I leaned it on the dining room table. The memorial candle for the last day of the autumn High Holidays was still going, although the wick was starting to sputter. Maybe that is how I imagined the exclamations and speech surrounding my hands. "Let me see! No! Me first." We all have these kinds of stored memories of childish sparring. In this case, it was quite plausible that not all my ghosts, both relatives and not, were memorialized in the single holiday candle. Or that I could leave them all behind and start in on the New Year, free of the ghosts of the past.

"Look at the little, tiny man whose image she has captured in this flat box."

"Indeed, he has a loud, mature voice, especially for such a small man."

"Is it a man?"

"Is it some kind of magic?"

And then the words rolled out in Hebrew, read from the tiny, digitized Torah scroll, set on the reader's table shown on the screen. "*Bereshis* ... in the beginning..."

More exclamations of wonder! "They are still chanting Torah after five thousand seven hundred and eighty-one years?" But the self-confidence in the reader's voice reduced anxiety. The tumult of "voices" quieted in the presence of the tuneful, sonorous chanting, even though it was only emanating electronically from online.

Wholeness

The Flowers of the Country

The forsythia comes to mind first: dead-looking branches carried to the city apartment in the depths of December and left to bloom in a large, centrally stationed vase. Such faith that they would bloom and belief that winter would pass. I made a pastel drawing of them in ninth grade, which was exhibited in a hallway at school. My social studies teacher bought it, insisting that she wanted to encourage me, as it was unlikely that I would find support at home.

"This is really very good," I remember her saying, and she proffered fifty dollars for it—a huge sum in 1961.

In April, the lilac bushes were also ruthlessly pruned to bring back to the city. Great armloads went to my father's two sisters' apartments, as well as our own. The fragrance even today reminds me of my father's joy in having such a gift to offer his willing recipients. My mother would chime in to me privately that the lilacs did so well because the area of the bushes was my father's favorite place to relieve himself outdoors when at the country house. The bathroom was in the house and upstairs.

The tiger lilies occupied an area the full depth of the garage: lush, green foliage and bright orange flowers. My east neighbor in Seattle has lilies too, and they make me homesick for the old hammock and the lilies by the garage. We read comic books and swung to and fro.

Poppies are always a surprise, and I cannot get over fretting that they might be addictive. I think one has to cook the centers first.

Shasta Daisies — my first wedding featured these

Queen Ann's Lace — create a scent of carrots at the roadside

Black-Eyed Susans — my Mom's favorite flowers, though not wild

Nasturtiums — orange, and grow profusely in Finland

Geraniums — my memories of Greece, sunlight

Tulips — I mowed down a whole row by mistake when I was about nine.

If I learn to name them, identify them, then they are a part of me. I own them.

"I found a fruitful world because my ancestors planted it for me. Likewise, I am planting for my children." —Talmud

A History of Bicycling

I always had a bicycle, even when I lived in a city apartment. I suppose I rode it in the park when I was small. Even if it was just on an exercycle, my desire to ride was so strong that I got myself thrown out of the physical therapy unit attached to the hospital. My attitude was unacceptable to the old dragon lady who ran the department. I would not accept her dictum that I would need to walk with a cane, nor her ban on trying out the exercycle every chance I got. I was told not to return.

Instead, I undertook my physical therapy with another, much-more-experienced amputee, who was more of an acrobat than any kind of licensed physical therapist. After meeting him in New York, my parents sent me to him and his wife for a month in New Orleans and at their summer home in Pass Christian, Mississippi. I found the moss hanging from the trees there to be ominous and mysterious and the weather oppressive. The only time my "trainer" spoke harshly to me was when I proposed sitting on the same back seat as a hired man for the ride home. I was crammed into the front seat, and I thought that segregation was ridiculous until my trainer yelled at me that I could get his hired man killed.

In Mississippi, I also learned to wade fearlessly out into the Gulf, to taste crab for the first time, and to drink bourbon with 7Up. Cubes of cheese were served up on toothpicks during our daily cocktail hour. The workout regimen was to try to keep up with my host: in and out of the car, up and down the stairs at the post office, as well as dedicated lessons in ballroom dancing, roller skating, and bicycling. The last one was the easiest. All he did was run beside me on an above-knee artificial leg and let go of the bike as soon as I had my balance. It only took the one time, and this was after the famous Dean Rusk Institute in NYC had advised my parents that it was impossible for me to ride a bicycle again! Modified for additional power with a slightly shortened pedal on the right side, I could again ride a bike in NYC with my friends. Later, I was able to ride to class across a large suburban college campus, even though people I had just had lunch with refused or simply could not recognize me as I reconfigured the number of legs I would appear with for different activities.

Early Educational Experiences

Dr. Chandler

Audiovisual education was offered in fourth through sixth grades in the progressive elementary school for gifted children. Dr. Chandler presided over a large collection of slides covering the world's art history but focusing mainly on European masterworks and the American Thomas Hart Benton. His work held a particular fascination because his two-dimensional paintings appeared three-dimensional. Apparently, he sculpted his scenes in clay before painting them! Dr. Chandler's enthusiasm, her excitement, really, was contagious in sharing her favorite images with us. I was interested.

Mrs. Lilienthal

In eighth grade, junior high in the same campus schools, Mrs. Lilienthal insisted on many things related to study skills and habits. We were to read the *New York Times* Science section every Tuesday without fail (or weekly); we were to review our class notes daily. We were to be close observers of nature and draw exactly what we saw, specifically botanical drawings of leaves and other structures, and we had to keep a bound notebook current with all of the above.

Art class(es)-The Elephant and the Forsythia

My main memory of art classes was that if I did anything outstanding, it would be taken from me. And so I lost the stuffed elephant I had designed, sewn, and stuffed. "You made it in my class, so it is mine!" the teacher insisted. She was the same one who had me write, "I will not talk in the art class," either 100 or maybe even 1,000 times (on lined paper) as a punishment for visiting with my classmates during class. That one stuck, and I had a reputation later on in art school for being uninterruptible and sort of aloof. I still hate to be interrupted when focusing on what I am doing.

A pastel drawing of flowering forsythia was displayed in a hallway near the art classroom. My ninth-grade social studies teacher purchased it. She stated that she was pretty sure I would get no encouragement at home and that she wanted to encourage me, that I "had something."

Years later, I stole a coiled clay pot I had made in my first pottery class out of a student art show. There too, the teacher wanted it for a sample of what was being made in his class. It was mine!

Flattest foot in the world

I was an ace student in solid geometry. However, no one pointed me toward architecture or structural engineering or related subjects as a career. I actually had tried to build myself a cabin at age nine, collecting enough stones for a foundation. At twenty-three, I drew and measured, ripped, and cut (using power saws) all the lumber for a 24-foot-diameter geodesic dome held together with wingnuts through predrilled holes. Even the final triangle slipped into place with no accumulated error.

Once, the math teacher called me to the blackboard to draw a geometric proof in chalk. It was too hard to deal with my crutches, so I put them down and stood, poised, as I worked. The relative quiet in the room became completely still as everyone waited for me to fall over. After a time, Mr. Gerber remarked that either I had the flattest foot in the universe or the most extraordinary sense of balance. His additional quip, to take good care as I "already had one foot in the grave" was less welcome as it was a new concept and metaphor to me.

At semester's end, my mother marched on the school to insist that my grade of 100 percent be reduced, as no one is perfect. My teacher, Mr. Gerber, replied that as I had done all the homework correctly and scored 100 percent on each of the tests, he had no choice but to grade me 100 percent.

Pansies and Nursing a Baby

Vincenz Panny, the German teacher, answered an ad that I posted spring of my freshman year that I wanted to work as a gardener. I really missed helping my father in the garden. We had a country place in upstate New York. And Mr. Panny wanted to plant some flowers for his wife. I don't think it was a surprise, but he said he had no clue what to buy and where to put it. I didn't have that much idea, either, but it was a very delightful job. It wasn't very long, two or three sessions at the most. But he would fetch me and we'd go to the plant nursery and buy a bunch of pansies and different things, and dig up the beds around the edges of his backyard and plant them.

They had a baby in the house. And it was springtime and it was one of the most formative things that happened to me at Reed was coming into his home with him with these trays of pansies. And his wife was sitting in the kitchen in floods of sunlight nursing the baby. And she was partially exposed, so we saw her shoulders. And she was the most beautiful thing. The whole picture was a beautiful picture. And he was so appreciative. He said, "Look at this." I don't know what he said, exactly. But it made a tremendous impression on me. It was probably the first time I'd ever seen anybody nursing a baby. And it looked good to me.

And it was terribly, terribly European on every level that she was half undressed, that she made no move to cover herself, that he wanted me to see this. He could have taken me in another door, or said, "Oops," and taken me around the back. But it was like entering a painting.

Aprons

What is with the aprons? Why did I always have to have one in my possession as I grew up? And why so many now? (Like nine to ten.) And what is with the guilt over finishing the embroidery designs imprinted on them? I have centralized all my extant handicraft "projects," including six aprons, one still from Russia (pre-1919). I have a small one from age four (one duck and one flower), a slightly larger one from age seven (two ducks and two flowers), one from age twelve (an abstract design), and the last one from home. Then there are the ones I bought or made myself: pinnies, like the southern maids wore for housework and I use for casting plaster, and dishwashing over-the-head-aprons for my second marriage. Then I have my mother's collection of half-aprons for cooking for company.

The best grandma picture I have of my own mother shows her in such a half-apron, lighting a Hanukkah candle while surrounded by her five grandchildren. I gave her a sixth some years after she had passed away. She would have been so proud of him, he is such a thoughtful, considerate, and organized person.

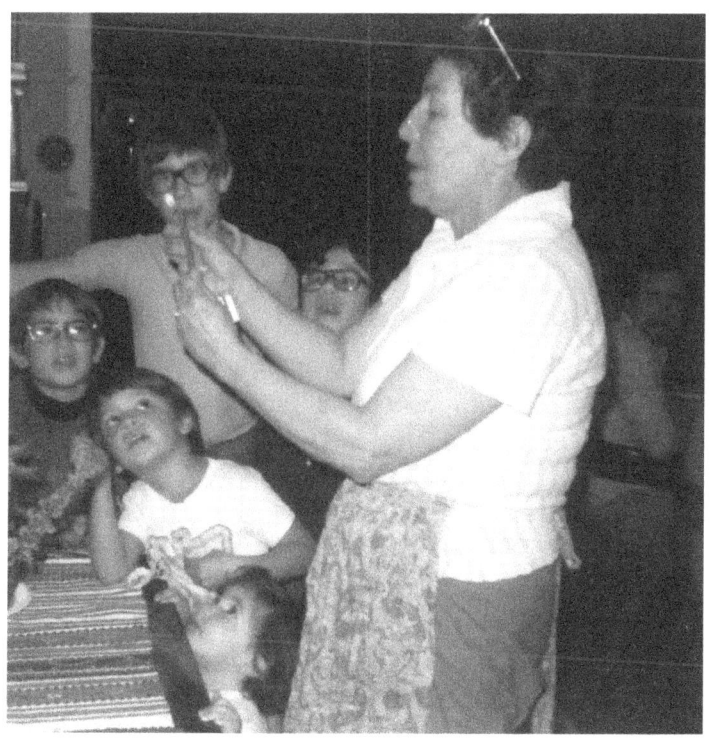

Hot Bronze

When the wet bronze scrap was mistakenly dropped unceremoniously into the crucible of already molten bronze, the steam released caused a mini-explosion. The crucible cracked, and a rivulet of bronze flowed out across the concrete floor. I don't remember who took up a shovel and dropped some sand in its path to stop the flow toward our feet, but I think it was me. The explosion also sent fragments of hot bronze onto the chest and shirtfront of the hapless student who had dropped the wet stuff in. Although he had gloves, he stood shrieking as no one moved to help him. I seemed to be the only one who could still think, and I grabbed a broom. I swept the glowing fragments off his shirtfront. Unfortunately, he simultaneously grabbed the waistband of his loose-fitting trousers and pulled it away from his body, allowing some of the fragments to fall down his pants. Thankfully, he was not burned as they fell harmlessly out the cuffs. That moment, when no one else could think, much less act, was more proof to me that splitting from consciousness is both a learned and a useful skill.

Building the tradition of Tzedakah

When I was little, we were each given twenty-five cents to add to the Keren Ami fund at Sunday school. I don't think I had any sense of where that money was going or that it even was my money. When I first noticed that my three-year-old had a tendency to hoard pennies, I put up a tzedakah box in the kitchen. It is still there. I made it out of a Barton's honey cake box, a tough blue cardboard container already decorated with Jewish symbols. I taped it shut and put a small hole in the back. Then I simply hung it on a nail. Teaching by example, I often put loose change in it and sometimes allowed my son the privilege of standing on a chair to drop my change in. I told him this would be money we would share with other children who didn't have any. He eagerly started putting some of his pennies in too.

Halloween would come around, with its special containers for collecting money for UNICEF, and I was able to put our year-round collecting in perspective, to tie it to something the rest of his secular world school did. After he would come home from trick-or-treating with huge amounts of candy, all for him, we would ceremoniously count the contents of the tzedakah box. I would then write a check to UNICEF. An unexpected side benefit would be my son's sudden desire to share some of his candy. A further unexpected conversation would be about the history of banking and how a check can be turned into money in another city.

Over the years, as his knowledge of the world increased, I would save the letters from various helping agencies soliciting funds and ask his opinion. So, some years we selected other groups and learned how hard it could be to have to choose, with limited resources, among worthy causes.

When we went to stores displaying collection canisters, I could reinforce the notion that we were not the only concerned people in the world. He started to notice and to care about what our local agencies were doing. After he started taking the bus alone, he would ask about the people who appeared to have nothing and wanted to know whether they had enough to eat and someplace to go if they needed help.

One of his concerns after his bar mitzvah reception at age thirteen was what would happen to the leftover food. When I asked him what he wanted to be done with it, he knew exactly where he wanted to take it—to the agency on Skid Row that distributes food. He also received some money for his bar mitzvah. With only the smallest hint from me about the reciprocal nature of gifts, he chose to give a portion of it away. Again, he knew which agency he wished to support and for what purpose: for temporary assistance for the unemployed.

Mentor Graphics

At the time I was hired at Mentor Graphics as a "technical illustrator," I was very much in need of a full-time job. I had been piecing together short-term projects with "artists in the schools" and with the "talented and gifted program", but then I had no income during school vacations. I was a divorcee and a single parent of a fourteen-year-old boy—a math whiz and scholarship student at Catlin Gabel School.

I had taken word processing (this was 1983) at community college with an eye to my general employability. I approached Mentor's documentation department with this certificate of completion as well as a portfolio of landscapes and figures. The manager who hired me recognized me from Portland State. More to the point, he needed someone who could rule lines with a Rapidograph type of ink pen. The software available could not yet draw a boundary around a "table" in an instruction manual. So, for the first release of software manuals I worked on, most of what I did was draw straight lines and correct any errors with White-Out.

My talents and interests were further utilized as I experimented with the basic drawing program to depict hardware drawn in perspective. This got people very excited until they realized it was art training, not the program itself, that created the drawings. I had also brought in a camera from home and took some photographs first to help me simplify the compositions.

The overall contribution I made to Mentor included effectively replacing three software engineers from Taiwan, who had been tasked with trying to draw the English alphabet. No one seemed to know that the field of typography even existed, nor that fonts could soon be bought from Adobe. My art school knowledge of fonts was helpful in creating readable manuals. In addition, I advised the Human Interface team in its early days regarding how to select contrasting colors for readability. For yet another task, the trained engineers did not seem to have basic knowledge of art disciplines as needed to research or to make effective choices for their own fields.

At the time I gave notice, I was actively looking for another job within the company and also outside it. After reporting my immediate boss for sexual harassment, I would essentially be leaving with no references. I accepted the marriage proposal from my suitor in Seattle and left Mentor on a one-year leave of absence. I rented out my Portland duplex and moved north. Later that year, I was informed by the office of one of the VPs that if I returned, I could be assured that I would not have to work for that same manager, so I suppose I was finally believed. I did leave behind an $80,000 art collection purchased and installed in four buildings by the employee art committee of which I was the chairperson.

I Wanted to Attend a Sculpture Conference and Ended up Speaking at the Smithsonian

So far as I am concerned, I had no choice but to be terrific. The hall was large. It held 300, and it was full. I was the next speaker in the parallel program of the biannual International Sculpture Conference. My topic was building and casting in masonry materials: strong, versatile, cheap.

The conference featured name artists such as Christo, but there was a track of parallel programs one could apply for, so I had done so. When I registered on-site, I was asked to sign a release that audio and video of my talk would now belong to the ISC and that it would be bundled for sale through the organization and for their benefit. I confirmed that, unlike Christo or whoever, I would not be receiving an honorarium nor travel expenses, and I refused to sign. I refused to be exploited. They argued (bullied) with me for a while but gave up and gave me my assigned room number. I assumed it would be a classroom with about thirty people, as promised. Apparently, though, a lot of people had indicated interest in the subject of my talk, and so I was assigned to have an auditorium and had an audience of about three hundred.

I could have fainted on the spot as soon as I entered the hall. Fortunately, I had just visited NYC and gone to a dinner theater performance. Two guys in loud plaid jackets had to hold the room of chattering diners without losing their humor, volume, or their cool. I decided to emulate them. I had to be fantastic: lively, entertaining, informative, but most important, "out there."

I was well prepared with a short technical talk, slides of the art of two other women artists working in concrete, and some of my own work. I had samples of materials to pass around, and names of suppliers. I was terrific! When I was done and applauded, the lectern was swarmed with excited artists, mostly women, who wanted to congratulate me and to exchange business cards, to ask questions, and to stay in touch. A smaller group bore me off for lunch (this had never happened to me before).

They were all so proud of me!

After I got home, I did two things. I started a monthly newsletter by subscription for artists working in masonry materials, using the business cards I had collected in Washington D.C. as a starting mailing list. (I wrote, edited, and distributed for that expanding list for two years.) Then I went to the audiovisual department at the University of Washington with my materials samples and my slides, put on the same lucky shirt, and gave my lecture again for a cameraman. I placed an ad in Sculpture magazine of the ISC for an instructional video copy of my talk for $30 plus shipping and quickly made more than $3,000—enough to cover not only my expenses but also a nice honorarium, which I attempted to share with the other two artists I featured (they both refused it). Anyhow, I had earned my share of my conference appearance for my own benefit and not that of the organization.

Artists are often treated like women, as too ignorant to protect themselves, and this was a political statement that I made to them in refusing to turn over my talk and my work for nothing.

Suitcases

My Mother's Suitcase
My mother's suitcase is large and heavy, with a stout lock and her initials, L. R. stamped in gold. It is an orange sort of leather, the same, actually, as her father's suitcase, also stamped with his initials in gold.

My Grandfather's Suitcase
I gave his away some years ago after emptying it of a large photograph of him and a set of bottles for cologne, hair stuff, and toothbrush. I kept the hairbrush. It had hairs in it. So, now I have his DNA from sometime before his death in 1955. If I knew what to do with that... It gave me quite a turn to open what I thought was an empty suitcase and find that large photo portrait!

My Suitcase
This one is really a nylon overnight bag, entirely filled with handmade productions made for nephews Alex, Ken, as well as Ben, by my mother, Lucie; by me, Joan for both my sons; and by a friend, Lynette as well as Estee's aunt Esther, for baby Zach.

Ben's Suitcase
This was my suitcase for family trips, maybe for college, always mine. Gray, strong, not too large. It has older-child clothing in it from Zach's childhood, intended for Ben's children.

Zach's Suitcase
This suitcase is thin, nylon fabric with bare cardboard reinforcement along the side that opens. It is filled with toddler clothes from Zach, intended for grandchildren. I have plundered the collection for several other babies who needed clothing, so only a selection of special gifts remains.

Faith

The blind man walked behind my car. The engine was running. How did he know I was not about to back up in order to turn around, striking him in the process? In fact, I was about to back up, out of the driveway I had turned into, in sheer frustration over not finding a parking space on the nearby avenue. What stopped me? Was my gaze caught by his white cane approaching? Did I notice a small plaid pattern in his shirt? Or his belt (unusual in such a young man)? Perhaps it was the angels of the young man: Michael, Gabriel, Rafael, Uriel. Before me, Uriel, behind me, Raphael, to my left, Gabriel, and to my right, Michael. Or perhaps my own angels, who warn me when a car is in my own "blind spot," and I am about to change lanes. (They do exist.)

B'shem Hashem, elohei Yisrael
B'ymini Michael u-smoli Gavriel
U-milfanai Uriel, me'acharai Raphael
V'al roshi, v'al roshi, Shechinat-El

(This song, also known as Reb Shlomo Carlebach's "Angel Song," unifies Jews from every corner of the world.)

Something protected the young blind man, and that certainty calmed some of my rage and frustration over being unable to park, over being late for my appointment. Certainty. Perhaps that is what faith is, the certainty that things will work out. It is OK to go forward, that the way will be smooth. Like ironing, faith takes out the wrinkles in our composure.

Pattern also protects. Plaids, stripes, embroidery all confer protection on the wearer. All those Scots cannot be wrong. The stripe has a more difficult history, as a mark of the lower classes as a rule, but also demarcating the heaven and earth. Watching over someone from the heavens is a concept found in many cultures, with angels being just one manifestation of the protective power of faith. Embroidery, especially stitches taken by hand, is probably older than either plaids or stripes. One feels at ease on hand-stitched pillow covers. A well-done darn on someone else's knee declares "this is my man" more surely than a wedding ring. I keep my hands off that man and tell him that his exquisitely repaired clothes proclaim him a liar and a married man.

The Threshold

Perhaps I should not have hugged her across the threshold of the front door. That is supposed to bring bad luck, although I did not know it at the time. My older son had called around 8 p.m. to say he would like me to meet his beloved—now, right now, tonight—to settle for her that she would be accepted, loved as he loved her.

I did not have much time to prepare before they would come. I could shower, cook, bake, or even clean the kitchen floor. They would be driving up, arriving just after 11 p.m. I made a vegetarian lentil soup. I baked a cake. I showered and put on PJs and a nice robe. I suppose I prepared "his" usual room, which held narrow bunk beds with clean sheets.

There was no time for the floor, which was, unfortunately, where she looked, rather than continuously meeting my eyes. She had opened them wide at the front door, just once. They were blue and full of pain. She appeared to be a runaway, fragile, waiflike. My son was her protector and rescuer, but as I knew only too well, the triangular dynamic of rescuer, victim, and persecutor would shift roles in infinite movement among the three positions, leading to vast unhappiness for all.

The beginning was simple and quite beautiful. He was lonely. He looked online for a partner. He traveled to meet her. She came to visit him. He went to fetch her and to dispose of her things, and she arrived with a small carry bag containing all her worldly possessions. My son's father and I outdid each other in providing her with clothes, a coat, and jewelry.

Tablecloth for the Broken Hearted

The two sisters, now elderly and one widowed, went directly to Portland, Oregon, when they arrived as children from Russia. In old age, they retained a sort of country girlishness, unspoiled by any stay on the East Coast. On a visit for tea and cookies, we sat around a big round table covered with a huge ecru crocheted tablecloth. I did not ask if it was dyed with tea. My own grandmother would dye dingy whites with strong tea to renew them. Also, brown tea was what was most likely to be spilled, so it would not show.

To crochet a tablecloth must take a long time and a good deal of patience. Girls, in particular, were schooled in patience in the old days. That was the point of making up a trousseau of largely handmade or crocheted or hand-embroidered items, to acquire enough patience to put up with a man and with a family.

When my oldest brother wanted to get married at twenty-one or twenty-two, my mother gave him her most tangled, fine and thin, necklace chain she had in her jewelry box, as well as a single straight pin.

"If you can untangle this without losing patience," she said. "Then maybe you are old enough to get married."

He did succeed with the necklace, and he did get married to his high-school sweetheart. They had two sons and divorced when the boys were both young teenagers.

On that first visit, the two sisters showed me the underside of the apparently clean and perfect tablecloth. Underneath, resting on the tabletop, were all the bread and cake crumbs from several meals, ready for sweeping when convenient. The elder sister crowed with delight over how the tablecloth itself reduced her housework, but I took an entirely different lesson. Let the crumbs go. Let them pass through. Keep the nuggets and any larger pieccs (Of bread? Of cake? Of the relationship?). Memory is available to us to revisit either the good memories or the bad. Look at the good ones, often.

Photo: Alex Strazzanti

Vi di yorn flien/Zach's Bar Mitzvah

We celebrated Zach's Bar Mitzvah in January with 135 friends and relatives and Zach's school classmates all gathered at the University of Washington Hillel. A poised Zach seemed to actually enjoy himself while doing extremely well with the Hebrew and original speech in English, and even a short thank you in Yiddish.

It was a "three-hanky" affair. There was also smoked white King salmon and Yiddish folk dancing led by the remarkable Strauss/Warshauer duo from New York. We're very proud of Zach and of the plans for the event, which not only worked but caused one participant to say it was the only such celebration she had ever been to where nothing came across as phony.

The event involved Friday and Saturday night dinners for family, Saturday lunch for 135 guests, Sunday brunch for out-of-towners, Sunday dinner for the remnant, new clothes for all of us, various religious articles, and as many fresh primroses as our van could hold. At this, it was considered too small to be worth bidding on by two of the possible caterers!

Vi di yorn flien! How the years fly by! The child we nurtured is growing into a young man!

"We take great pleasure in welcoming all of you to today's *Shabbes* (Sabbath) services and for the happy occasion of Zach becoming a Bar Mitzvah during the morning services. In Jewish tradition, *Shabbes* is a day of rest and worship and of visiting with friends and family. We appreciate the opportunity to hold the services in this beautiful new setting of the Hillel Foundation for Jewish Living at the University of Washington.

As you enter the auditorium/sanctuary, you will see the curtains of the Aron Hakodesh (Holy Ark) on your right. Above it is a light that never goes out, the Ner Tamid or Eternal Light. It reminds us that when things seem impossible, dark, or frightening, that there is always light and hope. The Ark houses the handwritten Torah scroll (or scrolls), which are calligraphed onto parchment, and contain the first five books of the Bible. The Torah is divided into weekly portions, and each week a consecutive portion of the Torah is read so that by the end of the lunar calendar year, the Torah has been read in its entirety. Today's portion of the Torah, which we will hear chanted in Hebrew, is being read in synagogues all around the world on this same day, linking us as a people and connecting us to the past as well as carrying us into the future.

Our choice of a 'traditional' service stems from a visit to Denmark a few years before Zach's birth. Joan attended synagogue one Sabbath in Copenhagen and was moved by the realization that this 'standard' service has been the same in every Western country where Jewish people have lived for the last thousand years. The Hebrew is accessible wherever Hebrew literacy is maintained, part of the objective of Bar Mitzvah training. (Joan was only totally surprised when the Torah explication was delivered in Danish!)

Zach's religious education in Seattle has been highly eclectic, hopefully demonstrating that there is more than one 'right' way to be an observant Jew. While this has included some exposure to secular and cultural Judaism, he has actually attended a Modern Orthodox synagogue regularly since age 3 ½ and is most familiar with the liturgy of today's complete traditional morning service. We would like to especially thank Cantor Boaz Pnini of Emanuel Congregation for tutoring Zach for his Bar Mitzvah and Jerry Gess for anchoring today's prayer service."

2006 Trip to Mexico

We went to Bucerias, Mexico (near Puerto Vallarta), for a week to recuperate. There were crocodiles in the local pond, but the ocean was gorgeous and warm. We got so relaxed that we were no longer sure which morning we were scheduled to leave. Zach saved the day by hovering near a (closed) cafe that had Wi-Fi. He was able to get ahold of our trip details and flight numbers on his Palm Pilot!

The spring was dominated by my one-woman exhibit, *Carving in Clay*, at the Manuel Izquierdo Gallery connected to my art school alma mater. It was exciting to show bronzes for the first time and to see old artist friends from Portland. In the fall, a back-to-school party at our corner pocket park featured relay races I invented to mimic the morning rush: "wash" (run with a full bowl of water), "eat" (balance an egg on a spoon while running), "dress" (put on costume clothing and hat and carry a briefcase, and "catch the bus" (get your homework into the briefcase and run for it). Parachute games were also popular with the grade-school set.

The search for a high school for Zach seemed analogous to a college admissions process. Two of these upscale independent schools give breakfast; one of them even offers breakfast to hungry parents who leave home before they have time to eat. Something seems really off balance in the lifestyles. At the end of eighth grade, Zach's current school planned on taking the class to China and Tibet for three weeks. They prepared all year with language, geography, and history classes. This was an enormous trauma for the parents to trust the trip leaders, but aside from some travelers' tummy, all went well. It turned out that Zach is a terrific traveler, and afterward, we realized it would be hard to intimidate an adolescent who had already been to Tibet.

I spent part of the next school year undergoing docent training at the Henry Gallery associated with the University of Washington. While this seemed like a good idea at the time, activating dormant public speaking skills, for example, at the end of the training, I decided not to be a docent, and for that matter, that contemporary art was not my niche of interest. For example, a visiting European artist was awarded $4,000 and an empty gallery room for a contemporary installation. He and his wife spent the money on designer purchases and displayed the (empty) shopping bags. I thought it was larceny, not art!

While Zach was at summer camp for a third season, Joe and I took a long-awaited trip to Alaska. Instead of a cruise, we opted for the state ferry, which had minimalist accommodations. The shower was so small, a washcloth served as a floor covering. We brought a cooler with a lot of our own foods and dined on burgers and ferry food the rest of the time. We did see lots of whales from constantly looking through binoculars. (We have seen more whales from places on the Washington coast.) The ferry had multiple stops along the way to Skagway, and I even got to see a totem pole carving in process. Mysteriously, above the work in progress, there was a hand-lettered sign in Hebrew characters reading *Barukh haba* (Blessed is he who comes).

The wheel of life seems to be rotating faster and faster as the weeks whip by, and then the years. Our kitchen calendar seems like a blur of weddings, births, Bar Mitzvahs, and, yes, death. Still, we traveled and "did" art, science, and high school, respectively. We are grateful for the gift of life, which allows us to keep connecting to one another. The year 2008 saw three new babies, four Bar Mitzvahs, two weddings, and one funeral of a close friend. An ongoing sadness is my older son, Ben, and his wife, who choose to remain at a distance. We can only hope that the situation may improve as they themselves grow older. Meantime, we have been enjoying the events in our larger families, both of relatives and of friends.

In 2009, I had another one-person show—this time in Seattle, at Gallery 6311 in Ballard. This installation involved many trips to bring all the boxes of terra cotta figures, some of which were painted in soft colors, as well as wall reliefs. There was a well-attended opening and a good response. For Passover, extended family came to Seattle for the festive meal. The two tables were arranged in a "T," so each of six men thought he was at the head of the table. I cooked the food and hired a server, who stayed to wash the dishes. In June, we went to Mexico City for the Bar Mitzvah of cousin Max. The party included two ukuleles, a tambourine, and a sort of dulcimer, plus singing and dancing. The lunch was kosher-style and Mexican, including a spectacular nut cake layered with whipped cream.

This is No Longer My Native Land

It is an old narrative for many peoples who have been dispossessed, the story of adapting to a new land. What does it take? A continuity of some things: of language, of feast days and holidays, and fellowship with people from "the old home" (der alter heym).

"Ikh dank dir Gott, far Amerike, di naye, fraye land." (I thank you, God, for America, the new, free land.)

If enough bad things happen in the new land, the old one looks better and better. The strange thing is that I no longer can relate to the trees and flowers of the colder climate of my birthplace, and stranger still, that I do not care for the summer molds and mosses and winter ice storms of my adult home. And now, even my current mature adult home is no longer home. I crave the Mediterranean, the sun, the light. I have never been as happy as when I swam parallel to the shore near Forte dei Marmi, Italy, in view of the marble-covered slopes of the Apennines. I was alone. I was free. I was one with the mountains and the sea simultaneously. I had no pain. I had no self at all—only a huge smile as I waved to the mountains.

This happiness came again toward the end of my stay. Alone I went on a tourist boat going north, parallel to the shore. As the boat surged forward and the wind rushed against my cheek, I had a moment of total, total happiness. I had launched, I was on my way, I was free—at one this time with the wind and with the sea, in sight of land but moving, traveling on my beloved sea again in sunshine and with speed. Free. Unencumbered.

2008: Italy

Even little girls, from the age of six, do a shift from hip to hip as they walk. Most of the men, just like the local bank manager, walk like orangutans, rolling their mighty shoulders forward as they go. When not on "display," they revert to waddling. Women display all the time, fixing their hair and preening. Both genders constantly seek to look at their reflections in store windows. Women in high heels flounce and sashay with their hips. There is a new, modern kind of shift while holding and walking with a cell phone and yet another type of hip shift walking on the beach in a bikini with a cell phone. They know they have something men want.

An old man pulls out into traffic on a mobility scooter while checking the angle of his hat in his rearview mirror. All Italians gesture, walk, and talk at the same time. Both genders sweep and mop floors and sidewalks. Maybe that's where they learn the hip shift (while smoking a cigar) and sweeping.

One day, when I wanted to see the local Museo de Bozzetti, I saw the hero of my imagination. I really wanted to see this museum, but there was a long staircase to get to the display floor. There was a stairlift, but the key was missing. My rescuer came into the lobby, a beautiful, smiling, fit man in a blue tank top. He grasped the situation immediately and gestured that he would go tell them upstairs that somebody needed the stairlift. I heard a tremendous tumult of argumentative Italian from up there. Apparently, they were telling him that one had to be paralyzed to be able to access the stairlift, and he was telling them not to be ridiculous.

A harassed-looking clerk came down with the key, and I got to see the wonderful exhibits upstairs. I never spotted my rescuer again, though I looked for him in all the rooms. Every night, we heard the high school band practice in the fields outside Forte dei Marmi. The donkeys who lived in the fields thought it was all for them and would pitch in with their braying. It was very amusing.

In the heat of summer, the church was a good place to rest a little after lunch. One day, having no one to speak to, I addressed the statue of the Virgin Mary. I argued with her to give me back my son, my older son, the one married to a Catholic woman who refused to let us all maintain contact.

"Give him back!" I said to the virgin mother, and she answered, I heard it, "I gave you," she said. I assume that referred to the gift of my younger son at not quite forty-five. I stayed out of the church after that. I found the local Jewish community and attended a Shabbat service held in someone's large and beautiful garden. The Torah was in a hard case like a Sephardic presentation. The people were of Lebanese Jewish origin (summering from Milan), which meant that they spoke French, so I could speak with them. The Hebrew prayer book was a comfort, and the fruit platter for kiddush was so beautiful that I went home and painted it from memory.

I have never been so thoroughly inventoried as by the good ladies of the congregation. I could see them passing their eyes over my ring (real pearl), my watch (gold with discreet diamond chip), my shoes, my simple summer clothes. They could not figure out who the heck I was and whether I belonged. I never went back there, either. Rich people do scare me, but I loved Italy.

The lifeguards were afraid to let me swim alone. They seemed to think I was casting myself into the sea and wanted to rescue me. My landlady, fortunately, told them that I was alright and that I would swim back. I would walk down to the edge of the sea on crutches, cast them down, and scoot my way into the water until it was deep enough to swim, and then swim away. The trick was remembering where the heck I parked my crutches when I came back, and also I had to crawl to get out, but I didn't care.

At the studio, when they wanted to find me an *artigiano* (artisan) to enlarge my small clay maquette into a larger stone sculpture, they sent someone to go to the plaza to ask among the cafes and see who was free and who wanted the job. The emissary went by bicycle. It was so quaint that no phones were involved. I know how to enlarge clay sculptures by eye. I thought perhaps learning how the old-timers enlarged in stone using geometry would be of use to me in the future. I wanted to see how it was done before everyone went to computer-aided enlarging. It was very interesting, but actually, I still enlarge things by eye using two sculpture stands, one for the small maquette and another for the larger piece. The artisans all wear paper hats folded out of newspapers. It is a simple design, a little different than a paper boat. I asked for and took one home as a model. The tradition is that when you finish a sculpture, you tear up the paper hat. That indicates clearly that this sculpture is finished.

After I paid my artisan when he finished enlarging my piece, he must have gone right out to buy shoes with it because the very next day, he showed up in a pair of brand-new Birkenstocks, which were very expensive locally.

The Italians seem to have a very rich sense of life, of tragedy, and of humor. Our landlord laughed himself silly at the story of Zach's birth when my labor nurse walked the perimeter of the room over and over when I was really ready to go to the delivery room. When I asked her what the hell she thought she was doing, she said she was looking for my other shoe! I then knew why I had had so little intelligent support during my labor.

When I got on the boat to go see the five towns of the Cinque Terre, the people on the pier shouted, "Brava!" There were a lot of steps on that pier. I think that it might have happened more than once that I was congratulated by a crowd. It wasn't really so nice when the sailors were ordered by the captain to catch me by the armpits and walk me on and off the boat. I couldn't manage crutches on a moving boat. When I traveled by myself by train, it was actually only French people who ever helped. The doors of the train would open, and I would see whether there were two steps or four and usually just fling myself and my knapsack and my crutches at the steps and then crawl up from there. The only people who ever helped me were French. The Italians just stood and watched like sheep.

My Dutch roommate upstairs at the duplex was a mixed blessing, generous with her tea and cookies but nasty to our landlady (not enough towels, too much noise, etc.). I drove to and from the studio with her for the first few days and then, with Joe arriving, went out to the airport to fetch our own rented car. This involved driving back from Pisa on the autostrada, finding our turnoff, paying tolls, etc. It was fairly hair-raising but actually less so than the one-lane roads with blind curves and masonry walls or ditches on the sides. Eventually, we got (longer) routes figured out to and from the studio in Pietrasanta, as well as to the store and the train station. It turned out the Italians have more *bonhomie* (geniality) than the French.

The *artigiani* were stunned by me, and they thoroughly disapproved of me sitting on the ground to work. (It was less dusty and noisy outside.) My sense of dignity had been totally erased already, having to ride on the bottom of a luggage cart out of the airport in Paris. There were not any visible wheelchairs or other wheeled conveyances!

We bought and learned cell phones, but we actually operated as a family with an agreed on plan and a watch, and we only used the phone once each.

So much summertime semi-nudity on the people increases the ability to undress with the eyes, which is useful for sculpting! My landlady's opinion of all of the (largely) religious statues carved in the local studios was that they were mostly for Mafia bosses and that the worse they were as people, the more religious they were. I told her about the beautiful life-size St. Sebastian being carved at "my" atelier. As soon as they got that torso smooth, they drilled it full of holes and put the bronze arrows in to depict the martyr's death. She was surprised I even knew the legend of St. Sebastian, and her reply was about her thirtysomething son's lack of religious training: "He doesn't even know who is St. Sebastian (sic) ... my mother would die!"

Our Italian Landlady often came by to see how we were doing. We were in her rental, not her house, although her husband kept chickens and a large garden, and was often to be found outside somewhere. I don't remember how she got in the kitchen door. I may have left it open, or just covered with the screen door. She had been very helpful in stocking the refrigerator before we arrived, even with some pecorino cheese. A day I remember I was about to put a chicken in the oven. She may have excused herself "with your permission" but in any case she took over. Looking for and finding a lemon, ruthlessly squeezing half of it into the cavity of the chicken. Then she had me follow her outdoors to show me the giant rosemary bush outside. She must have gone back inside for some clippers, as rosemary is tough. She clipped a significant bundle, stuffed it any which way into the chicken, and plugged it with the half of squeezed lemon. When I ventured to ask about string to hold the legs to the body she shrugged and pushed further on the lemon stopping up the bird. I think she put it in the oven for me too.

We spent a whole month in northern Italy, June to July 2008, and understand New York better than before. In fact, we are now interested in visiting Ireland sometime in order to add further to our understanding of three early immigrant groups and their respective cultures: the Irish, the Italians, and the Jews.

We rented a duplex near Pietrasanta, between Florence and the Ligurian Sea. The area we were in was very close (2 kilometers) to the sea and faces Nice, France. The beaches were white sand with many private beach clubs, each one with colored umbrellas. The sea was swimmable most days and plenty warm. Delicious. People were very tan and bathing

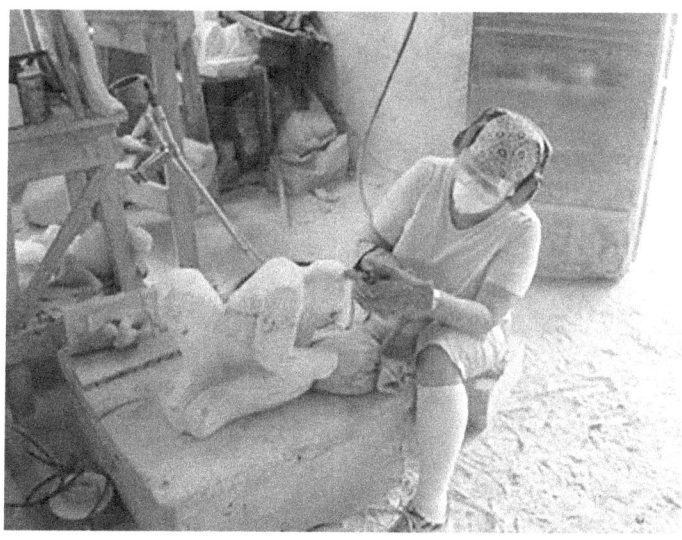

suits small. The duplex turned out to be a great find, roomy and airy. Zach figured out how to use the washing machine and dishwasher however we washed the dishes with water softener tablets for the first three weeks because we didn't understand the labels. The dictionary eventually solved this. The stone carving studio I joined was working on several interesting commissions during my time there including that life size St Sebastian. Meantime, Joe and Zach went on short trips to Turin, Oxford, London, and Lausanne. Zach even did a couple of short train trips on his own. The 310K wooden crate of carving marble arrived safely home to Seattle. Joan thought the crate would make a dandy creche and donated it to our next-door neighbors for their church.

Zach 13–19

I think of Zach's teenage years as having belonged totally to his care, but actually, this was a time for my own artwork as well. Some of my parenting involved ideas for independence training, which in turn led to hobbies of his own. I felt strongly that fifteen- sixteen-year-olds had no business driving cars, so around eighth grade, we began learning the buses—or rather, he did.

I would drive us to a library in some different part of town, stay long enough to be sure he was confident of the bus directions available on the library's computers, and leave him there to get himself home. Challenged by the wide geographical area where his high school classmates lived, he succeeded in finding bus routes these families had never used! Expert status conferred a different status than the family gift of a car, and we were grateful for the bus training when an astonishing number of these same classmates totaled their cars precisely at age sixteen.

This was shortly after the near-death of the sixteen-year-old son of Al Gore in a typical teenage car crash. Our compromise was a learner's permit and lessons (and insurance) at age seventeen, so he would have his license in the spring semester of senior year, at eighteen, and well after college applications were in. The positives that came out of all this city geography was a hobby called "geocaching," a combination treasure hunt and skill with a handheld GPS. Zach spent much interested time creating his treasures, hiding them, and checking on them. He also put our corner pocket park, Penguin Park, onto the city's maps and Google Maps, to the great puzzlement of the city's parks people. The park, thereafter, also became a favorite Pokémon GO destination.

As a family, we continued to go to the beach locally after summer camp. One of those trips was to the far Northwest, where we rented a cabin for a long weekend. There were no restaurants—in fact, no real towns—in the area, and as we passed what was probably the last diner advertising chicken strips, we resigned ourselves to our own cooking for the whole vacation. Fortunately, I had spied a simple cardboard sign that said "fish" nailed to a utility pole just a mile or two back. Convinced it was a fisherman with a local catch, we went back and found a pickup truck with a man just unloading his catch in a large picnic cooler. We bought a whole salmon, paid him to clean it, and bore it back to the cabin.

The fish was kind of large for the oven, and there was an outside grill and charcoal briquettes available. I had noticed the kitchen drawers were lined with aluminum foil and ruthlessly stripped them all out to wrap the fish for grilling.

Any skepticism we felt about the whole deal disappeared when we tasted the freshest, most perfectly cooked fish any of us had ever eaten. We did not tell the owner of the cabin about our escapade. Perhaps we thought the place was overpriced in the first place. There was no store nearby to buy them a new roll of foil and no energy to reline the kitchen drawers anyway. I still feel guilty about it.

Other Washington, Oregon, and Vancouver, BC, beach spots had their own quirks, but the enjoyments were surprisingly similar. Some apartments had more atmosphere than others—that is, not fancy, just offbeat like the Sou'wester Lodge in Long Beach. I'm not sure Zach understood the appeal of going downmarket for vacation: no dishwasher, no disposal, only one large cooking pot, etc. But for me, it was a return to simpler, more bohemian roots—less bourgeois, where a room with a Matisse reproduction became beautiful because of a pink bed sheet hung as a curtain. We were also not confined to our single cabin at the Sou'wester but had the whole beach as well as the run of the main lodge with its interesting owners, books, and fireplace.

On Credit

There was a balding watchmaker who worked with his curly-haired grown son in a small storefront watch repair shop near Lake City. The interior walls were covered in small wooden cabinets, drawers really, with tiny labels on each one and containing mysterious hidden contents: watch parts? The watchmaker always wore a magnifier centered on a band around his head as well as thick eyeglasses resting on his nose. This gave him the appearance of a very wise man. Perhaps he was really a religious "rebbe" even, with a sort of phylactery on his forehead, or an eye doctor about to peer into your eyes while clicking strange measuring tools and odd-looking instruments. Who knew who he was? His students at the local college would have said he was a fine instructor, loving really, in his warm, paternalistic fatherly way with them. His repair clients still speak of him as from another age, definitely from another culture.

There was the day I, myself, went in the store with a hat on. It looks like a hat for a colder climate, though the fur is just fake plush. My winter hat is black and round, with a turned-up plush rim. My winter coat has a black lining, so if I don't zip it up, the black lapels set off my black hat. I look like an Orthodox Jewish woman in this getup, even if I am wearing long pants and not a long skirt. Actually, it might have been the long black pants, short coat with black lining, and round fur-like black hat that caused the watchmaker to look at me with curiosity and perhaps a little alarm. His enlarged eyes, magnified by his thick glasses, took me in from head to toe, returning to the hat. Was I now the visiting rabbi from another century?

I asked for a new battery to be installed in my watch. I cautioned him that I had forgotten my large purse and had only a single bank debit card. I could suddenly see that his shop did not have the kind of card reader to accept pin numbers, and I knew my card was a simple debit card without a credit feature attached to it.

He replaced my watch battery in the time it took to caution him that I probably could not pay for the repair in cash right then. I was on my way to get groceries, I said. He ran my card through his machine with great force: one, two, three times, saying, "They always work if you've got money in the bank." I knew the card would not work without either a pin number or an imprinted credit logo. I offered to leave the watch with him until I could return with money from the store's ATM.

"Take the watch," he said, "I thought you had it on already."

He took hold of a business card, wrote "I.O.U $10" on the back of it, and slid it across the counter.

"I close at five, and I am out of here," he said.

Returning from the supermarket with two ten-dollar bills at five o'clock, by my watch, I found the store shuttered and dark. The next day when I returned, I almost expected it to have disappeared overnight like the relic of a bygone age that it was. But it was still there. I wore my green raincoat, by the way, and no hat. Nonetheless, "There she is!" He greeted me right away, accepting and then stroking the ten-dollar bill I gave to him—his eyes alight, his faith restored.

A Mother's Prayer

Yet again I looked to the *techinas* or women's prayers written in Yiddish, for guidance on how to wait in peace for my son's return from far away. This excerpt is about a son who has gone abroad and has not kept in contact.

...O Parent of All, hear my fervent prayer
And bring my child back to me
At the right time, full of joy and the vigor of life,
To be the pride and delight of my heart,
A blessing to all, and pleasing in your sight,
My God and Sovereign, Amen.

From the book *Hours of Devotion* by Fanny Neuda, 1855, updated by poet Dinah Burland after translation. Published in 2007 by Schocken Books, New York.

Terminal Illness in the Family

Each of my parents left me a memorable quote that I am sure they did not intend as last words. However, the fact that I remember them has to count for something.

On what was her last visit to me in Oregon, which went pleasantly, I suggested to my mother that she might like to visit more often. She replied, memorably, "But, darling, I am only on vacation because I am dying!"

(I resolved on the spot not to live like that.)

My father spent several of his last months at the country house, mostly on his own. He commented to me that he had developed a newly found perception of color, specifically green. (The surrounding hills and trees were green). "I always just thought of green as just one color, green. Now I see that there are many different kinds of green, and now that I can see it, I cannot imagine how I did not see this before."

(I thought this was a profound realization stemming from a time of peaceful meditation and contemplation.)

My eldest brother had a memorable last comment on viewing my Seattle studio with sculpture stands and tables full of plaster mold-making projects. "Bleeaghhh! Work!" he commented on my choice of profession.

(The tricky part of making art is to hold on to the contemplative while finishing off the practical involved in completion.)

Contemplation is an infinite activity and one I practice wholeheartedly as a valuable use of time.

Why I Like Housework, Into the Light

It is a relief to be in control of space, shelf, décor. This house is mine, and so is its upkeep, dusting, and display. When we have household help, I can be, or choose not to be, "houseproud." When we do not have outside help, the house and its work are all mine, including the right to let the vacuuming go until my husband cannot stand it and does it himself. I like the ownership more than the help. When I cannot control the world, or my friends and family, I can always restore a bathroom to its pristine state or rearrange my jewelry. Small, finite projects help me feel in control, certainly less overwhelmed. But they also isolate me, daring anyone to disturb the order I have created and now "own."

The prospect of one day emerging from the pandemic that is keeping us sheltering in our homes is kind of overwhelming. The boundaries between me, my things, and the outside world have all shifted. Perhaps I will stand in some new relation to the outside world, or perhaps I will not be going outside anymore at all.

I plan on hiring help to spruce up the backyard and make a better garden of it. That could be a bridge project. There is no telling how I will feel next season. Perhaps I will be able to tell by how I sound. Perhaps I will sing outdoors next summer.

Unity

Making the Outline, Ages 0–12

To make an outline, draw up the basic shape: beginning, middle, end. It is the same with any story. Where did it start? In what way did it continue? And how does it end? That is the most important part: how it ends—whether it is the line comprising a completed silhouette, or the boat returning to its harbor, or the protagonist meeting a long-awaited death. How does it end? Who can foretell the future? What will be?

Along the way, the rough volumes become apparent, the main storylines, the chief variations. The details describe only the surface, literally sketched on the outside of the main mass.

The texture of a life is like the finish on the outside of a piece of furniture, whether smooth and new, scratched, or worn down. The outline of a life remains the same in any case, a basic form, whole. It describes the surface, of a volume buried deep inside. To change the final outline, it is necessary to change the actual shape pressing out from within: the inner nature. The essence. What will show on the outside.

The lady clerk at the post office assumed I did not speak English. What was it in my good face that gave the impression of the immigrant? No makeup? No hairdo? My red, flowered, peasant scarf? She spoke to me slowly, clearly, distinctly as if expecting non comprehension and an accent. I was tempted to answer her in Russian.

In short, I am a Yid.

Roughing Out the Shape, Ages 13–25

Alts iz gut nor in der tzayt. "Everything is good in its own time."

The clear silhouette leads directly to a need for mass, for stability. The weight of this mass is what gives the figure solidity and endurance. While a figurative sculpture can be somewhat attenuated, its fundamental quality is the displacement of space. Without weight, the figure is literally insubstantial.

This bulk is synonymous with mass or volume.

The broad outline yields to some particular details of structure and, most importantly, to the perpendicular cross sections of the original silhouette. Without an idea of the thickness or depth of a piece, it remains a "cut out"—made in only one dimension.

Getting the general shape of a thing requires a loose hand and a firm mental focus. Clay can be squeezed into a mass like a fat whale or pinched into protuberances like a beak or a fin. To take it to the next dimension, the sculpture must enter the space around it. What is the overall "footprint" of a figure? Where is it in space? Hips over feet. Shoulders over hips. Head over shoulders.

For a teen to assume an adult shape, one has only to wait until puberty and add exercise. Sports options for girls in the 1950s-'60s were limited to roller skates and ice skates, bicycles, and dance. Undergoing an amputation for a mesenchymal sarcoma of the knee at age fifteen, eliminated the ice skating, but I learned how to roller skate, ride a bicycle, and dance again, albeit with some adaptations.

Growing breasts and a general shape noticed by males was almost as upsetting. It took me a while to regain my power as an independent woman. I married, produced a healthy baby boy, and divorced. During this latter period of dislocation, I briefly dated a sociopathic painter, whose work should have tipped me off to the level of detail he would add to what was essentially an assault. I retaliated with a painted egg (see story The Culvert Ran Pink), and I vanquished him.

Modeled or Curved Surface, Detailed or Not, Ages 26–38

To model something is to give it form. In order to reach the surface of the forms of a sculpture, material such as clay must either be added (additive sculpture) or removed (reductive sculpture). While clay can be worked in either way (up or down). most other traditional materials can only be removed—e.g., stone carving and wood carving. Another newer method is fabrication, such as welded steel or assemblages made of mixed media.

During this time period, I finished art school. I produced a first gallery show of new cast stone (fine concrete), figurative castings equivalent to a master's degree effort. I also orchestrated an over-the-top bar mitzvah gathering for my thirteen-year-old son. In addition to him conducting the service and then entertaining friends and distant relatives, we held the first such party with live local musicians in the Conservative synagogue on the Sabbath itself. I asked a life model of my acquaintance to dance in my stead, and he did so with the bar mitzvah boy atop his shoulders. I danced too, suddenly barefoot and with my hair unbound from its chignon.

All the excess caught up with me nine months later with a complete financial and mental collapse. I recovered to be able to regain full-time paid employment within a short time, back in my role of project manager, this time in a tech company's documentation department.

I always have more than one thing going on, so I can rotate among projects, preferably one material leading to the next. I leave work where I know what the next step is. And I take the next step, only the next step, one at a time. Small bits of clay are cut off a plug of clay with a paring knife and stuck onto previous layers. The first layers go on the axes (plural of axis), following the directions of the cross-sections.

Composition of a sculpture is a matter of curves and planes. The vertices of the angles define the planes. The points along the curves define the direction of the forms. Over a lifetime, the proportion and scale of each life event determine, ultimately, the surface of a life, and later, its details.

Finishing and Texture, Ages 39–51

What will the finished surface be? What texture can be perceived if you run your hands or eyes over it? Is the actual material valuable or not? (It was a good age for wearing silk, like my wedding suit, and wool sweaters for working in.)

Sculptural finishes may accentuate the planes, the places where life has gouged out deep hollows. Two hollows next to each other create a new, raised form. The amount of finish is like a declaration of status: harried or effortless in its attempt at beauty, elegance, line.

What is the difference between stylization and finding the Bezier curve(s)? According to sculptor Elie Nadelman, "All form and volume can be understood as swelling."

The overall composition of a piece is an approach to spirituality. Through the pursuit of beauty, a secular avenue is found. The tool marks left by modeling the surface is a texture all by itself. The marks of the tools form a sort of PTSD of the creation of each piece. Smoothness is not all! Sculptural forms create shadows, which read like shading in a painting. Each three vertices define a single plane. Form(s) represented by planes still need to keep their sense of line, of the outline.

What will the finished surface be? When I work I seem to nail the feet down and pull out the wooden supports made of skewers. I seem to have eliminated or minimized human faces in favor of patterns which can be read as faces.

What is the point of making human figures unless it is to represent something? Some quality of attention? Of connection? Of compassion? Usually, dolls have small feet. With large feet, however, we maintain hope—on earth and not just for heaven. We stay "grounded".

Color interferes with designing form. Like designing a car, one tries for nice lines, good curves. I am ready now to tackle the clay "rough" versions using only a crude linoleum knife. These are shaped like the "crooked knives" used by Native carvers in the Northwest.

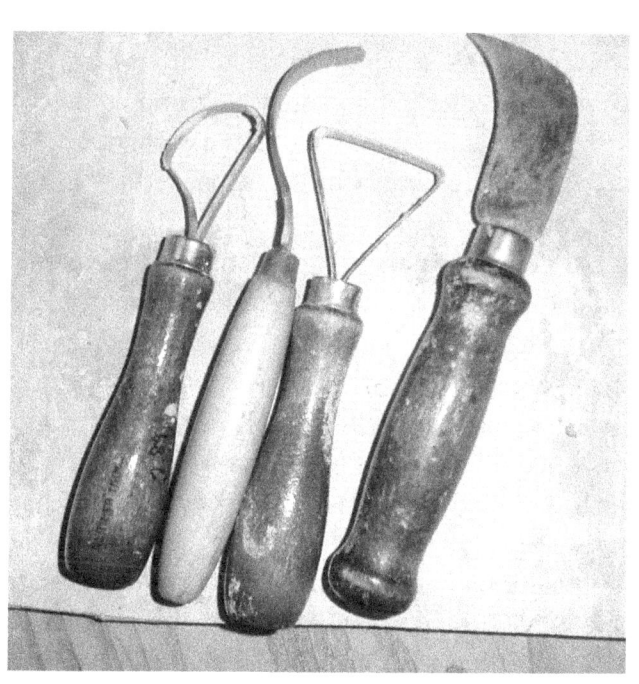

Color and Variegation, Ages 52–64

Color and variegation—which is having patches, stripes, or marks of different colors. Or, including many different things: full of variety.

During Zach's childhood, I rediscovered the uses and properties of color beyond clothing.

What were "they" wearing in New York City? That was the perennial question when planning a trip East, where it matters. There was always a new predominant color per season, which rotated precisely every thirty-nine to forty years, like deep purple or a warm russet. Movement, rather than color, is more my subject. So, silhouette and contour counted more than color for me.

When I was growing up, there were clothes to wear in the city and, almost more importantly, clothes to wear in the country. The country clothes were often hand-me-downs, boys' clothes from my brothers, or coats from my parents. These were clothes we did not have to be careful of, clothes we could play in, get muddy, spill paint on. I had a sort of split identity between the person who wore comfortable country clothes and the girl who had to look a certain way in the city. I recently bought a red plaid flannel shirt in a pattern that might be exactly one my mother had and wore only in the country. Whether it is the right plaid or not, having this shirt around makes me feel like my mother is around somewhere. On one of her early visits to me in Portland, she looked in my closet and said, "But my dear, you don't have any clothes." It was true. I only owned studio clothes, nothing in which I could go to work in or dress up to go out. She bought me some plaid pants I hated and sent me a simple, long gauzy dress I loved.

In my work, I could easily see that color interferes with designing form. Shading and edges by themselves both help to explain form. Once sculptures were completed, the ancient classical sculptors colored them. So did sculptors in the Middle Ages and of the Renaissance. Color is warmth and heat. It can feature and blur out the details of a thing. Color adds enough contrast to really see. Color and combining colors help me feel: my feelings. Color gives me pleasure; it pleases me. On sculpture, I usually just color the clothes and leave the hands and feet to show the raw clay.

Scale effects color, such as when my husband Joe brought a queen-size blanket—bright blue—instead of a receiving blanket, to pick up the infant Zach and take us home. The nurses had a field day with that one.

Visually, when moving around, I probably still notice letter forms and signs with words on them more than I notice color.

At one time, I went to a single session with a medical hypnotist in a dress suit. He helped me to visualize a golden tree beginning at the roots, growing upward through the trunk, and out along the branches. This visual image was one that I could return to if I felt unbalanced or deracinated. I don't know where the hypnosis came in. I think it was just plain creative visualization with relaxation, but it helped me a great deal.

To apply color to a fired sculpture, try dry brushing a lighter, oil-based color over a darker tone and then rub off the excess. This picks out details and adds depth.

Another recipe for color for terracotta in particular:

1. Apply two to three layers of milk (at least two percent fat).
2. Add tempera pigment to a mixture of water: white glue at 10:1.
3. Fix color with a layer of painted on white glue.
4. Move sculpture outdoors to large patch of bare pavement.
5. Sprinkle with isopropyl alcohol and set on fire with a tossed match.
6. Cool, and polish with floor wax.

Color can be used for harmony, logic, order, or lightness (whimsy and freedom).

In 2010, I fell down and broke my hip. I had to be quite forceful to get my family to call 911, and then the firemen insisted on carrying me down the bumpy front steps, even though I told them there were no steps down the side driveway, where it would have been more comfortable. Again, the medics would not take orders from the patient! After a metal plate was installed, I had to rest for 10 weeks without leaving the house.

It was a freedom I had never known – to rest and to do nothing, and to feel content!

Later on, I took a two-week summer watercolor class at Menucha (Creative Arts Center) with painter Paul Missal. He had the whole class cut up magazines to create the largest color palette we could within a given timeframe. This was made out of strips of magazine print, but I'm not sure I had ever seen the whole palette before in one place. The year before his death, my father had told me that he had just understood that there were many shades of green. He had been in the country house for some weeks and said he had somehow never noticed it before. My experience with the magazine palette was similar but much grander. I had never seen that there were so many shades of every color. In that class, we did a combination of drawing from a life model, painting, and collage. I've been doing those exercises ever since with great interest and amusement.

The Base or Foundation, Ages 65-77

Sculpture is always about mass or bulk and gravity. Gravity anchors everything, including us, to the earth even as it continues to spin. Sculpture can remind us not only of gravity but of timelessness. Of eternity. While all things of space eventually disappear, time itself remains. Sculpture can capture a moment of that eternity through its constancy of form and its presence.

As a sculptor, I always visualize the installation of a finished product first before it is even begun. (I knitted my first baby blanket when I was about fourteen, square by colorful square. I installed a mezuzah at child height before I was even pregnant with my second child.)

I know what ground is by this time of life, now. *Di erd is glaykh far aleman glaykh.* (The earth is level for all). It means that when we pass away, no one is actually greater than anyone else. The earth holds the idea of passion rock steady. The expression "grounded" means "well balanced, sensible, judicious, stable, at ease."

One plans all this in advance. First, find level ground or the floor where the sculpture is to be installed. What is the surface like? If attachments such as bolts or welds will be needed, this is decided now.

I can analogize the steps of planning sculpture with those of planning for family solidity and cultural transmission: the ground, the pedestal, the base, the plinth, and the sculpture.

For sculpture, one first considers what is the ground surface or floor: **the SEASONS**, and then what goes on top, such as a pedestal.

The pedestal is like **the HOLIDAYS AND FESTIVALS** (which take us out of ourselves) and which themselves have healing properties.

On top of the pedestal goes a solid base, such as **the FAMILY** (biological or chosen), and then,

Only then, is a piece of work installed (usually built or cast with its own built-in, stable plinth). The plinth represents the common **TABLE** around which family and friends will gather to share food.

Finally, the figurative sculpture's figures, integrated with their plinth, stand or sit together in **DIGNITY and in UNITY**.

That is how (and why) making and installing sculpture resembles family stability (and not anything negative or irreligious like "idol worship!"). One must work backward from the desired outcome and build forward, step by step, solid, from a firm foundation. Any deviation and there is the risk of a fall, of a smash, of a broken line.

As a parent, you "give them not what they want, but what they did not even know they needed."

And, when you yourself were a kid, you did not realize that your parents were still growing up.

Building solid is a question of building yourself solid first, so that all you do later can stand.

Into the Light, Ages 78–90

A Likhtkhn Gan Eden (A light-filled Garden of Eden) A parting benediction
is to wish someone "a light-filled Garden of Eden", ie in the other world.

Sculpture Thesis BFA 1977: Conclusion

"My work in art reflects a complex of intentions all of which I wanted to succeed at equally. I have established a certain form order and some basic techniques for producing somewhat permanent work.

I feel an enormous compulsion to focus on the human. I always planned to explore something of the range of human emotion within certain fixed formal elements of rhythm, and volume, and light. I wanted to be sure I could differentiate different mood states within the same set of limitations. These limitations were chosen very deliberately by me because of the way I experience perception of feeling and spirit as flow.

Light is the formal element which expressed this theme. Light falls everywhere. The forms of sculpture poke up into it and make the observer more aware of how light explains form.

I think my work can be seen and accepted as reference to any person's richness of humanity which for me also represents divinity. In either case the invitation to the observer is to become more human in feeling and response and therefore more valuable, and important, and unique.

When the human spirit is revealed in person or in art it is planted deep into the memory. I think I have succeeded in translating images of bodies into sculpture, drawings, and paintings whose rhythm allows the spirits depicted to be beyond things of space.

When I make choices anew for hallowing the human, in many moments of perception and notation I feel uplifted. Since art school days I feel I have made the beginning of a concentrated attempt to preserve that reality for myself and to transmit it to others.

I believe that my work celebrates my own particular quality of insight, which reflects an attitudinal choice for letting the sacred into the everyday."

Artist Statement

"Nemen keyar fun dayn mekhshirim un Got vet gefenen di arbet."
Take care of your tools, and God will find the work.

I can stand, run, skip, and jump all I want with my depictions of human figures doing the same. I have used clay to explore my feelings about human capacities for more than fifty years.

In my earliest works, grief, hollowness, and constriction are paramount. Slowly, over time, depicting healthy joy, centeredness, and movement, became my themes. There was also a long period during my single-parent years when all I depicted was repose! More recently, with carving into clay, I chose to depict connection, affection, and solidarity among my sculpted figures. I use Yiddish for many of my titles because the humor and resiliency embedded in this culture allow, at times, for "laughter through tears" (usually simultaneously).

Economy, vitality, and clarity and the values I strive for in my work.

Epilogue

Autonomy, physical tone, connectedness, and perspective are all needed to navigate life as well as to neutralize trauma and difficulties of various kinds.

I have experienced a lot of traumas over the course of my life. What I see from my writing is evidence that the essence of resilience and of survivorship comes from pairs of personality characteristics that exist simultaneously. These are always opposites, such as "soft" and "powerful." These characteristics could also be categorized as gendered, because soft is generally considered a feminine attribute and powerful to be a male one. In short, some degree of so-called androgyny in a person's personality seems to lead to enhanced survival. Following trauma, a sense of safety and trust must be restored. Support from peers and mutual collaboration with others strengthens the ability to make life choices, and hopefully, at last, to find one's own expression.

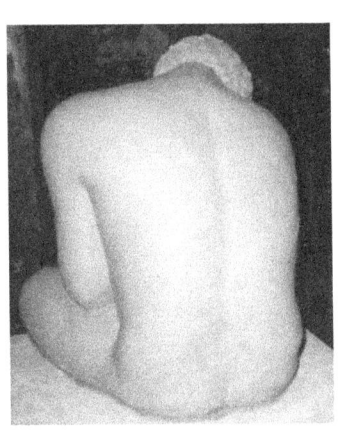

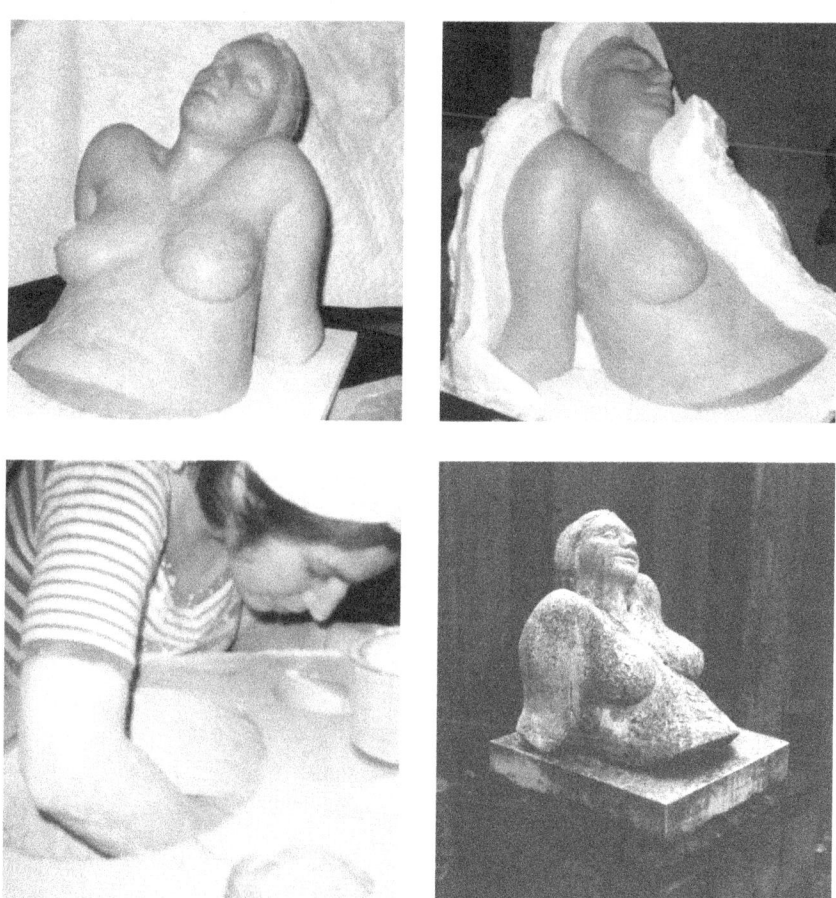

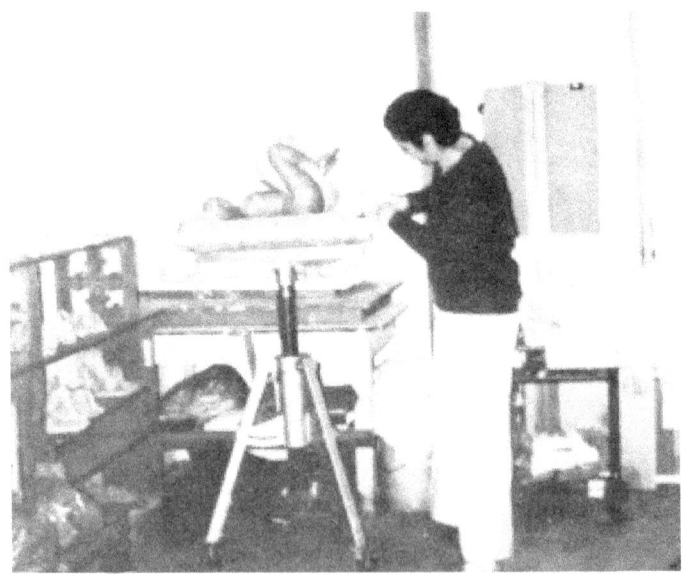

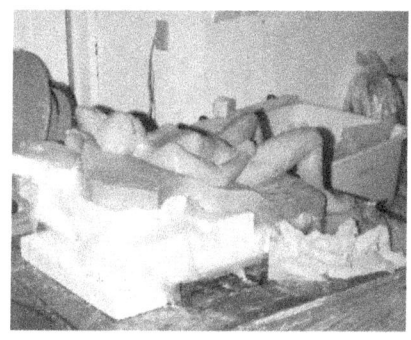 

435

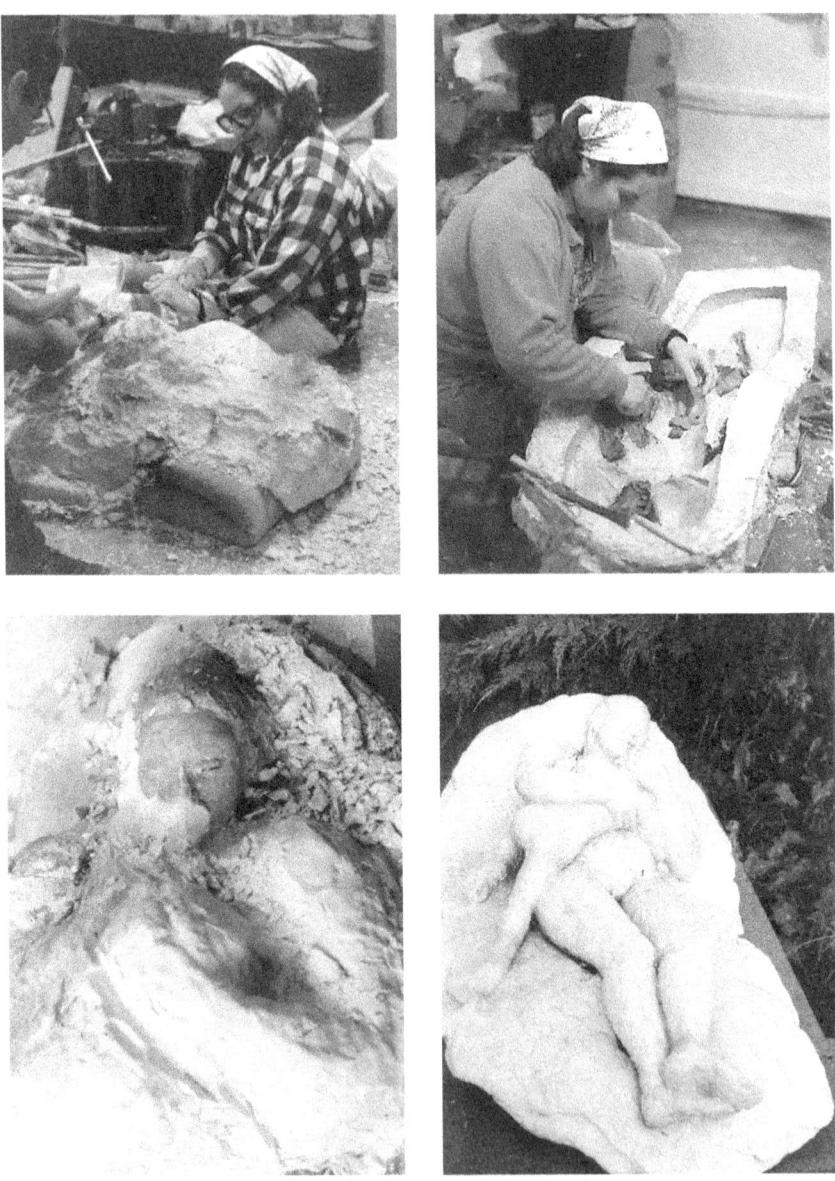

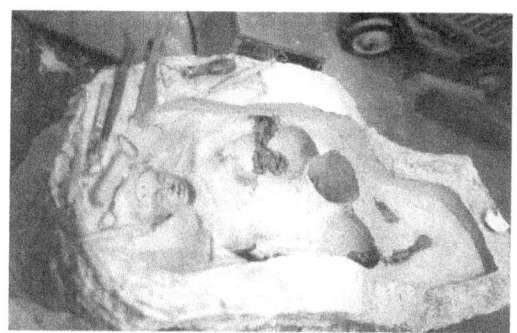

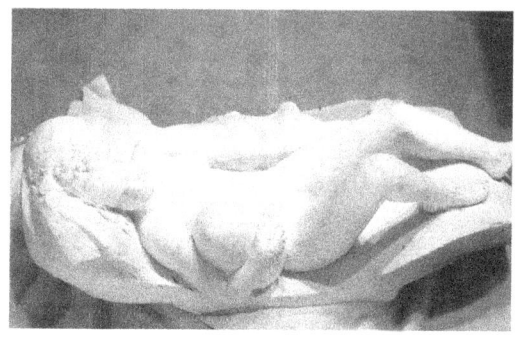

438

439

440

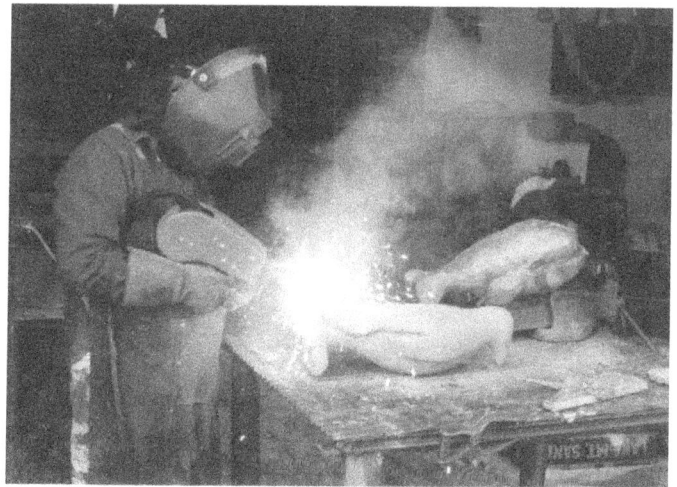

441

TSORES MIT YOYKH IZ GRINGER TSU FARTROGN VI TSORES ON YOYKH.

Troubles with soup are easier to bear than troubles without soup!

MIT EIN TOCHES, OIF TSVEI KHASENES KEN MEN NIT TANTSN.

With one backside, you cannot dance at two weddings!

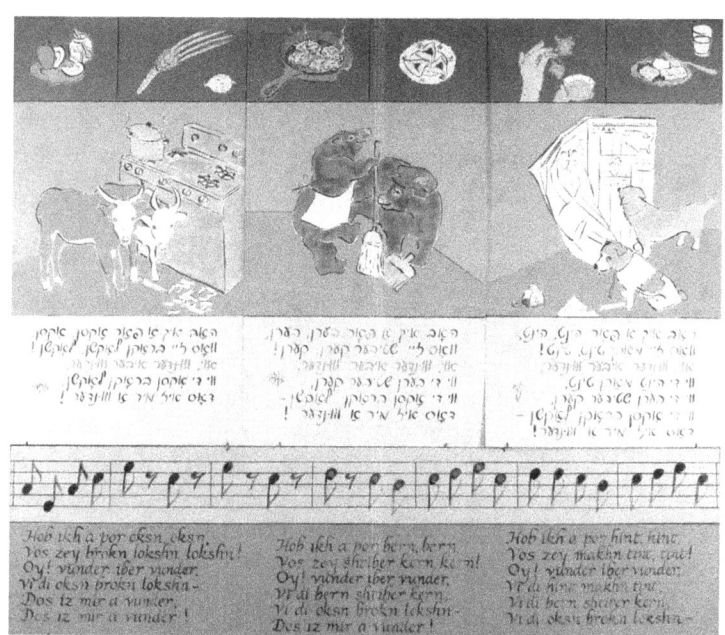

Hob ikh a por oksn, oksn,
Vos zey brokn lokshn, lokshn!
Oy! vunder iber vunder,
Vi di oksn brokn loksha –
Dos iz mir a vunder!

Hob ikh a por bern, bern,
Vos zey shraybn kern, kern!
Oy! vunder iber vunder,
Vi di bern shraybn kern,
Vi di oksn brokn lokshn –
Dos iz mir a vunder!

Hob ikh a por hint, hint,
Vos zey makhn tint, tint!
Oy! vunder iber vunder,
Vi di hint makhn tint,
Vili bern shrayr kern,
Vi di oksn broka loksha –

Kinder kert zikh um!

 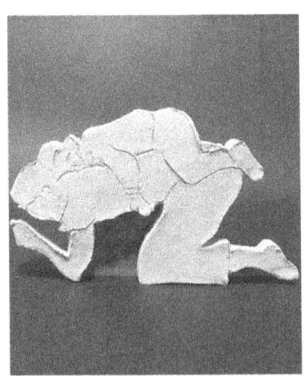

445

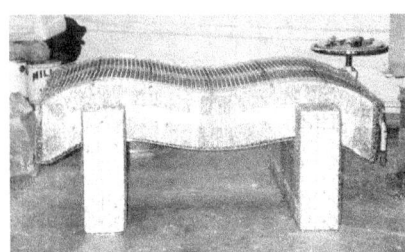

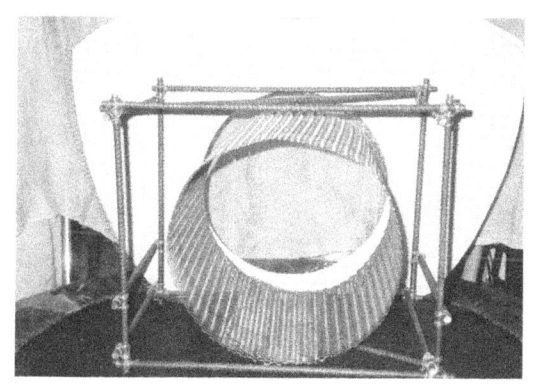

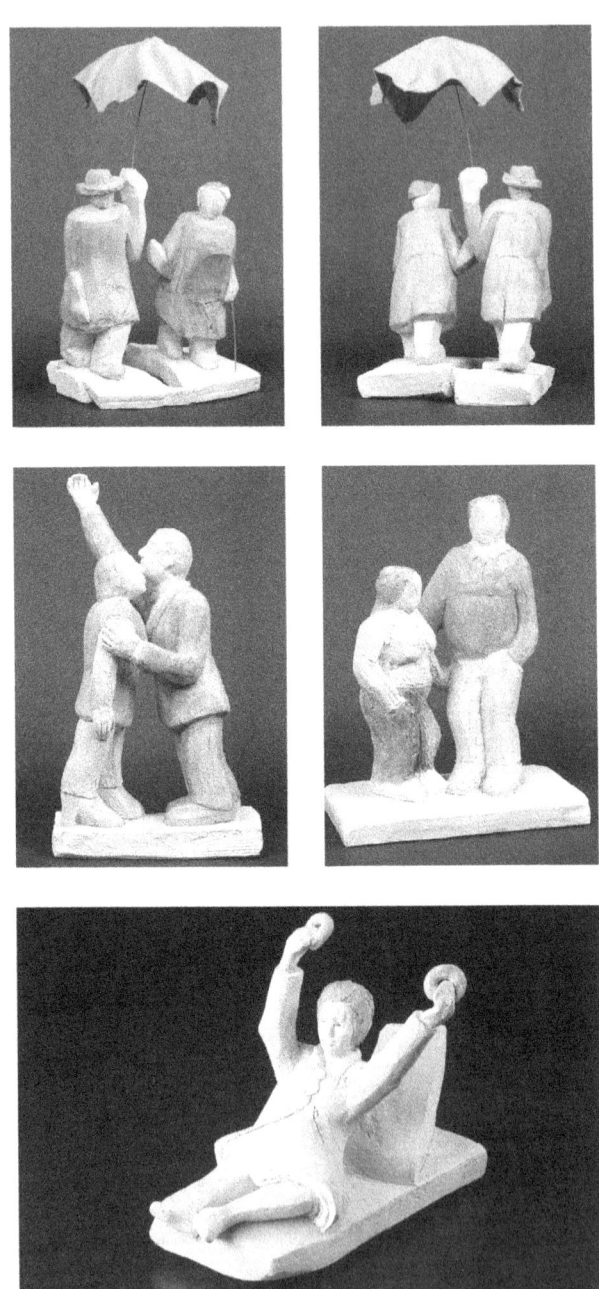

449

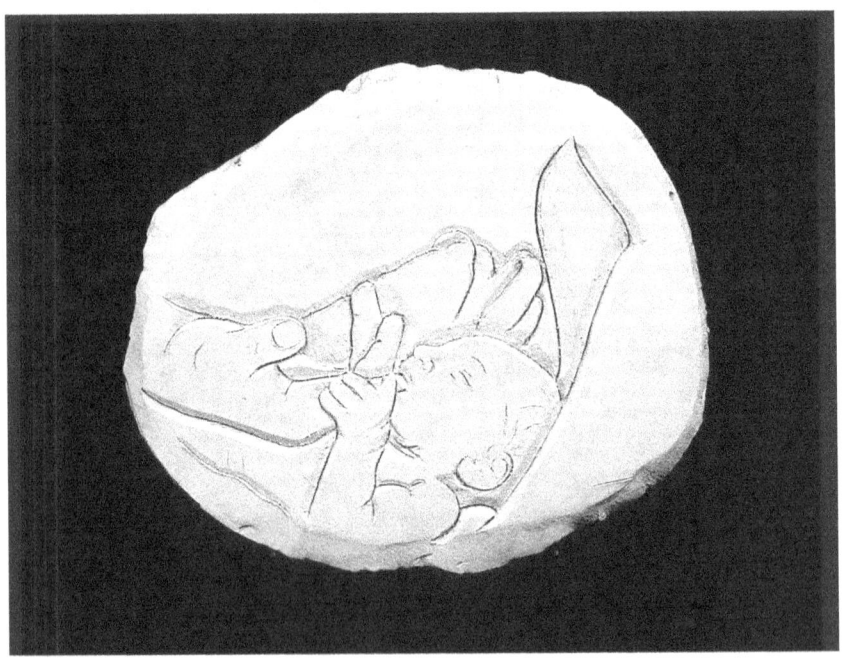

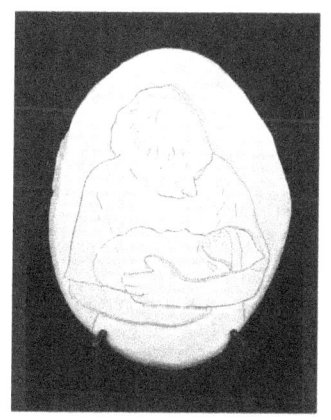

454

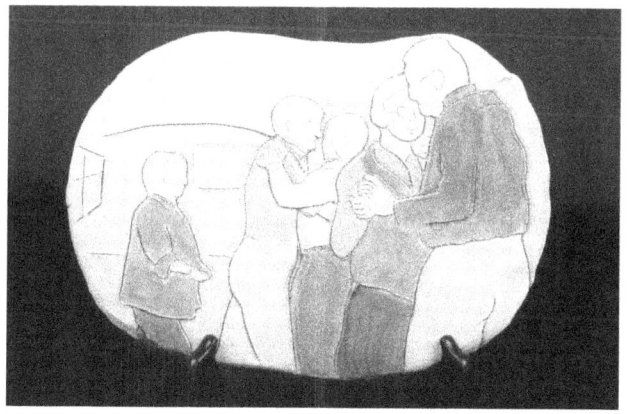

455

458

459

Appendix I: Chronology

1948: Born in NYC to refugee physician parents and grandparents

1952–1965: Attended "special" NYC public schools for gifted children

1958, 1961: Summer trips to France, Italy, Switzerland

1963: Forcible amputation of right leg for mesenchymal sarcoma of the knee

1964: President of Bronx and Manhattan Federation of Temple Youth

1965: Israel trip I, NFTY Mitzvah Corps working with immigrant children

1965-1966: Reed College in Portland, OR, studied art with Lloyd Reynolds

1965: Met first husband, Lew, at Jewish camp in CA

1966: Israel trip II, worked on kibbutz, stayed with Kalev family

1967: Transferred to Monterey Institute to study Arabic and to live with Lew

1967: Marriage to Lew (26), Joan (19) on trip to NYC, returned to CA, then moved to OR

1967–1969: BA Portland State University, graduation trip to Ecuador

1970: Son "Ben" born to Joan and Lew in Portland, OR

1970–1972: Living on the "Land" in summer and in a city commune in winter

1971: Lew moves to local ashram and on to California, no fault divorce

1972: Joan assaulted while on date with an older artist/painter

1971–1976: Joan single parent to Ben

1976–1988: Lew returns to Portland to see Ben every other weekend,

1976–1988: Joan continues as single, custodial parent throughout

1973–1977: Joan graduates Pacific NW College of Art, BFA sculpture with Manuel Izquierdo

1978: One-woman show of figurative sculpture, drawings at Mittleman Jewish Community Center, Portland, OR

1977–1983: Joan employed doing advocacy for accessible housing, for accessible arts venues, and as artist/teacher with talented and gifted programs. Also Manager annual Ski Expo Portland

1980: Gold medal in the slalom, women over 30, skiing three-track downhill, National Inconvenienced Sportsmen's Association, Winter Park, Colorado

1980: Joan's mother dies of lung cancer

1981: One woman show at The Don Conard Gallery in downtown Portland

1983: Bar Mitzvah ceremony and party for Ben

1983: Emotional/mental collapse at age 35 due to the many external and simultaneous stresses

1984-1988: Joan employed as technical illustrator/graphic designer at Mentor Graphics and creates corporate art collection (including a bronze by Seattle sculptor Phillip Levine)

1986: Met second husband, Joe, at the Vancouver Folk Music Festival in Canada

1988: Marriage to Joe (46), Joan (age 40) in backyard of Seattle home

1986-1993: Travel with Joe to scientific meetings in England, France, Scotland, Germany, Israel, Crete, Greece, Denmark, and Wales.

1988: Ben graduates high school, four years later 1992 graduates Carnegie Mellon BS in Math

1989-1992: Three miscarriages

1990: Month long sculpture residency with sculptor Rich Beyer in Pateros, WA

1991: Joan lectures at the International Sculptural Conference in Washington, D.C.

1992: Curator and organizer of a $10,000. Garden for Sculpture installed at Seattle Center's Bumbershoot Arts Festival

1993: Son "Zach" born to Joan and Joe. Joan's father is now terminally ill

1993: Emotional/mental collapse at age 45 due to stressful postpartum situation

1994: Joan's father dies of liver cancer

1993-2011: Joan shepherds Zach through 15 years of private schools. During this time, they went to Disney World once and attended 14 Yiddish programs

1998: Joan studies Yiddish at summer intensive in Oxford, England, Zach in daycare

1999: Ben elopes and marries

1997–2001: Joan organizes Yiddish language conferences in Seattle and paints 4 more murals of Yiddish folk songs in addition to 4 previous language murals for METRO, also exhibiting sculpture in group shows biannually

1999 Ethnic Heritage Council of the Pacific Northwest, The Aspasia Phoutrides Pulakis Memorial Award recognized Joan's work to preserve, document, and present ethnic heritage and advance cross-cultural understanding in the Pacific Northwest.

2005: Travel with Joe and Zach to France

2006: Joan has one-woman sculpture show Manuel Izquierdo Gallery in Portland

2006: Bar Mitzvah ceremony and party for Zach

2008: Joan has another one-woman sculpture show Gallery 6311 in Seattle

2010: Month long summer sculpture residency in Pietrasanta, Italy

2010: Teaching ceramics to seniors, Yiddish to kindergartners, Joan falls and breaks hip

2011: Zach graduates high school and moves on to University of Chicago

2011: Merit Award, "Di tfile di shtile" (The quiet prayer), terra cotta, Port Townsend Annual Juried Figurative Show, "Expressions Northwest". Juror, Gary Faigin

2015: Zach graduates University of Chicago and works at a startup in Chicago, then moves to live and work in San Francisco for another startup company

2011–2021: Empty nest for the second time, no less difficult than the first time

2013: Travel with Joe to Japan to receive award, we meet the Emperor and Empress

2014: Created Pop-Up Exhibit Jewish Cultural Heritage, Storefronts program funded by a J-Kick (Jewish Federation) Kickstarter and installed at Bellevue City Hall meeting space.

2016: *Passport to Washington* captures the stories of Jewish migrants to Seattle. It is now a traveling exhibit of the Washington State Jewish Historical Society exploring the unique stories of how 50 selected community members including Joan made their mark here in Washington State. Themes of this exhibit included arts, education, music, food and wine, science and medicine, public affairs, and technology.

2014-2019: Joan awarded monthlong residencies at Macfarlane Studio, Whiteley Center, Friday Harbor Labs, San Juan Island, WA, continuing with gouache/collage and clay

2019: Operation to remove large gallstone, diagnosed after laughing uncontrollably at a mime

2019: "Retirement" party and exhibit of paintings and sculptural maquettes by Joan held at the former Portland studio.

2020: Personal narrative completed. Some perspectives on aging amid the pandemic and isolation. Various reflections on mortality and memory.

2021: Matzke Fine Arts Gallery and Sculpture Park, Camano Island, WA, Small Works Show.

Appendix II: Stories from my mother prewar medical school

I finally found some of my mother's papers relating to her degrees from the University of Paris. I have color Xeroxed them and I was very touched by them because of my continuing contact with some of her medical-school-era friends, many of whom were still very much alive in 2002.

Of the ten we knew who graduated in 1939 and 1940, seven are still alive and perky at eighty-six and eighty-seven. In New York, Katia Lodyjensky; in LA, Lydia Kuhn; and in Paris, Lia Andler, Olga Fink, Colette Brisac Dreyfus, Helene Guerin, and Helene Severin. To me it is astonishing that out of those seven girlfriends they ALL finished their studies, and survived World War II. They all rebuilt their lives and practiced medicine. All but one had children, and in most cases, outlived their husbands. The three who are gone include my parents, Emmanuel and Lucie Lia Rudd, and their friend Jules Landowski (in whose honor I always wanted to learn the mandolin, which I have done.)

There are lots of stories about med-school survival. Jules's wife, Rosette, used to bribe him with fresh strawberries and cream for every exam he studied for. Helene Severin threaded her petticoats with colored ribbons the night before exams instead of studying. When asked what the hell she thought she was doing, she replied that she would probably faint on the morrow and wanted to look good on the floor. The girlfriends suggested she study instead. In May of 1940, Colette and her future husband, Claude, and my mother, Lucie, sat in a Parisian park and spun pipe dreams about their futures, all completely changed the following month by the Nazi invasion.

Colette passed for French and remained above ground in the Resistance, and Claude fought Underground and was ultimately captured. He survived his camp (Buchenwald) to return and marry Colette. My mother, Lucie, finished her studies but not her thesis by June 1940. Just one week ahead of the Germans, the family went south, first to Toulouse, ultimately to

Marseilles, and by boat to America. In Toulouse, the girlfriends wrote their own thesis papers and also many others (Lucie wrote four for the men they knew that were on the run or at the front.) The actual "degree" caught up to her only years later in America. In 1940, she would have been twenty-four years old. The auberge de jeunesse identity pass along with the other color Xeroxes shows her pictured in 1939. It was a serious world, but she traveled all over the south of France.

The dates might seem confusing. There is a baccalaureate from 1934 at age eighteen (this corresponds roughly to high school and two years of college), followed by the internships in general medicine, surgery, and obstetrics, the medical degree of 1940, and most emotional of all the ARRETE (stop) of August 1940 stating that because she was not "of a father of the French nationality." She could not practice medicine in France. Three years later in America, she was considered proficient in English and collecting references from her first job. It all seems a hard act to follow. I was always kind of intimidated, myself, but some qualities continue by inheritance, and some by culture.

All of my mother's girlfriends that I have met agree that they went to Lucie's house after school to study, to have tea, because her mother welcomed them and fed them cookies with their tea. To me, the bonds of friendship that survived sixty-plus years are, in a way, the greatest "success story" of all.

Appendix III: The slap ("patsch"), or Yiddish and longevity as we all become increasingly difficult

Next, for further perspective, a lengthy history of self-motivated Yiddish activities in Seattle over some years, i.e., the intersection of The Bronx, Reed College, and The Workmen's Circle:

1.) The Arbeter Ring (Workmen's Circle) had an actual building and a strong chapter presence here in Seattle's 1930-'40s, and some of its members were instrumental in starting Group Health and the PCC Food Coops. By the early 1950s, membership had dwindled, partly due to conflicts with the local establishment over the State of Israel. The more things change, the more they stay the same. The last chapter secretary, Ben Stein (z"l), donated some 400 books in and about Yiddish to the UW's Allen Library. A now-retired librarian, Janet Heineck, continued to purchase newer Yiddish texts and textbooks for the collection over many more years. The library is open to the public, and it is worth a browse. If you can park.

2) The Seattle Yiddish Group was founded by Charles and Kate Solin (z"l). Their daughter, Gale Lurie, used to live a couple of blocks from me and has moved to Vashon Island, where she is a potter. Two additional older couples, all social workers, relocated to Seattle from the Bronx. They were Murray and Sophie Meld, as well as David and Ruth Farber. Mr. Farber was the first director of Jewish Family Services. The Farbers' daughter, Annie Baldwin, was my good friend at Reed College, and we stayed in touch until her death several years ago. Annie played piano in one of the first NW klezmer bands, the Hester Street Band (they played at my older son Ben's Bar Mitzvah party), and were contemporaneous with the early Mazeltones group.

3) Murray Meld and his friend Frank Krasnowsky (from LA) took over running the Seattle Yiddish Group after the death of Charles Solin. There

were many wonderful people I met there, including Dr. Ed Flick, Ben and Ada Dortch, Seymour and Hilda Weingarten. I followed them all over to the small, friendly modern Orthodox shul, on NE 65th, which they attended (after we had become unhappy with the Conservative Beth Shalom, where some people were consistently rude to my patrilineal Jewish husband).

4) At the time, in the early 1990s, Ruth Peizer was teaching Yiddish at the offices of the Jewish Federation downtown. Wendy Marcus and I were both in her classes for some years, along with other wonderful people, some of whom went on to study at international Yiddish programs (Marna Sapsowitz, Linda Portnoy). Years later, Rita Katz (child survivor) taught an evening class in Seattle at Emanuel Congregation, but open to all.

5) Not everyone liked the format of the Seattle Yiddish Group, and there was an all-women's breakaway group that met at Diane Frankl's apartment every Friday at noon. Everyone brought some snacks to share, and the truly fluent, i.e., Diane (z"l), Hilda, and Rita Goldenberg (z"l), took incredible trips down memory lane about their upbringing (also in the Bronx). The rest of us (me, Annette Siegel, her sister Charlotte, Ruth Singer) just listened and occasionally asked for a translation. Some of the stories I remember were the costs of different foods in another era, the necessity of wearing gloves, how ice was delivered, and the incomparable taste of schmaltz on rye bread as a snack. These gatherings were very "heymish." At the time of writing, Hilda is still alive at ninety-seven and living at the Summit. Murray and Sophie (early nineties) are at Kline Galland. Frank lives somewhere on Capitol Hill.

6) What about that slap?

In 1997, Murray and Frank organized a script and a cast for a multimedia production called "Yiddish Lives!" I had a bit part singing "Hob Ikh a Por Oksn" (I have a pair of oxen) with younger son Zach (then age four) and some other kids and stuffed animal props, while blown-up images of my METRO mural illustrations of the same folk song were projected on a large screen behind us.

Murray and Frank would have been in their mid-seventies at the time, but one of the cast, at eighty-something, got mixed up with the pagination of the script. In frustration at appearing clumsy and foolish, and after this was pointed out to him, he hauled off and slapped Frank in the face. I decided it was time for a younger generation to direct Seattle Yiddish activities.

7) Also in 1997, Max Applebaum, who later romanced the widowed Ruth Farber (mother of my Reed musician friend, Annie), insisted that he wanted to see "Der Yiddish Mikado" when it was brought to Seattle. This was something of a pipe dream as there was no such plan. Murray assigned me to "look into it." I made the rounds of all the Jewish businesses, including Noah's and Starbucks. I got so incensed that the local Jewish-owned businesses would not support Yiddish culture (unless culture was for K-12) that I went rogue and just started selling tickets. I arranged for the auditorium at the old Museum of History and Industry which seated 400 and enlisted the JCC to help with ticket sales. Misha Berson wrote it up in the Friday paper, and the Gilbert and Sullivan Society turned up in force. Joe and I had visited the International District's fortune cookie company and placed an order. We then sold fortune cookies with Yiddish fortunes in them at intermission, and we made it, barely, with three performances, into the black.

8) Following this event and copycatting Mame Loshn (mother tongue) weekends back east were six Mame Loshn NW weekend conferences 1997-2002, with minimal funding by Arbeter Ring, largely to pay for national guest teachers such as Pesakh Fiszman (z"l). We were on the map. I worked alone the first year, then with Myra Rothenberg (z"l), then with Myra and Wendy Marcus. Eventually, Temple Beth Am's treasurer canceled the annual event as too costly. Once the paid band performances were added to the budget, the programs no longer broke even as they had in the beginning. The new, local Arbeter Ring chapter had to be disbanded too. We had the required minimum of ten paid members for a while, and this allowed us to receive continued seed monies of up to $1,500 for the

annual conference. However, people quickly tumbled to the fact that the member discount on the conference did not equal the yearly dues payment. It was a Catch-22 as we had to have a chapter to hold Arbeter Ring events with funding from them. Allying with any one progressive synagogue as a potential sponsor would have excluded both the secular and the observant from considering attending. *A shod!* A shame!

9) Myra's good friends Phyllis Grossman (genealogy conferences), Jeff Grossman (her Trilogy neighbor), and Joan (Mame Loshn NW) all connected with each other around the time of Myra's final illness and death. And Bernice gave me a ride home from the funeral. But it was Jeff who pursued a search for a Yiddish language teacher and began studying along with Wendy Marcus with the idea of forming a class. This varied over several quarters, first with Joan teaching beginners and Wendy the more advanced, then with Wendy teaching beginners and Ayn Dalgof teaching intermediate, then with Ayn teaching intermediate, and rotating "leaders" introducing new material, often from online.

10) Joan attended a Reed College alumni picnic shortly after one of the annual services in honor of Yiddish at Temple Beth Am. These had originated some years earlier with the untimely death of the son of TBA member Dena Dawson, who organized these services for the first years in his memory before she herself moved out of town. Presumably, the services continue in his memory as well as in honor of Yiddish (Does this kind of thing really depend on who pays for the kiddish?). At the Reed picnic, Joan was congratulated on her Yiddish reading by Judy and Billy Kreuter, who had been at that years' service.

11) Prior to the TBA group, but after the Friday group at Diane's, there was another weekly *tish* for conversation, which Joan organized, and which was held at Hillel with yet another breakaway set of people from the Seattle Yiddish Group. Elly Trepman, James Redfield, Jonathan Schwartz, Rita Katz, and Joan met for most of a year. The second year, Wendy joined us whenever her lunch hour allowed. This *tish* ended when

James married and moved, and Jonathan's wife had the first or maybe second of two young children. However, this was the first era any of us started using the Internet to translate and to learn. That was exciting. It was only 2011-12. Not long ago! James has persevered and has just published an English translation of stories by Mikhah Yosef Berichevsky called *From a Distant Relation*.

12) Another Reed College note was meeting the daughter (and granddaughter) of one of my favorite Yiddish poets to date: Abraham Reisen. His daughter had the most interesting face in the entire college dining area, and I went right over to see who she was. (The granddaughter was a Reed graduate who lives now in New Jersey.) The occasion was an installation of yet another college president and we had a very pleasant time over lunch sitting with the Reisen descendants.

About the Author

Joan Rudd emigrated to Portland from New York City at age seventeen to attend Reed College and study calligraphy, art history, and graphic arts with Lloyd Reynolds. Midway second year she transferred to an intensive Arabic language study program in Monterey, California. Reed would not accept those credits, so she transferred them to the Middle East Studies program at Portland State University (PSU), where she encountered her first organized antisemitism.

She then increased her number of art classes (ceramics with Ray Grimm, sculpture with Frederic Littman) and learned how to draw from life models. After graduating from PSU, she gave birth to her first child. As soon as he started preschool, Joan enrolled in the Museum Art School (now the Pacific Northwest College of Art) for another four years of college, culminating in a BFA in sculpture with thesis adviser Manuel Izquierdo (a former student of Littman and yet another WWII refugee, like Littman and like Joan's parents).

Her own creed has always been: "economy, vitality, and clarity" of form. However, elegance is less important than charm (kheyn) in her work, and economy more important than realism. She chooses to depict connection, affection, and solidarity among her sculpted figures.

Joan's work mixes references to art history, cultural history, and contemporary life. These include ancient Egyptian sculpture, cubism, the mid-twentieth century sculptor Elie Nadelman, and modern Japanese figures carved and painted in wood. Her knowledge of the physical processes of sculpting—clay modeling, mold making, casting, fabrication, and carving—all contribute to reinvigorating her art as she sets herself new challenge after challenge. There is a respect for materials in how she keeps her work surfaces and cares for her tools. Her calligraphic line quality is particularly evident in the incised work in clay reliefs.

Joan's images come from many sources, particularly from observing people in ordinary "poses," such as reading. She makes sketches on paper and in clay and holds onto ideas for what are sometimes long periods of incubation. Associating a pose with a fragment of song or poem for a title allows for a longer period of rumination. When building a sculpture up, she uses internal ribs to grow the forms to their final volume. When carving, she uses external curves to define and balance the mass. She makes use of templates, carbon paper, Xeroxing, pointing, and piercing to fix or to enlarge contours. She prefers to measure distance(s) by eye and can enlarge from a small maquette to a larger one without mechanical measurements. She changes the height and orientation of the sculpture stand frequently to change her viewpoint and takes photographs of each stage. This has facilitated learning when to stop working to avoid losing the essence of the abstraction.

She uses symmetry only to choose where to deviate from symmetry and confer more liveliness. She keeps a written journal of her goals, questions, and notes on how things are solved. She works clay with a limited number of simple tools and knives, including a prized wooden "crooked knife" she found in a Parisian art supply store to complement her standard linoleum cutter. This shape of the knife is sometimes still used in the Northwest by Native carvers.

In order to understand how Joan works, it is necessary to grasp the amount of planning, preparation, and simple labor involved in moving and manipulating her materials. The original choices to work in larger amounts of heavy clay and masonry materials necessitated an overhead hoist and a system of wheeled sculpture stands and stools. She likens this kind of necessary planning to cooking on a limited number of burners. The incubation of ideas is yet a different kind of process, often spanning several years while searching out the various elements. Joan's productivity in the studio (and at home) wastes little time but is often composed of many, many patient steps.

List of illustrations

Gallery pages

Contact www.joanruddsculpture.com for further information on availability and price

www.ingramcontent.com/pod-product-compliance
Lightning Source LLC
Chambersburg PA
CBHW071131130626
46553CB00004B/1331